Eat Shandong

A publication of The Ohio State University
National East Asian Languages Resource Center

Funded by

The. U.S. Department of Education

Pathways to Advanced Skills series, volume IX
Series General Editor: Galal Walker

Distributed by The Ohio State University
Foreign Language Publications & Services

Executive Editor: Galal Walker
Managing Editor: Minru Li
Copy Editor: Melissa Gruzs
Production & Design: Dan O'Dair
Distribution Manager: Gregory Wilson
Editorial Assistants: Xizhen Qin, Yuanyuan Wang

Eat Shandong

From Personal Experience to a Pedagogy of a Second Culture

Eric T. Shepherd

Pathways to Advanced Skills, Vol. IX

©National East Asian Languages Resource Center
The Ohio State University

Galal Walker
Executive Editor

This volume prepared and published by

National East Asian Languages Resource Center
The Ohio State University
100 Hagerty Hall
1775 S. College Road
Columbus, OH 43210-1340

614-292-4361 • fax: 614-688-3355
nealrc.osu.edu

Library of Congress Cataloging-in-Publication Data:
Shepherd, Eric Todd, 1968-
Eat Shandong: from personal experience to a pedagogy of a second culture /
Eric Todd Shepherd
p. cm. – (Pathways to advanced skills ; vol. 9)
ISBN 0-87415-351-4 (alk. paper)
    1.   Cross-cultural orientation—China—Shandong Sheng.
           2. Intercultural communication.
           I. Title. II. Series.

           GN345.65.S45 2005
           303.48'2—dc22

                            2005041554

Manufactured in the United States of America

Printed and bound by
OSU Printing Services, Columbus, OH

ISBN 0-87415-315-4

Table of Contents

Acknowledgments

Nearly all of the work on this book was completed while I was working as program officer for the US/China Links program. Without that opportunity provided by Dr. Galal Walker, I would not have been able to move beyond a surface level (mis)understanding of Chinese culture. Intellectually, I owe many of the ideas found within these covers to my time studying with and learning from him. Credit goes to him for both leading me in the right direction and for putting up with me for the last ten years. Also influential on my understanding of Chinese culture were two bona fide veteran players in a wide range of Chinese interpersonal games: Dr. Chung-min Chen and Dr. Xiaobin Jian. What I learned from watching and imitating these two elite players is immeasurable, and the thanks and respect I hold for both cannot easily be put into words. In addition to these three influential figures, I have relied heavily on Professor Mari Noda and Dr. Mark Bender for their expertise and guidance. I owe Noda Sensei a great deal for her meticulous reading of and detailed comments on an earlier version of this manuscript. During two summers I spent in the classroom with the SPEAC Japanese program at OSU, she also provided me with an unmatched model of how to construct performed culture environments in the classroom as well as how to elicit top-notch performance out of American learners in such language-learning contexts. Dr. Bender, himself an old China hand, has offered me his time and sound advice on how to go about both Chinese culture and my intellectual career. Because of my inexperience in the areas of folklore, oral traditions, and anthropology, I have relied heavily on his knowledge and comments to revise the earlier version of this manuscript.

The environment at the Department of East Asian Languages and Literatures at OSU has also enabled me to continue to grow both intellectually and professionally: graduate seminars on language pedagogy with Professor Charles Quinn, on modern Chinese culture with Professor Kirk Denton, and on East Asian scripts with Professor James Unger forced me to confront many of the issues found in this book with intellectual rigor, and talks with Zhiwei Bi honed my understanding of both Chinese culture and the teaching/learning process. The experience of learning Japanese with Professor Noda and Yuko Kuwaii not only allowed me to develop skills in Japanese but also contributed to my understanding of how languages are learned and taught most efficiently.

Several other individuals at Ohio State have directly contributed to my intellectual growth and thus indirectly contributed to the final version of this book. They include Professor Diane Birckbichler, whose comments on an earlier draft helped to narrow my focus and whose sound advice has enabled me survive graduate school. In addition, many versions of the various sections of this book grew out of smaller pieces written for a course on folklore taken at OSU with Professor Dorothy Noyes. My ideas of the fieldwork process that led to this book were also heavily influenced by a course taken at OSU with Professor Amy Shuman.

I also owe a heavy debt to many colleagues and classmates who have influenced my intellectual growth and understanding of Chinese culture. Although it is impossible to mention them all, I am indebted most to Lijuan Wu and Qingxin Wang, who edited the Chinese found in the text and who have spent many hours discussing Chinese culture with me. I would also like to thank Dr. Li Yu, Dr. Minru Li, Jingsheng Ren, Zhaoyi Bu, and Dr. Yi Li for their friendship, patience, and understanding. Other colleagues and friends at OSU who in one way or another made me think while compiling a memory of banquets include Yan Yang, Yulong Zhang, Lingjun Hu, Jing Yan, Stephen Horn, and Yunxin Zhang.

The staff at The Ohio State University Foreign Language Center has provided much-needed support for all of the projects that took me to China and allowed me to conduct fieldwork. Karen Sobul and Sheila Cowley deserve special credit for putting up with my antics and for offering valuable advice on life and how to stay sane. The Department of East Asian Languages and Literatures, in particular Debbie Knicely, has also supported my efforts while I was a graduate student and lecturer at OSU, and the Office of International Education has provided much-needed organizational and logistical support for study-abroad programs since 2002. Special thanks also go to Grace Johnson, Jenny Kraft, and Jeff McKibben for their support on China programs.

In addition to friends at OSU who have assisted in the development of this project, many friends and teachers in China have helped me by pointing out my cultural blunders and misunderstandings. Of special mention are Zhiliang Jin, Wu Yanguo, Ke Ding, Maizi, Huzi, my Older Sister Li (Ying Li), my Older Brother Su (Zhibo Su), Steven Lei Shi, my Chinese adopted mother Zhenfen Xie, Jianhua Sun, my Yantai family (the Wangs), Wang Jin, Jie Zang, Da Xiang, Professor Jingyao Sun, Weimin Jiang, Rong Song, Yuping Niu, Feng Bai, Jianguang Wang, Yuxian Li, Yajing Li, Yuehong Zhang, Jiancheng Dong, Minghua Du, Hui Xue, Dajiang He, Aiping Zhang, Jing Wang, Hongbin Qu, Benxin Xie, and Guilin Dai.

Melissa Gruzs and Minru Li deserve extra special mention for their multiple readings and comments that transformed a manuscript into a publishable document. Without their careful readings or patience in dealing with me, the ideas in this book would be even less clearly expressed than they are now. With their editorial help and expertise, I was able to significantly improve the quality of this book.

Finally, I would like to express my sincere thanks to my family, who have unquestioningly supported me in my China pursuits. My mother, Linda Bishop, my late stepfather, Jack Bishop, my sister, Lori Shepherd, and my brother, Bryon Shepherd, have always been there for me, and for that, I am deeply grateful. My late grandmother, Florence Beeler, also funded my first influential trip to Taiwan many years ago. Last, but certainly not least, I must thank Chih-Hsin Tai, who has made graduate school and the research to complete this book possible and whose undying love and support keep me going.

Foreword

If communicating in Chinese culture is conceptualized as games, what are the possible levels of participation for learners of Chinese to be engaged with these games? According to Galal Walker, there are six levels of participation: observers, spectators, fans, commentators, players, and shareholders. (Also see Chapter Five of this book for further discussion of these categories.) Examining the field of teaching Chinese as a foreign language in this country proves that what American university-level Chinese programs have produced so far are mostly observers and a few spectators and fans; American learners who can effectively play the game of communicating in Chinese culture are really hard to find. There are many reasons for this, of course. To begin with, one cannot ignore that many professionals in this field never envision their mission as training players, perhaps because they believe training players is either unnecessary or impossible.

For the coaches who want to train players, there are still many unsettling issues and questions: What does it mean to be a player of second culture games? What is actually involved in the process of a learner becoming a player? What can coaches do to create appropriate and effective learning contexts that are fitting for this process? To these ends, Eric Shepherd's book is as timely as it gets. Although his interesting, often amusing, and always pointed account of his personal experiences of both a learner becoming a player and a player becoming a coach is extremely revealing, his bold and firm-footed reconceptualization of the enterprise of learning/teaching Chinese as a foreign language is truly refreshing. A player who is seasoned in the game rarely provides theoretical insights through his rich in-the-field experiences. Equally rare is a researcher who also can effectively play the game. Eric's book has both sides of the coin. It presents alert observations, insightful and practical step-by-step how-tos, and keen analysis that come both from his extensive experience with the game as a player and as a coach and from his solid, cross-disciplinary research. Under Galal Walker's guiding notion of "performed culture," Eric explores a whole range of issues related to the process of becoming a player in second culture games. In particular, his analysis of enculturation, syncing, accommodation, establishing/interpreting intentions in a second culture, and compiling second culture memories is on target and very enlightening.

Since 1997, and under Galal Walker's guidance, Eric and I have been team teaching the course "Networking in China and America" and codirecting the US/China Links internship program. Through all the joys and frustrations associated with such a program, we are keenly aware that we can no longer delay rethinking the missions and approaches of the CFL enterprise and must redirect our focus on training and producing players who truly can play the game of communicating in Chinese. Eric's book is certainly a valuable and welcome contribution to this end.

Xiaobin Jian

Introduction

In my years of language study and interaction with Chinese people, the vital role that culture plays in meaning making has become increasingly obvious to me. In the context of language learning, language and culture are intertwined so intimately that separating the two during instruction is detrimental to any learner's chances for success. During my first stint in Chinese culture, while teaching English at Yantai University, I observed a number of students of English language who had mastered the fundamentals of the English linguistic code but who, nonetheless, were what I would consider unsuccessful in communicative interactions with native English speakers because they could not accurately interpret or establish their intentions.[1]

Conversely, while serving as the program officer of the US/China Links internship program[2] and the resident director of The Ohio State University's Qingdao and Shanghai summer language programs and while teaching Chinese as a lecturer in Ohio State's Department of East Asian Languages and Literatures, I have had the opportunity to observe American learners of Chinese who had

---

[1] See chapter six for a detailed discussion of intentions in culture.

[2] US/China Links is an independent organization coordinated by faculty and staff from the Ohio State University Department of East Asian Languages and Literatures that focuses on developing language and culture training programs for Americans and Chinese. US/China Links has created intermediate, advanced, internship, and teacher training programs in cooperation with universities located in Yantai, Qingdao, and Shanghai. All programs employ a performed culture approach to the learning and teaching of language and culture. Training is geared toward equipping participants with the skills necessary to integrate themselves into local communities in their target culture.

1

developed varying competencies with the fundamentals of the Chinese linguistic code but who were repeatedly unable to perceive their interlocutors' intentions. More important, typical American learners of Chinese also lack the ability to realize their own intentions in Chinese culture. Watching as learners establish intentions that are not viable in their culture of study has raised important questions in my mind and has guided much of my research over recent years. They include: How does an adult language learner approach learning a second culture so that he or she gains the ability to decipher and act upon the intentions of members of that culture? How do we develop the ability to realize our own intentions in another culture? And the underlying question, how do we integrate culture into the language curriculum so that our learners are able to achieve more advanced skill levels?

While struggling with these questions, I spent half of each year as a graduate student at Ohio State and half working in China's Shandong Province. Working and living in Shandong for much of my time in graduate school provided me with a unique opportunity to experiment (in real target culture contexts) with some of the pedagogical approaches I was learning about. And, because between 1995 and 2001, I spent more time living in China than I did in the United States, I was forced to try out various strategies for integrating into a nonnative cultural community. As point-person for our organization in China, I was repeatedly invited to banquets and professional interactions led to frequent encounters in local banquet culture. These experiences have led me to believe that there is a significant cultural emphasis on eating and eating contexts in China. This social importance of eating make banquets key situations all foreigners dealing with Chinese frequently encounter and thus must know how to negotiate effectively. An understanding of food, food contexts, and eating habits is vital knowledge for anyone going to China or interacting with Chinese people. Moreover, in all parts of China, eating contexts commonly serve as forums for managing interpersonal relationships and thus involve culturally defined behaviors and interaction patterns that are key in other contexts as well as to becoming a member of any Chinese community.

These unique experiences—periods of training in current Western pedagogical theory interspersed with extended periods of living and working in China—have led to this book, which is intended both as an attempt to answer some of the theoretical questions raised earlier and as a practical guide to participation in social eating contexts in Shandong. The design of the book may seem unusual to some readers because of the clear distinction between the two halves of the book—ethnographic description and pedagogical theory but this structure reflects my unusual path to these ideas as well as an attempt to appeal to multiple audiences.

Intentions and Cultural Frameworks
While interacting with Chinese in America and Americans in China, I have come to understand that because most people cannot accurately establish and interpret intentions in their second cultures, many find it difficult to become recognized participants in those cultures. That is, they are unable to integrate themselves into the communities in which they live. As a result, they often find themselves isolated in expatriate communities or, in the case of Chinese in the United States, limited to interaction with members of the local Chinese American community. With only infrequent plunges into target community activities, such individuals find linguistic improvement at best slow and inefficient. This raises the question of how to become an accepted and recognized participant in a second culture as well as the issue of pedagogical approaches that prepare learners to enter new cultural communities.

To assess and establish intentions, one must first become an acute observer of culture, meaning that one must learn the norms, both acknowledged and unspoken, of a new culture. Language learners must understand the contexts they will find themselves in as well as the possible meanings and available moves found in those contexts. They must have firsthand experience in target culture social interaction in meaningful roles. Once they are equipped with sufficient knowledge of a particular social event, learners can then begin to apply that knowledge while engaging in other similar target culture contexts.

However, being a good observer of culture is only the first step involved in developing cultural competency. Experience in the US/China Links program has shown that without training, most Americans have difficulty taking the cultural perspectives of others. Our in-culture training programs have shown that typical American learners are egocentric: they are focused on what is happening to them as individuals rather than on the people or events around them. However, learners must also develop personal memories of how each target culture context works. Moreover, developing a memory of the target culture works on at least two levels. First, repeated participation in target culture activities allows learners to develop experiential knowledge and achieve deeper understandings of each context until they become veterans who can perform in culturally appropriate ways without first thinking about their actions. Second, learners must *do things* in Chinese in order to develop such personal-level memories; doing things requires learners to create complex memories of the target culture that may sharply contrast with their own base cultural experience and worldview. These memories can then be used to make better-informed guesses when new situations are encountered.

In addition to personal memories of specific contexts, learners must develop an understanding of the cultural stories of those same events that native Chinese share. The cognitive anthropologist Michael Tomasello (1999) has shown that assuming available cultural roles is key in the development of native language and cognitive behavior. A similar pattern holds for the development of communicative and cognitive skills in second languages: to perceive possible intentionality, learners must assume roles found in the culture. Understanding the stories available in the culture provides useful road maps for how a particular context works as well as insights into how members of the culture establish intentions in that type of context. Being equipped with both personal stories of how a context with foreigners involved typically unfolds and the knowledge of Chinese stories of how similar situations should take place allows learners to perfect strategies that they can apply to a broader spectrum of situations.

The approach presented here is based on the ideas of a number of scholars working in a wide spectrum of academic arenas. First, the notion of performance as a mode of understanding drawn from the ideas of Richard Bauman (1977), Victor Turner (1987), and Dell Hymes (1964, 1968, 1974) provides a starting point for approaching learning: because of their social nature, all human activities contain significant elements of performance. In addition to the concept of performance, Michael Cole (1996) contributes the notion of the teleological being, which purports that all actors are intentional agents and that the establishment of their intentions is the key to interaction within a group. Working in the field of cultural psychology, Cole advances the notion that an individual's cognitive framework is formed by group culture through constant adjustment to the group. This insinuates that to successfully interact within a group, one must master how individuals go about creating and learning shared meanings. This is accomplished through intention management, or the interpretation and creation of intentions in ways recognized by the group.

In tune with Cole's notion of culture as a framework for interactions, Jerome Bruner (1956, 1966, 1990, 1996), also a cognitive psychologist, suggests the concept of folk psychology, which explains that culture is an emergent social phenomenon and that culture creates meaning for group members through a process of negotiation with the group. Bruner further argues that human action and experience are shaped by our intentional states and that culture, as a framework of basic default notions that constitute individuals' worldviews, provides contexts within which meaning is generated. This notion of culturally determined frameworks of meaning is crucial when attempting to establish intentions in a foreign culture. To accurately establish one's intentions in a culture, one must negotiate meanings that fit into that culture's shared frameworks of meaning.

Syncing

In *Geography of Thought*, psychologist Richard Nisbett (2003) demonstrates that individuals from different cultures tend to emphasize and value different cognitive skills and that each culture has its own distinct cognitive orientation. Thus, if we assume that each group has a unique set of meanings, the importance of adjusting one's way of interpreting information when interacting with members of a different cultural group comes to the forefront. Additionally, Edward Hall (1966, 1976) forwards the idea that individuals within a group make adjustments to "sync" with each other, a notion that can be understood as a strategy for becoming a member of a group.[3] If individuals native to a group *sync* with the group in order to be recognized by the group, this process should also be a focal point of nonnatives' attempts to integrate themselves into new culture groups. It is in this realm where we can find the negotiation of meaning that Bruner and others point out.

The approach suggested here also requires that individuals be willing to consider learning a new language and learning a new culture to be the same process. This is not a process of losing one's identity; rather it involves learning a new skill set and attempting to organize information in new ways. Language learners should not be learning just the linguistic code a group employs so that they can

---

[3]Here, I adopt Hall's *sync* as a verb referring to the active calibration of meanings and behaviors that individuals make when communicating with others.

engage in a process of translation, mapping, or decoding; they should also be attempting to build new worldviews that incorporate the frameworks of meaning pointed out by the likes of Bruner and Cole. Learners must learn the common stories a culture tells about itself and the knowledge structures used to tell those stories. To learn the knowledge structures that organize the world for the members of a particular culture, learners must actively participate in the contexts of the culture in roles available in that culture. After identifying roles and personas available in the target culture, learners can then begin adjusting behaviors to fit the patterns and rules dictated by the framework of that culture, in a process of constructing and assuming personas that are recognizable to the members of the target group.

Microcultures

The problem then arises that cultures are enormous conglomerations of overlapping groups that may or may not share frameworks of meaning. To determine how to select a group to focus on, we need to turn to Cole's notion that cultures are made up of various subunits, or microcultures, which provide the setting in which individuals obtain culture through the combined processes of enculturation and acculturation (Cole 1996, 301). [4] The notion of microculture is extremely important to language learners because the complexity of a cultural unit as large and diverse as Chinese or American culture necessitates the study of smaller, more manageable units. No one, not even the most educated natives of a culture, is capable of knowing everything about a culture, and no one is capable of becoming an expert in every domain of his or her own culture. Thus, expecting individuals learning a second culture to do the same is unrealistic. Because microcultures provide the smallest and most frequently encountered groups that individuals face and because the

---

[4] Microcultures are associated with places and groups of people who generate patterns of behavior based on repeated interactions. See chapters five and eight for a discussion and examples of microcultures.

shared meanings generated within microcultures are deeply contextualized and relatively stable, language learners should focus their attention on becoming competent in interacting in as many microcultures as possible. Confining attention to microcultures also facilitates access to domain-specific knowledge. Clifford Geertz (1983, 157) has demonstrated that knowledge is bound to domains even within our native culture and that not all members of a culture have equal access to or proficiency in every domain. Howard Gardner (1984, 257) has also shown that domain competence is culturally defined and that each culture values certain competences more than others. This is significant for the foreign language learner because it means advanced skills are possible only in certain domains of the target culture, and those domains that are valued in one's base culture may not be equally important in the target culture.

Simply encountering the microcultures of China, however, is not tantamount to learning the information and behaviors necessary to become a competent participant in Chinese interactions; an individual must also actively participate in the negotiation of meaning that occurs within particular groups. This means that to be recognized by their groups of study, learners must perform; otherwise, those groups will not attempt to incorporate them into their communities. In short, the group, or members of the group, must first see value in interpreting an individual's intentions before they will accept him or her as a participant in in-group activities. Once a group sees value in the individual, it will actively engage in enculturation and socialization processes that help to integrate the new member. The combination of the individual syncing, or adapting to the group, and the group enculturating, or socializing the individual, is key to achieving the deepest levels of cultural understanding and thus the most advanced levels of linguistic competence.

Performed Culture and Culture Games

Working in the area of Chinese language pedagogy and building on the ideas of Bauman, Cole, Bruner, and Turner, Galal Walker (2000) envisions cultural performance as completing a more or less involved process rather than a single deed or act. For Walker, performance is the conscious repetition of staged events, which allows performed culture to be viewed as observable behavior that can be models of actual behavior in the target group. Walker also espouses the notion that there are varying types of cultural performances, including games, or those performances involving a scoring system that provides a means for recognizing winners and losers. [5] By participating in games and becoming a competent player in such games, learners increase the number of tasks they can accomplish in a culture. Games are more global units of cultural analysis around which training can be designed. Because of the dynamic nature of cultural interaction, approaching language learning from the perspective of a game metaphor also prepares learners for changes that will be encountered in the flow of social interaction.

The significance for language learners is that individuals must change the way they are doing things when the game shifts. In other words, there is a different set of rules and a distinct way to play when playing second culture games. Just as a baseball swing on the golf course will not produce desired outcomes, American moves and rules do not apply in Chinese games even when the game is the same general category of game. For example, participating as a guest in an eating event in China while following American rules of dining etiquette will probably leave the impression that one is an arrogant, self-centered, inconsiderate guest no matter how *properly* one thinks he or she is behaving. The event is an eating game but a Chinese one, so American moves do not work and American rules and scoring systems do not apply.

---

[5] Other types of cultural performances include artistic performances.

Banquets as Games

Organized eating events in China can be understood as cultural games because they are situated social events associated with recognized spaces—banquet rooms—dedicated specifically for carrying out related activities. Banquets involve frames of meaning that are distinct from other social events and other types of activities. Moreover, banquets are categories of performances that involve participants in various recognized roles that have been institutionalized over time. That is, banquet goers assume available roles and participate within recognized frames of meaning according to established rules. An understood agreement holds among banquet participants to act in accordance with standards of etiquette and decorum associated with banqueting. Furthermore, participation in banquets is key to becoming part of local social groups, and is integral in accumulating valued community resources. It affects group members' status and their movement within the social order and ultimate success within the group.

Banquets involve prescriptions, [6] explicitly recorded or tacitly understood, for achieving desired goals. There are consequences for not following the conventions associated with such contexts. These *rules* can be spontaneous—in the flow of the game— guides for conduct as well as nongoal-related parameters on play such as the dimensions of the field, where the players are positioned, starting or reference points, what happens when someone does not act appropriately, what equipment is permitted, who is qualified to play, when the game is played, and rewards for achieving goals. In any case, rules associated with eating games are recognized and agreed upon by the players and are the culturally defined praxes that guide and constrain participants' behavior. Banquets, in particular, fit

---

[6] There are sometimes explicit restrictions on what you can do in a culture. There are also things that simply are not possible in a culture and there are things that are not traditionally accepted. There are explicit and implicit rules that guide behavior and there are also explicit restrictions on what one can or cannot do in some cases.

the game metaphor because there is a cultural mechanism[7] that recognizes good and bad performances—a scoring system. An extensive metadiscourse about good and bad performances as well as successful and unsuccessful banquets guides behavior in subsequent events. Finally, banquet behavior involves planned, spontaneous, and strategic moves that allow players to establish intentions and achieve desired goals.

By viewing games as learnable segments of larger cultural events, we are armed with a means to go beyond a single performance. If we equate learning to compiling a memory of an experience and if we view memory as being structured in narrative form, memory becomes the medium through which the one-time or short-term experience of a game is transformed into the long-term experience of sagas, or ongoing systems of games involving multiple microcultures.[8] Because cultures are made up of a number of games, participating in games can be seen as the means through which we become individuals in society. Thus, becoming a competent player in the games of a culture entails compiling a memory of the knowledge—procedural, declarative, and intuitive—associated with those games. Game playing provides a means of accessing the shared reality of the group. The personal stories compiled through game experience can then be called upon to sustain performance in future games.

---

[7] The mechanism is not one that can be seen or touched in most cases. It is shared ideas. We all know who wins and loses. In status games, we all know who gains status, who is liked, who is not, and who is making a fool of themselves. Culture, being part of a group that has shared behavioral patterns and customs that dictates norms, does this. The exact criteria may vary from game to game but other members' reactions to our behavior, our interpretation of what their reactions will probably be, and shared expectations shape our behavior and inform us who wins and loses in any cultural game.

[8] See Bruner (1990, 1996) for the relationship between narrative and memory. *Narrative,* rather than referring to written narrative, is employed here in the sense used by both Bruner and Walker in that individuals organize their experiences in story form. See also Roger Schank (1990). The notion of *saga* comes from Walker's lectures in language pedagogy at The Ohio State University (cf. Walker and Noda, 2000).

Organization and Layout

As mentioned earlier, one purpose of this book is to provide a detailed description of banquet culture that American learners and professionals can use as a practical guide for negotiating such contexts. The first four chapters are written from this perspective and with this goal in mind. However, my experiences—teaching in China, socializing in banquet culture and being trained in pedagogical theory—have also led me to some conclusions about successful approaches to teaching and learning culture. Thus, another purpose of this book is to suggest a perspective for approaching language and culture. I believe that my knowledge of banquet culture is an example of how the performed culture approach works. The behaviors that I have written about here may not all appear to the native as purely Chinese and they certainly should not seem to be typical American behavior. However, they should be recognizable to anyone familiar with Shandong banquets. They are game-specific. The idea is that when interacting in other cultures, one must shift their perspective to that of a player if they are to successfully integrate into that particular culture. The last four chapters of the book are my attempts to theorize about such an approach. Finally, it is also hoped that this work will provide the ancillary benefit of shedding light on social phenomena and modes of thought in Shandong as well as serve as a source of data for Chinese cultural and linguistic analysis.

Guide to Banqueting in Shandong

The first four chapters of this book analyze banqueting, a specific game involved in gaining social status in China's Shandong Province. These chapters provide language learners with a practical example of an individual game as well as an instance of a compiled narrative of a game. The game of banqueting has been selected for its relevance to American learners whose goals are to become successful players in Chinese culture games. The frequency with which foreign actors are faced with this and closely related games while conducting professional, academic, or government-related business in China makes understanding the knowledge involved in such games a prerequisite to successful interaction in Chinese professional contexts.

This first section is also a detailed ethnographic account of professional banqueting in Shandong Province, including modes of participation, rituals of introduction, seating rituals, toasting practices, drinking etiquette and strategies, verbal jousting, eating etiquette, smoking, guesting, and hosting. The works of three scholars in different fields are heavily cited for comparison and explication purposes. Michael Harris Bond (1991), a psychologist who has done extensive work on Chinese personalities, provides insights into the motivations and behaviors of the players in the social status games associated with banquet settings. Anthropologist Mayfair Yang (1994) has conducted work on social relationships and banqueting in Chinese culture, which is used here for comparative purposes to flesh out what is unique to Shandong cultures. Finally, the work of Andrew Kipnis (1997), an anthropologist who has conducted research on banquets in western Shandong, is discussed as the only English-language work dealing with banquets in this specific region.

The highly structured nature of Shandong banquet culture necessitates that participants regularly perform in roles determined by the group in a gamelike setting in order to make moves—establish and interpret intentions—that allow them to be recognized as individuals. In the game of Shandong banqueting, all participants are forced to participate on some level or they are not recognized as having been part of the event. Thus, if an American is going to conduct business in Shandong, he or she will not only frequently encounter this game, but will also be required to participate to some extent.

An additional reason for selecting the game of banqueting in Shandong stems from the cultural importance the region places on doing things in the "correct" manner. That is, Confucian tradition emphasizes the correct performance of ritual social etiquette and values a strict observance of the behaviors associated with that code of etiquette. For foreigners learning to perform in accordance with such behaviors, following the rules of the game explicitly facilitates acquisition. The abundant metadiscourse about social rules also provides insights that serve as a starting point for learners. The fact that the rules of etiquette are more strictly enforced in Shandong than in the same games in other regions of China offers the chance to learn in an environment of strict enforcement. Knowing how to play the game in Shandong's stringent environment facilitates participation in similar games found elsewhere in China where less emphasis is placed on adherence to ritual etiquette. It is easier to adapt behaviors to similar games in the less rigid environments in other regions of China than it would be to become accustomed to participating in environments where learners do not have to adjust their own behavior and then subsequently move to where failure to adjust to the expected behavior has greater social consequences. Combined with the importance of culinary contexts, eating in culturally appropriate ways becomes a survival skill for learners of Chinese. Finally, because of the abundance of ritual performance, Shandong banquets also provide an ideal practical example of a "real-life" game, complete with rules, winners, and losers. If participation in cultural games is the way in which we organize reality and if intentions are the means by which we make meaningful moves in those games, then to integrate ourselves into a new culture or game, we must develop skills necessary for participating in those games.

Chapter One clarifies what is meant by the term "banquet" and provides a description of banquets as events as they have developed over time. Chapter Two begins a discussion of how participation is achieved in banquets and introduces the modes through which some players become recognized and achieve desired goals. Because drinking and eating are the primary modes of play found in banquets, Chapter Three isolates some key concepts and moves necessary for successful participation in any banquet. Chapter Four then analyzes characteristics of speech as a mode of banquet play.

Theorizing About Learning Culture

Following the description of the game of banqueting and the modes of play associated with it, Chapter Five provides a detailed discussion of the concepts of performance and performed culture in order to flesh out a pedagogical approach to learning a second culture. Using ideas put forth by Cole (1996), Bruner (1986, 1990), Turner (1982, 1986, 1987), Roger Schank (1990), and Walker (2000), culture as a framework of meaning within a group is shown to be the basis for dealing with new pieces of knowledge; new information must be interpreted through the appropriate cultural framework to accurately assess intentions or to establish acceptable intentions within the target culture.

To describe the importance of correctly establishing one's intentions within the target cultural framework and to highlight the importance of ensuring that all players are working from the same framework for meaning, Chapter Six addresses the relationship between language and communication. Many practical examples taken from personal experience point out some of the problems that are encountered when communicating in a foreign culture as well as show the inherent difficulty in dealing with such interactions. However, because it is impossible to obtain all of the information involved in a game in a single experience and because learning one game is insufficient for becoming a player in all the games found in any culture, Chapter Seven confronts the notions of learning and memory. The works of Bruner (1986, 1990), Cole (1996), Schank

(1990), and Walker (2000) support the view that memory is story based and is constructed over time by repeated engagements with games followed by rearrangements of worldviews to incorporate the new knowledge encountered in those games.

Chapter Eight explicates the process of becoming a player in a culture game by delineating strategies for both learners and pedagogues. Although each microculture is unique and although every game has its own set of rules, some of the same strategies suggested here will be applicable in other microcultures and/or games.

CHAPTER ONE

The Game: Banqueting in Shandong

Food Is Heaven

In Chinese culture, eating is a way of life. Among other things, enjoying fine cuisine plays an important role in making friends, fostering the goodwill between relatives, showing respect for seniors, maintaining the flow of social relationships, and celebrating the course of daily life. A Chinese proverb sums it up nicely: "For the people, food is heaven, *mín yǐ shí wéi tiān* (民以食为天)." Anthropologists Frederick Simoons (1991) and Kwang-Chih Chang (1977) have noted that the Chinese believe food plays a central role in life. As evidence of the cultural importance of food in China, Simoons cites the wide range of dishes and types of cuisine that exists in China, the elaborate protocol associated with eating contexts, the fact that food is a dominant topic of Chinese conversations, and the presence of typical greetings framed in culinary terms, such as "have you eaten, *chī le ma* (吃了吗)? "

Simoons also has noted that social gatherings in China invariably involve a meal. He cites Arthur Wolf (1974), who has shown that a family's social standing can be discerned according to the people with whom the family will eat, and E. N. Anderson (1988), who argue that in China, the frequency of eating out was traditionally a good barometer of a person's rank in society. Chinese humanist Lin Yutang (1935, 313) also has written that Chinese people consider eating food to be one of the rare joys of living to which they are more devoted than religion or the pursuit of knowledge (Simoons 1991). Factor in the tremendous amount of time and resources expended in preparing for and engaging in eating events in China and it quickly becomes apparent that such events are both important venues of social activity and repositories of folk beliefs.

Eating as Social Events

Chinese culture, particularly Shandong culture, associates positive connotations, notions of group pride, and aspects of identity to hospitality and the entertainment of guests. This is evidenced in the fact that when describing themselves, Shandong people often use phrases such as "warm and hospitable, *rèqíng hàokè* (热情好客)," "straightforward and outspoken, *háoshuǎng* (豪爽)," and "kingdom of etiquette, *lǐyí zhī bāng* (礼仪之邦)." As a result, entertaining guests is a skill that plays a vital role in Shandong social, political, and economic life.

Eating- and drinking-related events are often the forums for entertaining guests. They are used, among other purposes, as both a site and a mechanism for facilitating the flow of social capital, a forum for the exchange of feelings, a means of displaying status, a key to accessing the group, a strategy for managing social relationships, a way to confer face, an instrument of reciprocity, and a method for balancing social harmony. Moreover, prestige, honor, and social status can be associated with successfully conducted culinary engagements. In a context where strict norms of etiquette dictate public interaction, food is a valued cultural artifact, human relationships are emphasized, and a balanced social ledger is the ideal, events associated with eating, drinking, and food hold special social significance. The cultural importance assigned to eating and the significance of eating as a social activity in Chinese cultures are necessary backdrop for an understanding of banqueting in Shandong.

Tradition of Proper Etiquette

As early as the Zhou dynasty (1045–256 B.C.), the *Book of Rites* (礼记), *The Book of Rituals and Etiquette* (仪礼), and the *Rites of Zhou* (周礼) recorded in extensive detail that social activity among virtuous men was governed by strict codes of protocol and that without an understanding of ritual and etiquette, one could not become a functional member of society. *The Book of Rituals and Etiquette* gives detailed instructions for formal behavior and manners including marriage, hospitality, banquets, archery contests, state affairs, audiences with the emperor, mourning rites, and funeral arrangements. The *Book of Rites,* on the other hand, is a comprehensive guide to state administration, compiled in the first century B.C. by Dai De 戴德 and Dai Sheng 戴圣. This compilation enumerates specific procedures for funeral rites, mourning practices, sacrifices, archery contests, ceremonies, weddings, drinking, banquets, state affairs, and the rules of propriety. The presence of these and other classical works indicates that culturally defined norms of etiquette have since very early in Chinese history delineated an intricate web of social roles, spelled out responsibilities associated with those roles, and shaped public behavior and hospitality in China.

The elaborate codes of etiquette in the *Book of Rites* that dictate the structure of banquets and drinking also indicate that as early as the Zhou dynasty, banquets were recognized forums in which professional and social transactions were carried out. They were held, among other reasons, to entertain guests, express gratitude, affirm friendships, and celebrate special occasions. It is also readily apparent that from early on, the focus has been on the participants and their interaction rather than on the acts of eating and drinking: literally, "not to focus on eating and drinking, but to implement the rituals, *fēi zhuān wèi chī hē yě, wèi xíng lǐ yě* (非专为

吃喝也, 为行礼也)."[1] Etiquette and ritual were seen as modes in which gentleman, *jūnzi* (君子), interacted, and banquets were the format in which these modes were actualized. Examples of banquets are ubiquitous in traditional Chinese literature. Much of the action in three of China's four great novels—*Romance of the Three Kingdoms, Dream of the Red Chamber, and Water Margin*—takes place in or revolves around banquets. In Chinese, banquets have been variously labeled "entertainment seat, *yànxí* (宴席)," "mat and seat, *yánxí* (筵席)," "alcoholic entertainment, *jiǔyàn* (酒宴)," and "entertainment gatherings, *yànhuì* (宴会)," with the most common contemporary term being the latter. Although eating events have undergone significant changes over time, the elaborate traditions surrounding banquets provide the cultural backdrop that frames contemporary Shandong eating events. When asked to summarize Chinese hospitality for a reference work, I wrote the following:

> As China moves into the twenty-first century and social relationships continue to deepen in complexity, acknowledging hierarchy, knowing one's place in the social dynamic, reciprocating, exchanging *gǎnqíng* (feelings), and maintaining social harmony are still behaviors recognized and maintained through the Chinese system of etiquette. These behaviors constitute a large part of the repertoire of skills socially competent Chinese draw on to manage interpersonal relationships and are, therefore, an integral part of hospitality and social life. (Shepherd 2002)

Chen Si (1996), author of a contemporary book on social engagement in Chinese culture, states that banquets are an important form of interpersonal interaction, and anthropologist Mayfair Yang (1994, 137) notes, "Banqueting in Chinese culture is not merely a

---

[1] *Lijì, Xiang yin jiu yi* (礼记: 乡饮酒义).

tactic in the art of *guanxi*, but it is also an important ritual in the social sphere." Yang further characterizes banqueting as "a medium of not only social, but especially economic and political exchange." These statements point to the important role that banquets still serve as a ritual forum for social, economic, and political interaction in Chinese culture. As such, banquets are often an arena in which the game of gaining social status takes place (see chapter 5). In post-2000 Shandong, banquets are still conducted with a varying array of underlying purposes:

> to welcome a friend home or see him off on a journey
> to gain or give face
> to introduce two or more unfamiliar parties
> to establish and strengthen relationships
> to reaffirm familial ties
> to request assistance
> to reciprocate for help received
> to celebrate important occasions such as weddings,
>   holidays and promotions
> to express gratitude
> to repair strained relationships
> to get together with friends and consume rare foods
>   and fine spirits.

Regional Variation

Because of its vast size and enormous population, China is characterized by tremendous cultural variation and regional diversity. As a result, it is useful when dealing with cultural China to think of "China" as a plural noun, meaning that there are many Chinese regional subcultures that to greater or lesser degrees maintain general underlying themes and values. Many scholars have noted that the numerous minority ethnic and cultural subgroups inhabiting much of China's periphery often maintain distinct social practices, but Western scholarship has overlooked the tremendous regional diversity that exists within and across Han-dominated areas of China. This regional diversity is particularly evident in the behavioral realms of etiquette and eating customs. The degree to which traditional protocol in the entertainment of guests is adhered to in developed, urban centers such as Beijing and Shanghai varies drastically from that found in conservative, rural areas such as Shandong and much of inland China. Banquets in public settings in southern Cantonese culture often are forums for reaffirming familial bonds, whereas individuals from northern Chinese cultures such as that found in Shandong rarely expend family resources for hospitality of in-group members except during major events such as weddings. Similarly, the amount and type of alcohol consumed, the foods eaten, and the procedures of etiquette found at a banquet conducted in centrally located Wuhan certainly differ from what one might observe in coastal Shenzhen. That is not to suggest that eating events and social protocol in other regions of China is any less important or complex. The idea is that the underlying theme of attention to the shared flow of feelings is the same, but the manner in which people go about accomplishing that goal varies from place to place. In the Shanghai region, for example, there is less pressure to drink, and the banquet atmosphere is more subdued than the raucous northern banquets examined here. However, hosts pour drinks for their guests and place food on their guests' plates. Participants make toasts, take food from the edge of dishes rather than from the center, refrain from eating the last portion of a dish, try not to eat too fast, avoid infringing on the hosts' role as controllers of the event, and attempt to establish and maintain relationships during the banquet. The suggestion here is merely that because Shandong banquets have been less influenced by regional and international interaction, they maintain more traces of traditional cultural patterns of behavior.

Shandong Banquets

"From 8 to 5, I read the paper. From 5 to 9, I get things done." This quote stated to me by a local government official in response to my query about the reason for the frequency and importance of banquets reflects both the tremendous amount of time professionals spend in banquet rooms consuming scrumptious delicacies and fine spirits and the social importance assigned to banquets in Shandong, a densely populated (population in 2003 was 91 million), culturally conservative province located on China's northeastern coast best known as the home of Confucius, Tsing-tao Beer, and the home appliance juggernaut Haier. In Shandong, banquets are large-scale cultural performances involving copious amounts of food and spirits that serve as the primary venue for the management of *guānxi* (关系), or interpersonal relationships. [2] Banquets are a form of social interaction that is still ubiquitous in Shandong culture: some professionals are forced to attend as many as three or four banquets in a single day.

Shandong banquets are also what Erving Goffman (1959, 9-10) has called focused gatherings. That is, there is a "set of persons engrossed in a common flow of activity and relating to one another in terms of that flow." It is true that the participants of banquets fluctuate—it is rare to have the same participants at multiple banquets—and no two banquets unfold in exactly the same manner. However, because the participants are members of the same community and thus are situated in the same hierarchical web of

---

[2] The concept of *guānxi* includes a multiplicity of meanings as well as corresponding discourses related to those meanings. Two of the more frequently encountered meanings: first, *guānxi* as "connections," which carries negative connotations associated with corruption, nepotism, personal gain, and unethical behavior; second, *guānxi* as "interpersonal relationships," which carries positive connotations associated with friendship, shared experience, closeness of sentiment, group loyalty, and brotherhood. The focus here is on the latter meaning, which is referred to as "interpersonal relationships." For more on *guānxi,* see Mayfair Yang's (1994) *Gifts, Favors, and Banquets: The Art of Social Relationships in China* and Andrew Kipnis's (1997) *Producing Guanxi: Sentiment, Self, and Subculture in a North China Village.* "Management of *guānxi*" suggests that in the Chinese context, significant time and effort are spent establishing, strengthening, repairing, and maintaining large, complex networks of interpersonal relationships. The best Chinese language book on *guānxi* from a practical perspective is Jingsheng Ren's (2003) *Cong dong dao xi kan guanxi.*

relationships, rather than thinking of banquets solely as a process that recurs independently of previous events, it is more useful to think of banquets as part of a more global network of multiple processes.

Because Shandong banquet goers are all part of the same sociopolitical circles, what happens at one banquet may affect what happens in another. Discussion at banquets frequently includes comments such as: "I heard *this* happened at *that* banquet." "I heard you drank ten bottles of beer when you were with Zhang San, so you should drink at least that amount now to show your sincerity." "Will you tell story 'x' again?" Additionally, the cultural emphasis placed on reciprocity requires that participants remember in minute detail what other hosts have done for them, how much money has been spent, and what they liked to eat, drink, and do. This is vital information so that guests are able to return in kind in a timely manner. It is of note that Shandong people feel extremely uncomfortable when the social ledger of accounts is out of balance in someone else's favor. The ledger is never in balance for people from Shandong. It is either out of balance in favor of other people or out of balance in favor of you. Even if you reciprocate for something done, it is important to try to do a little more than what was done for you to tip the scales the other way. The important thing for Shandong people is to never allow the ledger to be in someone else's favor, to never be in debt to someone else. Some people even attempt—the other parties try not to accept or they do everything they can to tip the scales back as soon as possible—to place as many people in their debt as possible so that they can call upon them for assistance in times of need, but tend to reciprocate as soon as possible so that they themselves are not in debt to others. In fact, many how-to books on interpersonal relationships and social etiquette suggest this as a desirable strategy for social advancement, described as "learning how to take a loss, *xuéhuì chīkuī* (学会吃亏)." Shandong people also often try to "one-up" what others have done for them to tip the scales in their favor, a practice that creates a vicious cycle requiring the expenditure of increasingly large amounts of social capital.

Professional Banquets

In addition to a variety of purposes for banquets, there are myriad banquet types. Banquet types in Shandong can be roughly organized into three major categories: professional, casual, and celebratory. Because they are the most frequently encountered type of banquets for foreigners operating in China, the focus here is primarily on the professional variety, which differs in size and level of formality from the casual (among in-group friends) and celebratory (weddings, holidays, promotions, and birthdays). "Professional" indicates those social events engaged in by businesspeople and government officials during the conduct of job-related and social transactions (Yang 1994). This type of banquet differs inherently from casual banquets, which commonly involve intimate friends and are usually less elaborate, smaller in scale, and less formal. Participants in casual banquets tend to ignore or only cursorily observe ritual aspects such as seat taking and formal toasting that are frequently found in other types of banquets. Professional banquets also differ in nature from celebratory banquets, which are held for weddings, holidays, or birthdays (Kipnis 1997). Celebratory banquets are festive occasions that involve large numbers of people in open settings, which are conducted in large open areas such as the dining room of a restaurant where others not necessarily involved in the banquet may be present or may pass through. This type of setting contrasts with the closed setting of professional banquets, which are usually more controlled: because they involve fewer people—typically five to twelve people—interacting in private rooms in the large hotels or in the back of restaurants. Such settings create an event in which people not involved in the banquet cannot enter as they please because there are doors and walls separating them from "the crowd".

In Shandong, the flow of social, economic, and political capital hinges on what happens in professional banquets. Although status and relationships can be gained or lost during casual and celebratory banquets, professional banquets are both the public stage for performance and the principal mechanism for accumulating reliable *guānxi* by people in key positions who have access to resources and who can be called upon in times of need. This process of *relationship maintenance* is a socially accepted and culturally recognized means of gaining social status. In describing Balinese cockfights, Clifford Geertz (1973, 417) notes, "As much of America surfaces in a ball park, on a golf links, at a race track, or around a poker table, much of Bali surfaces in a cock ring." Similarly, banquets, as a repository of Shandong folk ideas and behaviors, tell us a great deal about local social norms and practices. As a microcosm of Shandong society, banquets are conducted with particular emphasis on conforming to the proper norms of etiquette, with themes of modesty, sincerity, and mutual respect framing behavior.

Banquets as Entertainment

In addition to being arenas in which social status is won and lost, banquets serve as a form of entertainment, especially when held to host foreign guests and business clients or when arranged for holidays and festivals. Eric Barnouw and Catherine Kirkland (1992, 50-52) define entertainment as an event intended to absorb the attention of the audience and to leave them with agreeable feelings. In Chinese culture, there is a tradition of combining eating, drinking, and entertainment that dates at least to the early imperial period when emperors and court officials engaged in large-scale, festive activities involving food, drink, and professional entertainers. In contemporary Shandong, where there are very few other options for entertainment (although this is changing rapidly), banquets serve as one context in which participants can escape from the reality of long, hard workdays and the complex, pressure-filled interpersonal relationships of the workplace.

The role of banquets as entertainment also reflects recent social trends. Because many Chinese organizations exhausted significant amounts of public resources to finance extravagant banquets during the 80's and 90's, banquets and the notion of *qǐngkè* (请客), or entertaining guests, have come to be associated with waste and corruption. In the recent past, most firms and government agencies had personnel whose sole responsibility was to handle what is referred to as *gōngguān* (公关), or public relations, and much of the money spent on banquets was *gōngkuǎn* (公款), or public funds. The focus of public relations work is tending to the relationships of an organization, and banquet rooms are where much of this work takes place. Many *gōngguān* workers are hired specifically for their banqueting skills, and nearly all companies allocate significant portions of their budget to maintaining relationships. However, in response to complaints about Party corruption, public funds have been more tightly controlled in recent years. Additionally, many banqueters are beginning to feel that the number and frequency of banquets are actually a burden (in terms of time, resources, and health), and sufficient alternative sources of entertainment such as movies, bowling alleys, VCDs, malls, and discos are becoming available. However, restaurants around Shandong consistently remain filled with banquet goers.

Banquets as Performances

In addition to being forums for maintaining relationships and a form of entertainment, Shandong professional banquets are also cultural performances. This is true on at least two levels. First, on the macro-event level, banquets are elaborate productions that involve the five criteria commonly associated with cultural performances: (1) specified time, (2) specified place, (3) recognized roles, (4) scripts, and (5) audience (Bauman, 1977). Second, to view a banquet as a single performance would be to ignore that it is composed of numerous smaller-scale performances; Victor Turner (1987) has referred to these compositional performances as "cultural media." On the sub-event level, participants of Shandong banquets interact in various cultural media when they toast, speak, sing, take their seats, or engage in any of a number of culturally defined modes of communication.

Because sub-event performances often involve an individual performing before a small group, they are extremely personal in nature. Performing at this level requires both revealing something about oneself to the group and sharing in the experience of the group. Exposing part of oneself in a public setting can be quite an unnerving experience; this is especially the case with novice performers who have yet to develop strategies for coping with this form of stage fright.

Performing breaks down barriers between unfamiliar participants because it shows a willingness to reveal or share a part of themselves with the group. It also shows that they are willing to take a risk on behalf of the group and are not trying to hide anything from the group. By performing, the person makes a commitment to the group, which is what Michael Harris Bond (1991) labels an act of trust. Thus, because interpersonal relationships are based on intimacy and trust, a revealing performance is often the first step in developing a new relationship. In this way, performances serve as a basis for further interaction. In Shandong culture, where the default approach to interpersonal interaction involves elaborate self-protection mechanisms and revealing only as much about oneself in public situations as is absolutely necessary, self-revealing performances carry added significance.

Shared experience also creates and enhances interpersonal bonds. In the banquet context, performance reduces the gaps that exist between participants by integrating them into the group at the same time that it differentiates individual performers —when they perform, individuals contribute to the group atmosphere while displaying their unique styles and abilities (Babcock, 1977).

Banquets as Games

As culturally valued social performances involving players engaged in complex moves toward recognized goals within the framework of agreed-upon rules on a predetermined playing field and governed by a shared scoring system that determines successful and unsuccessful performances, banquets provide a concrete example of what is discussed later as a culture game. The frameworks of meaning associated with and created by game play create order for the participants and generate shared social reality distinct from any other Chinese reality. Natives who frequently attend banquets have internalized a version of the cultural rulebook, although the skills and knowledge associated with banquets are clearly behaviors learned by natives through trial and error participation in such events. [3] Therefore, experienced banqueters not only know the rules, but by playing, they also agree to follow them. In addition, more experienced players have developed meta-discourses about those rules. Banquets, it is important to note, differ from other types of culture games in that play is not always voluntary. That is, there are cultural repercussions for not playing. For government officials and businesspeople in Shandong, failing to frequently attend banquets

---

[3] In Shandong culture, parents take measures to protect children, especially students, from the ills of society, so even college-age students frequently lack a deep understanding of how these settings work and the rules associated with them. Children may have general event schemas about banquets stored in memory—they know many of the reasons for banquets and what general themes may be if they have attended similar occasions with their parents—but young people learn the specifics once they leave the university and begin professional life. The head of the human resources department in a large state-run conglomerate in Shandong once suggested to me that after their company receives new employees, it typically takes approximately two years before those employees are fully-functioning contributors to the company. He stated the complexity of interpersonal relationships and the difficulty of handling banquet settings as two of the reasons for this long transition period.

leads to missing out on the social action. They must attend in order to stay in the information loop as well as to maintain relationships with people of status and controllers of key valued resources. Not attending key banquets with socially powerful people can also cause people from Shandong to lose face. In situations where invitations have been extended, failure to attend is a direct affront to the host's face regardless of whether the reason for not attending is beyond one's control. In cases where people have been requested to serve as escorts, failure to attend signals that one is undependable and/or is unwilling to sacrifice for others. Finally, subordinates are frequently given explicit orders to attend banquets by their superiors in the government and/or companies.

The scoring system in this particular game entails rewards for success that come in the form of ease in conducting affairs through continued relationships, recognition by the group, and potentially in the form of economic gains. In other words, through the efficacious management of interpersonal relationships, an individual is capable of accessing the resources valued by the group. Hwang Kwang-Kuo (in Bond, 1988, 215) analyzes the manipulation of these relationships in the following terms: "The Chinese cultural norm of *li* demands that an individual interact with people across different *guanxi* in accordance with various standards of social exchange. Thus the manipulation of interpersonal relationships has long been a strategy for attaining desirable social resources in Chinese society." As one gains more social status, the influence associated with that status increases, which, in turn, provides the means to accomplish other goals more easily than would otherwise be possible. *Guānxi* can be both a means to and a result of social status. In sum, knowing the right people can help a person get ahead and, once ahead, others will want to associate with him or her because of the status that they have achieved.

The game of social status also has mechanisms for marking unsuccessful performances. These mechanisms most often come in the form of rejection or ridicule from the group or failure to achieve one's goals. Without social status, it is extremely difficult to accomplish any task within the society. However, participating in status-generating games is risky: one must be willing to suffer the consequences of losing, which can be emotionally devastating.

Modes of Play

There are myriad modes of play available to banqueters, including hosting, guesting, drinking, eating, singing, speaking, smoking, joke telling, verbal jousting, dancing, and storytelling, that are addressed in chapters 2 and 3. Banqueters all have designated roles and expectations about which modes of play are appropriate for those roles. Roles also have recognized responsibilities attached to them: hosts are expected to include everyone in the interaction, guests must participate to maintain the harmony of the event so as not to damage the face of the host, and escorts are invited for the express purposes of entertaining guests and assisting in the construction of mirthful atmospheres.

What is of significance is that all of the available roles require participation in the shared event. Nonparticipation is not an option if participants do not wish to pollute the atmosphere or create what is called a "cold situation, *lěngchǎng* (冷场)." At banquets I attended where banqueters chose not to perform, other participants attempted to include them in a variety of ways, such as through toasts, conversation, and requests for performances. This was especially the case for hosts, whose responsibilities include involving everyone in the action. When attempts to adapt the interaction to accommodate nonparticipants failed, those individuals were often ignored.

Many foreigners operating in Shandong approach banquets as if they worked in the same fashion as Western dinners. They participate when and how they wish to failing to realize the need to fundamentally adjust their modes of participation. This is precisely what got my American students in trouble while they were in Shandong. They just ate (and only what they liked) as they would in America. They did not change their American way of participating in an eating event even if when they spoke they were using Chinese grammatical structures. They did not engage the other participants in culturally recognized ways so hosts often did not even remember them being present. When they did hosts thought that they were not being good hosts because their guests were not participating in the festivities even though they were there and were eating. Still other hosts categorized American banqueters who did not partake in the action in expected ways as "ugly Americans" who saw themselves and their behavioral patterns as more sophisticated than those found in China. In the eyes of Shandong people, if participants do not banquet in a Shandong manner, which involves extensive verbal interplay, partaking of everything presented, toasting, verbal jousting, singing, dancing, and being part of the collective flow of feelings, they are seen as not having participated by natives of Shandong even if they were present physically. Post-banquet interviews I conducted with hosts revealed at least three views of guests who failed to participate: Some hosts remembered nonparticipating guests precisely because they did not participate. Of these hosts, some were concerned that they may have been inadequate hosts. Others believed the nonperforming guests did not wish to interact with them. Still others believed that nonparticipants were unable or unwilling to participate on the group's terms. Worse yet, some hosts did not even remember guests who failed to participate in recognized modes. These reactions suggest that performing is the primary means through which individuals become recognized as participants in banquet interaction.

The importance of this point was revealed to me when a close friend, an experienced Shandong banqueter, attended an American-style party at another friend's apartment in Beijing. She repeatedly commented on the party's lack of exchange of human feelings and concluded that American parties "lacked the flavor of human feelings, *méi-yǒu rénqíng wèir* (没有人情味儿)." The fact that people stood around chatting in groups of two also struck her. She said she sensed a huge gap in feelings, *gǎnqíng* (感情), between partygoers. To her, there was no order and no group. As a result, she had difficulty determining the roles of the participants, including who the host was. This participant felt that there was nothing for her to be a part of.

The above story reveals a cultural difference frequently ignored by Americans who interact with Chinese. Americans don't see the necessity to generate personal bonds with everyone who attends a party. We may have a small group within the group and our attention is typically focused on maintaining interpersonal bonds with those people. In Shandong banquets, however, there cannot be "a group within the group (or at least it is not proper etiquette to allow such distinctions to be observed by others)." Banquets are collective endeavors. Banquet goers partake of the collective flow of feelings that they see as the point of holding such a gathering. It's not about the drinking, smoking, dancing, singing, eating, or talking. The whole point is to partake of this flow of feelings among all participants. Americans don't view parties in the same manner, at least, based on the observations of the banqueter mentioned above. The point is that in Shandong participation is only recognized in distinct modes and those modes differ from participatory modes in similar events in American culture. Most Americans operating in Chinese culture at best stop at this level of awareness. However, to be successful in Shandong culture it is not enough to merely be aware of cultural differences. Americans—anyone not from the area for that matter—must make changes in the way they do things to incorporate interaction techniques recognizable to Shandong people. On numerous occasions I have observed Chinese from other areas of China who failed to adjust their behavior while conducting business in Shandong. In such situations I have heard them offer statements of frustration that they cannot get things done in Shandong and I have also heard negative remarks made about them by locals after their departure.

Mirthful Atmospheres

At a successful banquet, the goal of all participants is to facilitate the creation of a harmonious event with a positive collective effervescence—Durkheim's (1995) term for the increased intensity of interactions and feeling of the more powerful force of the collectivity over the individual that occurs when individuals come together and perform the same activity. A similar phenomenon is associated with banquets in Shandong and is described emically as a "lively atmosphere, *huóyuè qìfen* (活跃气氛)." Such an atmosphere is associated with a festive, mirthful occasion that facilitates personal interaction and the flow of *gǎnqíng* (感情). A mirthful atmosphere involves a group of people sharing an experience of belonging to a whole greater than the sum of its parts. All participants partake of the event, and there is an exchange of positive feelings among participants that fosters a sense of connectedness.

Durkheim (1995) noted similar phenomena in Western social contexts such as concerts and religious revival meetings, and the notion can be extended to football and NCAA tournament games. He described the feeling of being carried away by a group spirit as the collective effervescence of an event. In Shandong banquets, the likelihood of creating a positive collective effervescence and a mirthful atmosphere is extremely high, because multiple modes of atmosphere creating can coexist. Both the importance of creating mirthful atmospheres and the ease with which they can be created in the banquet setting explain, in part, the frequency with which Shandong people engage in banqueting. Furthermore, if the group doesn't recognize an individual as a member, he or she does not "exist" in terms of the group. Thus framed, the various modes of play are also modes of existence (Foley 1990).

Depth of Play

In addition to the game-like characteristics mentioned here, banquets involve a hierarchy of intensity that ranges from casual engagement to deeply intense emotional involvement, described in Shandong by terms such as "casual, *suíbiàn* (随便)," "happy, *gāoxìng* (高兴)," and "dynamic, *huóyuè* (活跃)."[4] It is the host who ultimately determines where a particular banquet will fall on this scale and guests must adapt their behavior accordingly. Although Shandong banquets do not involve monetary gambling, Clifford Geertz's (1973, 431) notion of *deep play* seems to be a particularly appropriate description. Participants in *deep play* banquets do gamble social capital; in particular, they risk face, reputation, and status.[5] Unlike in Geertz's "deep play" cockfights where status is at stake only symbolically and where no one's status is actually altered by the outcome of a cockfight, banquet goers can (*and do*) lose or gain the favor of key controllers of and gatekeepers to social resources, which can result in losing or gaining actual social status based on their performances in Shandong banquets.

Participants in Shandong banquets determine the depth of significance of the event—that is, whether to participate, the amount of effort they exert, the amount of preparation time, and how much they drink—based on the possibility of gaining or losing social status. This depth of significance is also reflected by the amount and types of foods served, the amount of preparation time, resources—

---

[4] In Shandong, "dynamic, *huóyuè* (活跃)" is pronounced similarly to the term for "gunpowder, *huǒyào* (火药)" with only a difference in tone on the first syllable, so there is an interesting play on words that banqueters employ to describe the raucous—sometimes explosive—atmosphere characteristic of banquets in the region.

[5] It should be noted that banquets in Shandong are missing the violence and aggression found in cockfights, even though aggression occasionally exerts itself in the heat of drinking wars. However, the local code of etiquette mandates the control of emotions in public. Aggression and excess in public settings are negative attributes in most Chinese cultures.

money, connections, social debts incurred—expended on the activity, duration of the event, the time of the event, and the guests invited. In terms of drinking, the hierarchy involves different types of spirits and a different pace and intensity of drinking depending on who is present. In terms of status, the hierarchy of intensity is played out in seating rituals, rituals for ordering food (see chapter 2), linguistic registers, and ceremonial toasting. Attempts to move the event toward a deeper level of meaning, intensity, and involvement often involve collective or inclusive performances, such as group toasts. An example of a common inclusive toast is described in local parlances as "conducting the electricity, *guòdiàn* (过电)." In such a toast, participants tap their glasses on the rotating table (or Lazy Susan) in a symbolic gesture of coming together before drinking; the connection of all of the glasses on the table at the same time is supposed to allow the feelings to flow among participants in the same way that electricity passes through a conductor. Alternate forms of this ritual include "stamping the seal, *gài zhāng* (盖章)," from a period before widespread electricity and referring to the traditional use of official stamps to legitimate any official document, and "getting on the net, *shàng wǎng* (上网)," which appeared after the Internet was imported from the West and is used as a metaphor for linking in a network of feelings as if the parties involved were connected on line.

The depth of significance is also reflected in the language used to talk about banquets. A banquet connected with social responsibilities that require a reluctant player's attendance and perceived as a burden might be described as a "social engagement, *yìngchóu* (应酬)". Social acquaintances that players frequently encounter during those activities are described as "meat and liquor friends, *jiǔ ròu péngyou* (酒肉朋友)" because the bond that ties them together is the banquet table. Conversely, banquets that an individual attends willingly and enthusiastically are commonly described as "activities, *huódòng* (活动)," "eating, *chī fàn* (吃饭)," or "get togethers, *jùhuì* (聚会)," and involve "good friends and relatives, *qīnpéng hǎoyǒu* (亲朋好友)" and "intimate friends, *zhījǐ* (知己)."

Flow of Feelings

In Shandong, an important cultural theme revolves around the phatic bonds (*gǎnqíng*) that govern interpersonal relationships (*guānxi*). This cultural importance ensures that the processes through which such shared feelings or sentiment are constructed, *jiànlì gǎnqíng* (建立感情), and the exchange of those feelings over time, *gǎnqíng jiāoliú* (感情交流), comprise a large portion of interpersonal interactions in every social realm. Interpersonal distinguishes these types of exchanges from the interaction between parties engaged in professional transactions involved in the government and business world, which are not always viewed as exchanges of feelings. Business exchanges conducted between individuals that do not involve feelings are referred to negatively as "transactions, *jiāoyì* (交易)." In Shandong, relationships work differently than they do in America. The social and professional spheres of life are much more closely intertwined than in the US where we have work worlds and private lives that can be quite distinct. As mentioned above, people in Shandong view themselves as nodes in a societal network—a hierarchical web—of relationships that is present and must be tended at all times. As soon as a person from Shandong walks into a room, he or she quickly assesses the both the relationships present and the hierarchy that exists in the room. That information then dictates how one should speak and act. If someone leaves the room or someone new enters, then a reassessment takes place and the hierarchy shifts.[6]

---

[6] Even intimate friends and relatives are ranked hierarchically based on age, which is reflected in and acknowledged through the use of titles such as "older sister, *dàjiě* (大姐)," "older brother, *dàgē* (大哥)," "younger brother, *dìdi* (弟弟)," "younger sister, *mèimei* (妹妹)," "second brother, *èrgē* (二哥)," "third sister, *sānjiě* (三姐)," "oldest uncle (paternal), *dàshū* (大叔)," "third uncle, *sānjiù* (maternal), (三舅)," "uncle (father's older brother), *dàda* (大大)," and "uncle (father's younger brother), *èrda* (二大)." Children are indoctrinated into this web of relationships early and

There can and are relationships that do not involve personal feelings (*gănqíng*) but in the professional sphere, people in Shandong prefer to conduct business with people they trust and they trust those with whom they have established *gănqíng*. I have been told on countless occasions that locals would rather take a deal with a friend that would make less money than accept one with a stranger that would make more. Of course, some of this is cultural pride that tends to get exaggerated but the point is that locals in Shandong trust those with whom they have personal relationships that have withstood the test of time and that have been fostered through shared experiences and interaction. Moreover, whether or not two individuals have such bonds between them is a major factor in determining whether or not a person from Shandong will continue interacting with someone as well as how they will go about that interaction. This includes business transactions, political exchanges, and academic cooperation. Banquets are one mechanism used to achieve these desired relationship states and because of time constraints they are sometimes used to speed up the process of developing relationships.

An example is when one of my former students was working as a sales intern in a local Internet company. She and a coworker had a lunch banquet with a prospective client during which they hoped to

---

often. Every time they accompany their parents during interactions their parents tell them to verbally acknowledge people using the appropriate title in the hierarchy in an exchange such as:

> Parent: "Say hello to uncle (literally 'call uncle'), *jiào shūshu* (叫叔叔)."
> Child: "Hello, uncle, *shūshu hăo* (叔叔好)."

These terms are used in the fictive sense as polite titles for both acquaintances and strangers so that *shūshu* is used as a generic title for men the same age as one's father, *āyí* (阿姨), for women one's mother's age, *dàgē* for young men (usually the same age or older but occasionally for those slightly younger as a means of showing added respect), *dàjiě* for middle aged women, *dàyí* (大姨), for women one's grandmother's age, dàyé (大爷), for men one's grandfather's age. Children are commonly addressed as "little friend, *xiăo péngyou* (小朋友), "young little brother, *xiăo dìdi* (小弟弟)" and "young little sister, *xiăo mèimei* (小妹妹)" by those older than them.

sell their company service package to the manager of a local company. During the course of the banquet, my student went out of her way to do the little things necessary to show she both understood local norms of etiquette and that she was interested in becoming friends with the manager. At the end of the banquet, the manager told her that although he had not planned on purchasing any services when he came to the banquet, he would purchase the most expensive package because he had come to like her during the course of the banquet.

Gǎnqíng (感情) refers to the sentiments between and among people (or between a person and a place) that play an integral role in interpersonal relationships. *Gǎnqíng* are generated through phatic interaction that builds trust and combine with *miànzi* (面子) to form the basis of any relationship in the Shandong context. When two people meet for the first time, no *gǎnqíng* exists between them because of an emotional or interpersonal gap. The state is described as "having no feelings, *méi-yǒu gǎnqíng* (没有感情)." That is, the individuals have no "ascribed commonality" (Yeung and Tung 1996). Mayfair Yang (1994, 140-1) refers to the same notion as "the gap between the inside and the outside." She employs the term "transformation" to describe the bridging of the gap between the inside and outside that occurs when two people "have feelings, *yǒu le gǎnqíng* (有了感情)" or have "built feelings, *jiànlì le gǎnqíng* (建立了感情)." In Shandong, good relationships cannot and do not exist without *gǎnqíng,* and people with whom one does not share *gǎnqíng* do not exist within the one's in-group world. That is, one has no social or moral obligation to such people. Thus, there is no need to apologize to strangers you bump into in public settings such as bus and train stations because they are not members of your circle of feelings.

Investing Feelings

Although *gǎnqíng* can simply happen between two people who share an experience, most often, *gǎnqíng* are consciously developed and nurtured to in a process referred to as a "feeling investment, *gǎnqíng tóuzī* (感情投资)," in which both parties commit to the relationship in some way, whether it be emotionally, monetarily, with actions, or in time. Once two people have *gǎnqíng*, they are recognized as individuals[7] and exist within a shared in-group. In the early, shallow stages of *gǎnqíng* development, these new acquaintances are treated with politeness devices such as honorific titles and phrases such as "please, *qǐng* (请)," and "thank you, *xièxie* (谢谢)." They are also complimented and told what they want to hear. This often is a stage of feeling out when participants determine if others are worthy of deeper investments in feelings. Later, once they are accepted as members of the in-group, individuals are treated with direct comments, brutal honesty, strong support, extreme loyalty, and offers for assistance that come even before assistance is requested. Thus, in-groups emerge from collective performances, are formed by people who have developed *gǎnqíng* created through everyday interaction, or among people who are united by common interest. If they are unaware of the cause, foreigners interacting with Chinese tend to find this shift from polite acquaintance to in-group member frustrating, unnerving, or shocking because it may entail sudden direct demands or harsh criticism intended to help make them better people.

Displays of Sincerity

It is only after both sides have displayed sincerity, *chéngyì* (诚意), that a relationship can move to the next deeper stage and true *gǎnqíng* can be exchanged. This notion of displaying *chéngyì* is critical to developing reliable, long-term relationships in the

---

[7] These people as individuals are recognized as participants in the interaction of the group and as personalities unique from others in the group.

Shandong context. Displays of sincerity can be accomplished in numerous ways, including through verbal statements backed up by actions. That is, declarations of sincerity are not enough. In Shandong culture, words are seen as carrying less weight than actions so a banquet goer may make a claim that he or she views the bond with another person as a bond of friendship but then he or she must do something to show that he or she is sincere such as filling his glass with beer and drinking the entire thing in one drink. Or, he or she must take other measures to prove his or her sincerity such as pouring drinks for others or revealing something about him or herself. Other examples of actions that can be displays of sincerity include giving gifts, providing assistance, expressing inner feelings, revealing personal information, and harming one's self on the behalf of another person. A local proverb best expresses the spirit underlying such displays of sincerity—to show sincerity in interpersonal interactions one must be willing to go to extreme lengths: "Cut out two ribs for a friend, *wèi péngyou liǎng lèi chā dāo* (为朋友两肋插刀)."

In brief, building *gǎnqíng* involves making a human connection or creating commonalities that serve as points of reference for developing personal relationships. This can be done only through shared experience and often is achieved only through prolonged personal interaction. Although the conscious desire to construct feelings with a range of people is strong, according to Shandong cultural norms, maintaining interpersonal distance is a commonly employed self-protection strategy when interacting with out-groupers. Moreover, maintaining distance also is a culturally coded signal that one does not desire to develop deeper feelings with another person.

Field of Play
Before discussing what is involved in banquet action, I must add a word or two about where these dramas unfold. I have attended

banquets in a wide range of restaurants and hotels, but because banqueting is a means for displaying one's social status, professional banquets most often take place in expensive restaurants. One characteristic that remained consistent, even if the quality of the restaurant varied, was that banquets always took place in a private room called a *dānjiān* (单间). These private rooms serve as locus for banquet play while molding the events that occur within their confines. *Dānjiān* are always isolated from the public eye and from the noise of large dining rooms. Thus, they are frequently situated in the private upper levels and rear areas of restaurants. This simple fact speaks volumes about the role of banquets in determining status: it is extremely important for banquet guests to be separated from regular customers in this way. Even in situations in which my host was not able to afford a banquet at an expensive restaurant, he would perform a ritual of arranging a private room, which often entailed loudly stating that he had a foreign guest to entertain and therefore needed the best available room.

In Shandong, this type of behavior is elevated to a level of importance that distinguishes it from merely "putting on a show" or "making a production." It is behavior that is part of a set of responsibilities associated with the host role and must be performed—completed—for all important guests. There is a prescribed cultural script for carrying out such acts and the addition of the foreigner merely increases the importance of carrying out the act.

In more extravagant restaurants, private rooms were equipped with anterooms complete with private washrooms and sitting areas furnished with leather couches. Many were also equipped with televisions and karaoke machines. As many as seven or eight waitresses catered banquets in such rooms. In less elegant restaurants, there was, at minimum, a room large enough to hold the focal piece of the environment, a round banquet table for eight to ten people. In every instance, hosts either informed me of the high level of status associated with the restaurant or made excuses that although the physical conditions were not ideal, the quality of the food served there was well known or the scenery was unique.

Some large companies that maintain enormous interpersonal and institutional networks establish designated restaurants for company-related banqueting so that their frequent patronage ensures lower rates and better service. Others buy or collaborate with restaurants to cut into the costs of banqueting. Still others go so far as to construct *dānjiān* in or adjacent to their offices; on several occasions while I visited companies in Shandong, after handling business in meeting rooms or offices, my hosts escorted me to banquet rooms in the same building for lunch, dinner or mid-afternoon banquets.

The Players

Professional banquets typically involve five to twelve people, usually business professionals and government officials. The resources required to host a banquet limit participation in Shandong banquet culture to those individuals with access to social, political, or financial capital. This group is made up of four general types of players: businesspeople, government officials, members of the media, and intellectuals. People from Shandong engaged in business participate in banquets out of the necessity to maintain connections and good relations with the people who control policy or who may have influence over their particular industry. Players must both host banquets for and participate in banquets hosted by individuals of high social status if they wish to maintain sufficient status to accomplish their goals. Additionally, banquets are a common means for establishing and maintaining business connections.

Shandong businesspeople vary greatly in their backgrounds, education levels, and characteristics. Because the Chinese economy has relatively recently begun its transition from solely state-run industries to multiple forms of ownership, most of the people now operating in the business sector have come from other sectors. Cao Tiansheng (1997) distinguishes four types of Chinese businessmen, a paradigm that with slight modification can also be applied to the Shandong context:

- official-businesspeople, *guānshāng* (官商), who use the power and resources of position to engage in economic activities;
- intellectual-businesspeople, *rúshāng* (儒 商), who either have failed in their pursuit of a career in academia or have been enticed by the prospects of economic gain to leave academia for the commercial world, a process referred to as "plunging into the sea, *xià hǎi* (下海)";
- officer-businesspeople *jūnshāng* (军 商), military officers who use their special status and privileges to engage in commercial activity on the side; and
- orthodox businesspeople, *zhèngshāng* (正商), who, because they have no other means of existence, rely solely on their ability to operate within the system to engage in business.

Irrespective of their backgrounds, the Shandong businesspeople who are regular players in professional banquet culture have one characteristic in common: they have been successful at achieving some level of social status within society, or they are attempting to forge such status for themselves by interacting with the people who already enjoy it.

Participants from other social strata also engage in banqueting, although less often. Intellectuals and people who see themselves as refined or cosmopolitan view banquets as "behind the times, *luòhòu* (落后)," "vulgar customs, *lòuxí* (陋习)," "wasteful, *làngfèi* (浪费)," and "unrefined, *tǔ* (土)." Finally, in Shandong, drinking is viewed as a man's activity, so women's roles are limited.

However, banquets are not exclusively male-oriented events; women can and do participate.

The Roles

The two major roles that frame the strategies people adopt for joining in banquet activities are guest, *kèrén* (客人), and host, *zhŭrén* (主人). These roles frame the modes of participation that are available as well as individual performative strategies. Roles are always dependent on those present and can change if a player is added or leaves during the course of a banquet. The standard rule that underlies all hospitality events is "guests follow the host's wishes, *kè suí zhŭ biàn* (客随主便)." Thus, hosting involves a significant burden of responsibility but affords enormous interactional power.

Yang (1994, 138) suggests that both guests and hosts at Chinese banquets are subject to a set of cultural etiquette. She also remarks, "There is a constant chatter by hosts of how modest and simple the meal is, and by guests of how sumptuous is the repast laid out before them." Thus, while hosting, hosts do things culturally associated with hosting such as placing food on guests' plates, pouring alcohol and tea, leading toasts, telling stories, guiding and maintaining the pace and flow of interaction, apologizing for inadequate hosting skills, and urging guests to consume food and drink. Likewise, while *guesting*, banqueters do the things guests are supposed to do such as eat, drink, compliment, display modesty, sing, toast, and reciprocate (Common forms of reciprocation include compliments and toasts during the event, taking actions to give the host face during or after the event, hosting a banquet or doing something for the host at a later time).

The primary responsibility for hosts of Shandong banquets is to create a festive group atmosphere that facilitates inclusion and enjoyment for all participants; the goal for guests is to display respect and appreciation to the host by partaking of the festivities. In fact, cultural expectations require guests to project the image that they are enjoying themselves as a result of the host's hospitality even when a host's hosting skills are subpar. Guests literally subject themselves to great pains and discomforts in order to avoid spoiling the atmosphere, *qìfen* (气氛). On numerous occasions, I was witness to guests' attempts to sneak away from the activities for momentary breaks or in order to get sick in private from drinking too heavily. These guests certainly did not appear to be enjoying themselves. I have also accompanied both guests and hosts to other locations for pre- and postbanquet snacks, which suggests that eating is not necessarily a primary concern at banquets. The idea is that both guests and hosts achieve their respective goals through cultural performances. By partaking of and contributing to the collective effervescence in at least one culturally recognized mode, participants fulfill the obligations associated with their respective roles and are recognized by other participants as having fulfilled them.

Hosting

Hosting is often referred to as "serving as (the host to the) east, *zuò dōng* (做东)," and hosts are called "the host to the east, *dōngdàozhǔ* (东道主)."[8] The host role can be subdivided into principal hosts, *zhǔpéi* (主陪), assistant hosts, *fùpéi* (副陪), and escorts, *péikè* (陪客). Hosts often feel obligated to spend significant amounts of time planning the event, preparing the site, and learning guests' tastes. This pre-event behavior may involve calling friends of the guest to inquire about preferences for types of food, drink, and entertainment. In addition to bearing all costs, hosts arrange everything and accompany guests at all times, a practice many Western visitors to

---

[8] The origin of this term is the *Zuo Zhuan*. It comes from a story in which the armies of the Kingdoms of Jin and Qin had surrounded the Kingdom of Zheng. A messenger dispatched by Duke Wen of Zheng said to Duke Mu of Qin that if he spared the Kingdom of Zheng and allowed it to serve as the host to the east, Zheng could provide Qin with all that it needed and Qin would not be harmed by doing so. "若舍郑以为东道主，行李之往来，共其乏困，君亦无所害。" (Yang 1990, 480). Thanks to Minru Li for providing this reference.

China find stifling. They arrive early, welcome guests, lead toasts, order dishes (including what the guests will eat and drink), issue self-deprecating remarks, serve food, pour drinks, and control every aspect of the interaction. The set of responsibilities associated with hosting include arranging a suitable time and location, sufficient food and spirits, an interesting and harmonious group of guests, transportation for guests, seating assignments, and entertainment. Hosts also have the duty to maintain the hierarchy of the event,[9] create a festive atmosphere, lead conversation, maintain harmony, facilitate the exchange of feelings, and ensure a pleasant experience for every guest. The expectation in Shandong is that hosts also have the responsibility to make offers to eat, drink, and participate with particular vigor, because the default assumption is that guests will politely decline offers of hospitality even if they plan to later accept; the typical pattern is to refuse two to three times before accepting anything offered.

Principal Hosts

The principal host is normally the person of highest social stature among the hosts and therefore is the person who dictates the flow of the activity. He or she is typically the player with the most at stake because of the significant list of responsibilities associated with the role. Local pride and emphasis on hosting and hospitality skills create pressure for hosts to perform the duties of hosting to a high standard. In particular, for reasons that will become clear later, the principal host is responsible especially for the two guests with the highest social status.

---

[9] Hierarchy plays such an important role in determining speech and behavior in Shandong, every event whether it be two individuals greeting while passing on the street or a banquet that involves three hundred people is viewed as having a hierarchy. People assess the rank order of individuals involved and this knowledge directs their speech and behavior. In the case of banquets, participants begin assessing this hierarchy prior to the beginning of the event. They find out who will be present, what their rank in the government bureaucracy is, and make preparations accordingly.

A foreigner may find it difficult to assume the role of principal host in Shandong culture. Although a foreign player may host a banquet, the same expectations for performance as a host do not apply—the culture simply does not allow foreigners to be viewed in such a role. In situations in which a foreign player attempts to act as host, the rules of the game are altered. For example, one of the guests often assumes the responsibility of dictating the flow of the interaction. This is done very subtly by repeatedly lauding the foreign participant's hosting skills and understanding of Shandong etiquette so as to avoid causing damage to the foreign host's face.

Assistant Hosts

The assistant host, *fùpéi* （副陪）, also plays an important role in Shandong banquets, one that is usually designated to the person deemed by the principal host to have the best social skills. Because the assistant host aides the principal host in all aspects of entertaining guests and settles the bill, principal hosts often appoint their most trusted subordinate to this position. The assistant host pays the bill with the host's money so that the host never has to leave the guests unaccompanied. While the principal host sees to the needs of the two most important guests, the assistant host has the responsibility of attending to the needs of the third and fourth most important guests.

Kipnis (1997, 52) notes that this responsibility entails "orchestrating, or at least initiating, eating, drinking and smoking." I would add to those the responsibilities of maintaining a positive atmosphere, helping to guide the flow of conversation, and, most important, protecting the host's face. Through toasting, smoking, and dialogue, assistant hosts aid hosts in their efforts to ensure that guests are comfortable and are having a good time. Assistant hosts also check on dishes that are taking too long, add dishes when needed, pour drinks, adjust air conditioning or heating, and handle anything that might call for someone to leave the room or that might distract the host's attention from the guests.

Assistant hosts are also expected to sacrifice themselves when the host's face is jeopardized. The importance of this role is clarified in the discussion of drinking that follows, but it should be noted that when the principal host is incapable of drinking or has drunk so much that he[10] can not continue to function as a proper host, the assistant host is expected to drink for the host or, at minimum, deflect the guests' attention while the principal host can regroup. As a result, assistant hosts are often formidable drinkers and rate highly in the group for that skill.

The duty of the assistant host to sacrifice his or her own face for the host can be seen in an incident in which I was the guest of a mid-level government official in Qingdao. After drinking several glasses of the infamous Chinese *báijiǔ* (白酒), a clear liquor of 140–150 proof, my host stated that he was not feeling well and could no longer drink with me, but that his assistant host was feeling up to the task and would drink for him for the remainder of the banquet. After that, the host continued to toast me, but the assistant host drank for him each time, forcing both the assistant host and me to drink a tremendous amount.

Another incident in which I was the guest of a village party secretary reveals the notion that the assistant host must take over should the principal host become incapacitated. After several rounds of toasting and drinking, the party secretary began slurring his speech and slipping into the local dialect. Without a word, the assistant host took control of the banquet, toasting the guests and regaling me with stories of his interactions with foreign guests. At that point, I stepped out to use the washroom. When I returned, the party secretary was no longer present, and the assistant host was in his seat. He gave apologies that the party secretary was called to a meeting with officials from the city government. This was unlikely because it was a Sunday afternoon, but it also meant that I was in for

---

[10] This is not acceptable behavior for women in Shandong culture.

a long afternoon. In any event, in the absence of the principal host, the assistant host took over as if he had organized the banquet from the beginning.

Péikè

A third category of participants that assists in the hosting process is designated as escorts, *péikè* (陪客). *Péikè* are usually invited because of their rhetorical and social skills, which they are expected to employ to create a lively and stimulating atmosphere for the guests. Kipnis (1997, 40) relates that one such individual was selected because "she really knows how to talk, guests are comfortable with her." Kipnis alludes to another important reason for the presence of *péikè* when he states, "Host reps were chosen to match the most honored guest at each table in age and sex." A host may also invite certain *péikè* to prove to guests that he or she is capable of assembling an interesting and lively group of people.

Péikè often attend because they want to be seen with the host at a social event, but the host normally wishes to invite *péikè* whose presence lends prestige and legitimacy to an event. In this way, hosts utilize the prestige of other players to enhance their own status in the eyes of other players. Furthermore, Shandong hosts feel the need to have a well-balanced group of people with similar interests so that they all enjoy themselves and feel a part of the group. As a result, a host may invite *péikè* of the same age, occupation, or sex as the guests simply to provide company for guests that he feels unable to entertain adequately.

When organizing a banquet for some acquaintances, I learned the importance of selecting appropriate *péikè* from the close friend I had asked to serve as my assistant host. Only one of my guests was female; she was an important guest because she had arranged for me to give a lecture at the training center she managed. My assistant host said that we could not put her in a situation in which she would have no one to talk to; this would be worse than not inviting her. Thus, we invited my assistant host's wife, who was of comparable age and social status, to act as a *péikè* so that our manager friend would have someone to converse with during dinner.

Guesting

A hierarchy also characterizes the arrangement of guests and is clearly reflected in seating arrangements as well as in the order in which individuals talk and the amount of time afforded for talk. This hierarchy is reflected in the discourse[11] about guests that includes the terms "main guest, *zhǔbīn* (主宾)," "honored guest, *jiābīn* (嘉宾)," "important guest, *guìbīn* (贵宾)," and "number two guest, *èrkè* (二客)." The general terms for *guest* in Chinese are *kèrén* (客人) and *bīnkè* (宾客), but the word for *being a guest* is literally "to do or be a guest, *zuò kè* (做客)," which is in contrast with "to do or be a host, *zuò zhǔ* (做主)" and suggests the active nature of the role and the responsibilities associated with that role. General *guesting* responsibilities include displaying respect for the host, giving the host face and showing appreciation by participating in the interaction, and partaking of the food and drink the host has provided. Guests are also expected to lavish the host with repeated compliments on hosting ability, amount and quality of food, atmosphere, guests assembled, and location. Complimenting the host on hosting skills is an indispensable part of guest etiquette. If a guest fails to deliver such compliments in a timely manner, the host may either become nervous that he is failing in his role as host or be offended to have invited an ungrateful guest.

Kipnis (1997, 52) suggests that another aspect of guest etiquette is that guests should not help themselves to food and drink: "People drank only during toasts and ate only what someone else put

---

[11] By discourse, I mean formal discussions of guests or their way of talking about guests that can be found in their conversations. They discuss banquets and guests at length in analytical and reflective ways and have a particular way of talking about guests that involves certain ideas, proverbs, phrases, sentence structures and words.

on their plates." The notion is that a cultural theme reflected in guest behavior is the display of modesty and gratitude. Although the host will tell guests that they should help themselves and the guests will repeatedly say that they can take care themselves, the ritual is performed again and again, often as a display of the principal host's hosting skills. However, this is the case only when guest and host don't know each other well or have never heard of one another. Otherwise, the guest who protests and waits for the host to take care of him or her would seem insincere, *xūwěi* (虚伪).

Etiquette for guests also includes projecting the image of being happy and of enjoying themselves even when they are in a bad mood, being polite to people they don't like, eating things they don't particularly like, and drinking when they don't wish to drink. This is a nonverbal manifestation of Bond's (1991) affective style, or a person's attempt to adjust to the feelings of the other parties in a communicative event. Judgments are made about participants' personalities based on behavior exhibited during banquets, so both guests and hosts pay particular attention to everything they do and say. For example, eating too much of one dish indicates that a person is greedy, and taking food from the center of a dish rather than from the side indicates that one is selfish.

The Positions
The specific seat in which individuals assuming particular roles sit is fixed in Shandong culture. The principal host is seated in a position that allows him or her to be the first person guests see when they open the door. Thus, the principal host faces the door and sits directly opposite it. Forming a straight line with the principal host, the assistant host sits with his or her back to the door directly opposite the principal host after all banqueters sit down. In most instances the assistant host greets the guests at the door and leads them into the room. The first person the guest sees upon entering the room is the host. Everyone then rises when the guest (s) enters the

room, introductions are made and the seating ritual begins. A variation that is beginning to enter into some Shandong communities is that the principal host is seated facing the source of entertainment. Whether that be an ocean view or a karaoke video screen, the room is arranged so the host can face both the door and the source of entertainment if possible. This is an example of what Bauman (1977, 37) refers to as the process of emergence, or "the interplay between communicative resources, individual competence, and the goals of participants, within the context of a situation." One quick way to tell where the principal host's seat is located is to look at the shape of the napkins found in place settings. In most restaurants, napkins (or cloth hand towels) are folded and placed either on top of each plate or in each glass before guests arrive. The napkin at the principal host's setting is typically folded so that it is either a different shape or it stands higher than the other napkins so that it is easily located.

Yang (1994, 138) observes that in the "protocol of seating, guests of honor always sit farthest away from the door." In Shandong culture, the number one guest is seated to the immediate right of the principal host and the number two guest to the immediate left. Because the principal host typically occupies the seat facing the door, the guest of honor's seat is also located at the farthest point from the door. The same principle applies to the seating of the number three and number four guests, who sit to the right and left of the assistant host. Again, right is always superior to left. Any additional guests and *péikè* sit, alternating guest and host, between the number one guest and the number four guest on the right and between the number two and three guests on the left. No two guests sit beside one another. They are always separated by *péikè*. The pattern is guest-host-guest-host.

Because of the importance of food and because they are social events that in large part determine status for people in Shandong, banquets are extremely important events. In addition, the local tradition of proper ritual and etiquette requires that banqueting be done in the correct manner. One experienced official suggested to me that it's getting the little details right that makes all of the difference. He informed me that if one does little things such as lowering his or her glass to show deference to others or taking the lower cigarette out of two offered, people in Shandong will look at him differently. "If you get them [the small details of ritual and etiquette] right, others will think more highly of you, *názhǔn le, duìfāng jiùhuì gāo kàn nǐ yì yǎn* (拿准了, 对方就会高看你一眼)." Most important, participation in banquets is viewed differently than in other areas, and nonnatives must calibrate their behaviors in order to be recognized as participants in Shandong banquets. Performing in the recognized modes of play, including carrying out the ritual behaviors associated with prescribed roles, allows people to partake in the action as recognized participants and thus to become someone in the eyes of the members of the group.

CHAPTER TWO

Playing the Game

Getting It Right

Before starting the game, it is important to discuss two other notions
that have a direct impact on the way the game is played in Shandong.
First is the idea that we are all relational beings tied together in
reciprocal and hierarchical webs. We cannot stand alone because
who we are and what we do are intimately related to whom we know
and what they do. The second idea stems from the first: the
importance of social harmony. Knowing one's place in the social
dynamic and fulfilling the obligations associated with that role are
critical to fitting in. The result in the Shandong context is that a
cultural theme of maintaining surface-level harmony has emerged.
Significant value is placed on proper conduct and the avoidance of
anything that disrupts the balance of social harmony. That is, doing
things in the prescribed manner, at the right time, and with the right
people is stressed. This is played out through etiquette and ritual
behaviors, which are a cultural guideline for activity and the
mechanisms through which hierarchy, social order, feelings, and
relationships are maintained. This cultural emphasis on surface-level
harmony regardless of underlying tensions is referred to negatively
as "formalism, *xíngshì zhǔyì* (形式主义)" and guides and constricts
moves within the game of banqueting. As a result, people in
Shandong tend to express the expected, avoid critical assessments in
public settings, and negotiate difficulties outside the public eye.

Introductions

Because they serve as the basis for any interaction that is to follow, introductions are highly important in all cultures. If an introduction is smooth and effective, it can facilitate the flow of an interaction; on the other hand, a poor introduction can intensify the tension and awkwardness present at the beginning stages of most relationships.

Introductions are rituals that normally begin banquets involving unfamiliar players. Generally speaking, introductions between players in the game of banqueting in Shandong provide three main pieces of information. The first is a person's name. Second, but possibly more important to the participants, is a person's title. The title informs the interlocutors of the person's social rank, which determines how the other banqueters will attempt to interact with him or her. The final piece is a bit of information about the person that is relevant to the event at hand; examples include the person's work unit, reason for participating, and background information that will allow the listeners to identify him or her in some way.

These three bits of information inform all listeners how they should address the person, what forms of speech should be used, and what types of discourse can be employed. The length and content of introductions vary according to the situation and the social status of the person being introduced. Formal contexts, such as business negotiations, lectures, and meetings, tend to require lengthier introductions in which more detailed background information is provided because such venues do not provide the same ready means of obtaining additional biographical information that a banquet setting offers. Because of the time constraints involved in the banquet setting and because of participants' cultural expectations, shorter introductions are the norm.

Modesty is normally observed in self-introductions, but significant manipulation of information may take place when introducing a friend, colleague, or superior. For example, although it has lost some of the original connotations and is now equivalent to "what is your name," the most common way to ask for a person's name in Chinese, *nín guì xìng* (您贵姓), is literally equivalent to the English "Of what noble family are you?" When asked for their name in this manner, Shandong people, almost without fail, employ a set response, "Dispense with the 'noble,' I am Wang," using the morpheme *miǎn* to deflect the honorific in a display of modesty, *miǎn guì xìng Wáng* (免贵姓王). However, although Shandong people tend to deny their own accomplishments, they often boast of the accomplishments of others present, especially their friends and acquaintances. Xi Changsheng (1996) sees this as a culturally appropriate method of self-representation that stems from the collective nature of Chinese culture. This tendency is shifting, however, especially among younger Chinese who have studied English as well as in areas where Chinese have had significant interaction with foreigners.

   Chen Si (1996) notes that a basic principle to bear in mind when introducing oneself in formal settings is to display humility by using generic titles rather than lofty sounding ones. I witnessed the following examples that bear this principle out during banquets in Shandong. The head of personnel in a particular organization introduced himself as someone working in personnel rather than as the head.

A. Correct: 我是海尔搞人事的。
            Wǒ shì Hǎiěr gǎo rénshì de.
            I do personnel work for Haier.

   Incorrect: 我是海尔集团的人事部长。
            Wǒ shì Hǎiěr jítuán de rénshìbù bùzhǎng.
            I am the head of personnel for the Haier Group.

Similarly, a professor would never initially introduce him- or herself as a professor, but rather as a teacher.

B.   Correct: 我是烟台大学的老师。
                                  Wǒ shì Yāntái dàxúe de lǎoshī.
                                  I am a teacher at Yantai University.

          Incorrect: 我是烟台大学的教授。
                                    Wǒ shì Yāntái dàxué de jiàoshòu.
                                  I am a professor at Yantai University.

To avoid appearing pretentious, members of the younger generation and those who have yet to obtain high social status should not use titles with their own name. When pointing out the differences between Chinese and American cultures, a Chinese colleague commented to me that a young American teacher affiliated with our organization signed his e-mails as Teacher "x," a practice that he stated Chinese would never do because it would be perceived as arrogant.

      Additionally, hierarchy is displayed in the order in which people are introduced. When several people are to be introduced, the highest ranking is accorded the first position, with subordinates[1] following in rank order. Furthermore, people of lower social status often receive cursory introductions from superiors, and subordinates tend to spend more time "building pedestals" for their superiors when charged with introducing them. If a person changes positions, retires, or for some reason no longer holds a particular title, he or she is usually addressed by the title of the highest position ever held. Thus, a man who had been the head of a bureau in the Yantai city

---

[1]"Subordinates" is used in the sense of the hierarchy of the Chinese political and cultural system in both instances. People may not actually work together, but they nevertheless view themselves as superior or subordinate to one another based on rank in a system.

government, although he had been retired for nearly ten years, was afforded the courtesy of his former title by everyone, including the current bureau chief. In addition to this practice, some people consciously employ former titles to show intimacy and to mark the length of personal interaction. Thus, one individual continually addressed his former office manager by his previous title even though the manager had been promoted to bureau chief.

For players in Shandong banquet culture, status-identifying information is noted and analyzed instantaneously, because status identification is part of the basic expressive repertoire shared by people living in the region.

Exchange of Business Cards

The ritual of exchange of business cards, *míngpiàn* (名片), is a subcategory of introductions. The role business cards serve in Shandong culture should not be underestimated; their importance can be seen in a small experiment I conducted in 1997 while working as program officer for US/China Links. I had two sets of cards printed: one contained our organization's name, my name, and all relevant contact information, but no title. On the other set of cards, the title "Program Officer" was added.

Over the course of six months of interactions with various government officials and businesspeople, I alternated using the two styles of business cards; the reaction to the two types of cards was remarkably consistent and therefore quite revealing about the importance of titles as a referencing device within the hierarchical culture of the area. When I distributed the card not bearing a title, my interlocutors often meticulously examined it, looking several times at both the English and the Chinese sides. The amount of time that elapsed before they addressed me was noticeably longer than when using the cards with a title. Often parties would wait for someone else to address me before adopting the form of address used by others present at the event. On occasion, however, a more extroverted interlocutor would approach this problem by directly asking "How should I address you, *wǒ zénme chēnghū nín* (我怎么称呼您)?" They asked how to address me despite the fact that my full name appeared on the business cards I gave them, which suggests that it is the title that is key in determining how to address someone.

When I presented the business cards containing the title, the actions of my interlocutors were strikingly different. After accepting a card, they usually looked quickly for my surname and title. Once they knew my social position as designated by the business card, interlocutors were able to determine which forms of address and types of discourse were appropriate. The result was that they were able to open dialogue with me without the hesitation noted in the interlocutors who were unable to determine my relative social position.

Furthermore, I was also afforded more respect than when I used the cards without my title. Interlocutors more frequently employed the term of address "Mr., *xiānshēng* (先生)," when aware that I was coordinating the US/China Links program; conversely, when they were unaware of my position, my full Chinese name without title was often used, as was the term *xiǎo* (小), which is often used when addressing younger people who have no bureaucratic rank or social status.

The business card contains the information often delivered in introductions only in written form, which serves as a reference until name and rank are committed to memory. During the course of interaction, it is more important to address someone with appropriate titles and status markers than to maintain the smooth flow of interaction. The ideal situation is that you can remember every person's name; however, in banquet situations where you may be meeting ten or twelve new people at once, there are certainly going to be instances when you cannot remember everyone's name and title. The way to handle such a situation is to place all of the business cards you receive on the table in front of you in the order in which the people are seated. Then, if necessary, it is acceptable to pause to quickly check information on those cards during interaction. I have observed locals consulting cards they have received just prior to addressing others on several occasions during both banquets and meetings in Shandong. Furthermore, it is clear that business cards provide information necessary for culturally appropriate interaction, specifically, the position a person occupies in the hierarchy of the room. This position then partially determines the roles to be played during a banquet, which, in turn, determines how players interact. The role in which actors see themselves combined with knowledge of the roles of other actors involved in the interaction determines both their behavior and their speech.

In his 1918 classic short story, *Diary of a Madman, Kuángrén rìjì* (狂人日记), Lu Xun (1994, 8), one of China's greatest modern writers and social critics, depicted people through the pen of the Madman as: "fierce as lions, timid as rabbits, and sly as foxes, *shīzi sì de xiōngxīn, tùzi de qièruò, húli de jiǎohuá* (狮子似的凶心, 兔子的怯弱, 狐狸的狡猾)." This analogy has been employed by some people from Shandong to characterize three of the potential attitudes players adopt once they become cognizant of their place in the hierarchy of an event. First, if an actor perceives himself as the highest-ranking player among those present, he often speaks loudly and confidently, sometimes being condescending toward others of lower status. This type of player speaks more frequently, dictating the flow of interaction. On the other hand, a player who feels that he occupies a less important position normally behaves in a very reserved, even timid, manner, deferring to higher-ranking participants. Finally, those players who are unable to determine or who have yet to identify the hierarchy of the event adopt self-preservation strategies incorporating characteristics of both lions and rabbits mixed with cunning attempts to improve their own position. Of note for nonnatives observing such behavior is that people can play each of these roles in different banquets depending on the company they find themselves in.

In determining hierarchical ranks in any Shandong game, players follow the postulate that government is bigger than business, *zhèng dà yú qǐ* (政大于企), and the Party is bigger than government, *dǎng dà yú zhèng* (党大于政). "Government" refers to anyone holding an official position such as village head, mayor, and all of the positions that make up the government bureaucracy. "Business" refers to anyone engaged in commercial activity such as factory heads and managers. "Party" generally refers to party secretaries who hold the number one position in most organizations. The implications of such a rule are that when the manager of a large Chinese corporation and a government official are both guests at a banquet, the government official takes the higher position. Furthermore, on the rare occasion when the mayor and the party secretary of a city are simultaneously hosting an event, the party secretary always acts as the principal host, and the mayor serves as the assistant host.

On a more practical note, business cards normally are delivered when being introduced or when introducing oneself. If seated, one should stand, regardless of whether the receiver is standing or seated. Cards are passed using both hands and holding the card between the index finger and thumb of each hand so that the receiver can read the information on the card without turning it over. These particular acts are performed as much to display an understanding of the rules of etiquette to members of the audience as for the convenience of the receiver of the card.

Players who perceive themselves to be in relatively high positions will not pass out their cards until they have determined the social status and character of their interlocutors. If they determine that actors are of appropriate social status and character to be worthy of a relationship beyond the encounter at hand, such high-status players will exchange business cards with them or obtain contact information through other means. The philosophy that dominates the thinking of modern businesspeople in such situations can be seen in the following statement a Qingdao businessman made to me: "I definitely take care to properly manage relationships with people that are of use to me or possibly could be of use to me in the future. As for those people who are of no use to me, I do not bother maintaining relations with them."

If such actors deem a person unworthy or of no practical use to them, they may employ the excuse that they have forgotten to bring their business cards with them. I once observed a mid-level government official tell another guest at a banquet that he had forgotten his card. Later, he made it a point to accompany me to the washroom so that he could speak with me in private. On the way, he presented me with his business card and asked me not to tell the other guests that he had given me one because they would only add to his workload if he were to give them one.[2]

Seating

The second order of business following introductions in Shandong banqueting is the complex ritual of seating. Neither guests nor hosts can simply enter a banquet room and sit down; seating must be arranged in a ritual that establishes the hierarchy within the room and

---

[2] People of lower social status view obtaining business cards from higher-ranking people as a means to continue interaction with them. Such interaction would allow them to take advantage of whatever power, resources or influence the higher-ranking person had access to so business card exchange, from their perspective, is viewed positively and as a minor goal of initial interactions. On the other hand, some people of significant social rank and some in positions of authority are reluctant to distribute their business cards precisely because it is a means for continuing the interaction. From this perspective, giving out business cards is viewed negatively because the number of people merely interested in gaining access to power or influence outnumbers those one could ultimately be capable of becoming friends with. I know of people who distribute both generic and serious business cards depending on who they are meeting. I have also known people with as many as four cell phones, the numbers of which are given out selectively—a work number that appears on cards, friends' number that does not, as well as numbers for family members or significant others that may or may not be given out.

therefore determines the roles to be played by each person present. Yang (1994) notes, "When it is time to be seated, there is often a minor ritual struggle over who is to occupy the seats of honor." Kipnis (1997, 52) records similar practices in western Shandong: "Though Fengjia banquet procedures did not constitute political hierarchies so directly, banquet seating was still negotiated and was still relevant to problems of reproducing and recreating specific hierarchies." It is often the case that everyone present at a banquet knows who should sit where, but the ritual is conducted nonetheless.

The original meaning of the word for "banquet," *yánxí* (筵席), consisted of two characters that meant "bamboo mat" and "a pad for sitting." There were no tables or chairs so when entertaining guests, Chinese placed a mat on the ground for cleanliness reasons. Thus, entertaining guests was known variously as "arranging seats on the ground and sitting, *xí dì ér zuò* (席地而坐)," and "arranging mats and setting up seats, *sì yán shè xí* (肆筵设席)." These terms were reserved for the entertainment of guests, which suggests that seats were arranged only on occasions that involved important guests. This simple etymology reveals some of the importance associated with seating positions at banquets. The frequency of the descriptions of arranging seating at banquets in China's literary tradition, including numerous occasions in the novel *Romance of the Three Kingdoms,* hints at its importance on such occasions (Zhou 1996).

The contemporary version of the seating ritual involves the principal host designating seating assignments based on political or social status. When hosts suggest that a particular guest should take a seat of honor, the guest is expected to decline in a display of modesty, *tuīcí* (推辞). Even in situations in which the guest of honor is known to all, the guest will attempt to defer to another guest— hosts never allow important guests to decline this type of offer in Shandong. The default assumption that hosts work on is that hosts know that guests will decline, so they will continue to insist until each guest is seated in his or her proper place. On numerous occasions, I witnessed guests continuing to refuse while hosts literally dragged them to their proper seat and forced them to sit down. The seating ritual can be time-consuming because the host must repeat it with each guest until everyone is seated. To avoid conflict, disagreement with the way the host orders the seating is not brought up during the banquet. However, players dissatisfied with the arrangements discuss such topics afterward, commenting on the appropriateness of the arrangements.

    The following chart presents the seating arrangement for a typical banquet.

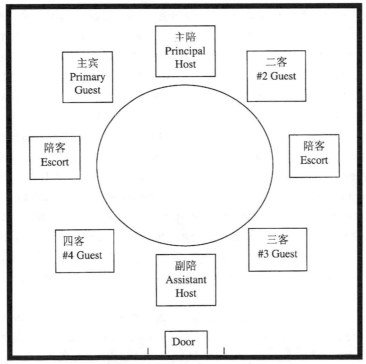

Typical Banquet Seating Arrangement in Shandong

Ordering

Once all guests are properly seated, the game can begin in earnest. All Shandong banquets are conducted in one of two formats: either the host makes arrangements with the restaurant in advance for a set dinner, or the dishes are selected from the menu once all guests are seated. The hosts determine the set dinner, and the guests don't participate in the selection of dishes to be eaten. In this format, a number of cold dishes, *liángcài* (凉菜), will be on the table before the guests arrive.

If the host decides to allow the guests to participate in the selection of what to eat, the ordering ritual begins with the host passing the menu to the most important guest; this guest will attempt to defer to the host by saying that the choice of dishes does not matter. Anticipating this, the principal host will insist that this guest choose something that he or she enjoys eating. The guest, not wanting to impose on the host, will then select a relatively inexpensive dish. The only person the host is obligated to consult is the highest-ranking guest. Some hosts, however, wish to please everyone, so they allow all participants to choose something they like to eat, which requires that the menu be passed around the table. I have witnessed numerous guests respond to this approach by asking what the host likes or wishes to eat when they are uncertain. When they are more familiar with their host's preferences, guests often simply order what they know the host likes while stating the reason for choosing that particular dish.

After all guests have had the opportunity to select something from the menu, the principal host, knowing that his guests were "too modest" to select any expensive dishes, will order a dish that is more expensive than any the guests have chosen. Usually, the host will then order several expensive dishes, balancing out the number of seafood, vegetable, and meat dishes. The number of dishes ordered always depends on the number of guests, but is usually eight, ten, or multiples of three. Eight is a popular number because the morpheme for "eight," *bā* (八), is a homophone in Cantonese for the word "to get rich," *fā cái* (发财). The auspicious connotations are also connected to the number eight in Shandong. Similarly, ten is appropriate because the morpheme for "ten," *shí* (十), is also used in an idiom meaning "perfect," *shíquán-shíměi* (十全十美). Multiples of three, such as nine and twelve, are also common because three is considered an auspicious number by some people in Shandong. Banquets of fewer than eight dishes are rare. In all cases, cold dishes are ordered first.

The final component of the ordering ritual involves determining what to drink. As is explained later, it is given that men will drink alcohol; the only question is what type. According to Shandong etiquette, the principal host allows the honored guest to choose the type of alcohol. However, if the principal host has a habit of drinking a particular type of alcohol and the guest does not select it, the host will often attempt to persuade the guest to change his mind. (In Chinese culture, male hosts do not typically attempt to get female participants to change their mind in this type of situation. Women have the luxury of declining; men do not.) For example, the host wants to drink a particular type of alcohol, such as whisky. The guest cannot stand whisky, so he refuses. Because the host really drinks only whisky, he then tries to get the guest to drink whisky because he does not want to drink anything else.

This is a major difference between Chinese and American culture: Americans generally would not force a guest to drink what he or she does not want to drink, and would allow the guest to choose what he or she wanted. In Shandong, I have seen hosts force guests to drink alcohols the guests do not like. In sum, the host will make the decision on what to drink despite protests from the guests. Normally, everyone drinks the same type of alcohol (They all drink beer or they all drink *báijiǔ* (白酒)), but this custom is changing in many urban areas, so it is possible to see several types of drinks poured at the same sitting. Shandong people have five choices when it comes to alcoholic beverages: *báijiǔ*, *huángjiǔ* (黄酒), wines, beers, and foreign liquors. Communist party members and men over the age of forty tend to drink *báijiǔ*, whereas younger men, and some women, choose beer more frequently. During the cold winter months, Shandong men enjoy drinking heated *huángjiǔ*. Those people who see themselves as urbane, many women, and some men who have a low tolerance for alcohol drink white or red wines. Finally, a small percentage of men of high social position who either have gone abroad or have interacted with foreigners enjoy brandy and whisky.

Women are not obligated to drink or smoke. Nevertheless, although they have the option not to drink, women who have the ability to drink are respected and even feared if they can consume more than their male counterparts. I met a number of women who realized the importance of drinking as a social skill and, as a result, had developed considerable capacities to drink. However, because it is considered more ladylike for women to abstain, most Shandong women opt not to indulge in alcohol. I frequently heard the phrase "drinking is men's business, *hē jiǔ shì nánrén de shì* (喝酒是男人的事)." Although I have witnessed young women smoking at banquets in Shanghai, I never observed women smoking at a banquet in Shandong. I know of women who smoke in more private settings, but because smoking is deemed "unladylike" in the region, it is rare in public settings.

Serving

As noted earlier, the first course of food always consists of cold dishes. In cases where the host has either called ahead to make prior arrangements for the menu or arrived ahead of the guests to place the order, cold dishes are placed on the table a few minutes before guests arrive. Another frequently encountered situation involves the host, honored guest and server—who jots down which dishes are being ordered—walking through areas of the restaurant designated for the display of meats, vegetables, live seafood, and sometimes live insects or animals such as scorpions, grasshoppers, pigeons, quail, pangolins, and prior to SARS, civets. In cases where guests participate in the ordering of the dishes, cold dishes are served all at once immediately after the order is placed. Once guests have enjoyed the cold dishes, hot dishes are served one dish at a time. Servers usually place a new dish on the opposite side of the table directly across from the most important guest, which requires guests opposite the honored guest to lean to the side to allow servers access to the table. Tables in most Shandong restaurants are equipped with a large rotating Lazy Susan, made of glass or wood. After placing a dish on the Lazy Susan, the server then announces the name of the dish and rotates the Lazy Susan toward the principal host until the dish rests before the number one guest, who is extended the courtesy of the first sampling. In less formal banquets, hosts simply wait for the honored guest to take the first bite and then begin eating themselves. In more formal cases, the dish will be rotated to a point halfway between the principal host and the most important guest. I have also noted people sitting in the seat of honor adjust the position of a dish, so that it rests halfway between themselves and the host. Then, a principal host normally uses what are called "public chopsticks, *gōnggòng kuàizi* (公共筷子)" to serve both the number one and number two guests before partaking of the dish himself. When hosts (or host representatives) place food on guests' plates, guests typically respond by picking up their plates with both hands and moving them so that it is easier for the host to make the transfer from the dish on the table to the guests' plate. "I'll get it myself, *wǒ zìjǐ lái* (我自己来)" is a polite verbal response acknowledging the efforts of the host that accompanies the lifting of the plate. The Lazy Susan is then rotated clockwise so that everyone can take a bite-sized portion from the dish and place it on the small saucers that are used as plates in Shandong. Chen Si's (1996) guide to social etiquette advises waiting for a signal from the host before moving one's chopsticks to eat. Once servers have filled all glasses and the first toast has been made, hosts normally pick up their chopsticks and motion for everyone to eat while saying, "eat, *chī* (吃)," "please, *qǐng* (请)," "enjoy, *qǐng màn yòng* (请慢用)," "eat while we chat, *biān chī biān liáo* (边吃边聊)," or "let's eat first, *xiān chī cài* (先吃菜)."

The remaining hot dishes are then served one at a time. After the principal host has taken his or her first helping of a hot dish, the Lazy Susan is then rotated to the right so that each person can sample the dish. As each dish makes its way around the table, guests are expected to partake whether they wish to or not. It is pertinent to add that hosts are very keen observers who will discern immediately what dishes guests like and dislike by the amount of a dish they eat and the speed with which they eat it. Consequently, hosts typically do not ask whether a guest likes a dish. Finally, when the dish reaches the assistant host, he or she first serves the number three and four guests before serving him- or herself. All dishes that follow are handled in the same way. Once the first bite has been taken by the honored guest and the host, then everyone eats as the dish arrives in front of them.

A local proverb states that a dinner event is not a banquet unless a fish is served, *wú yú bù chéng xí* (无鱼不成席). The serving of the fish signals the end of the round of hot dishes. Again, the sound of the Chinese word for "fish," *yú* (鱼), is homophonic with such sounds as the word for "excess," *yú* (余), having the connotation of an abundance of food. Following the fish, a soup is generally served. Then, the guests are asked what kind of staple food, *zhǔshí* (主食), they would like to end the meal with. Standard staple dishes include rice, dumplings, noodles, and any of the various flour-based biscuits, *bǐng* (饼), found in the region. The staple food is served only after the hosts determine that their guests have had enough to eat of the nonstaple foods, *fùshí* (副食), which include meats, vegetables, and seafood, everyone has had sufficient amounts of drink, the goals of the banquet have been accomplished, and a ceremonial final group toast has been made. Finally, as a signal that the banquet is nearing a close, fruit is served. Typical fruits served at banquets include sliced oranges, pineapple, star fruit, kiwi, and watermelon. In most restaurants, the fruit is served on a fruit plate, *guǒpán* (果盘), that includes a mixed variety of these fruits. Guests then use toothpicks to take individual slices off the fruit plate.

Smoking

Although not as pervasive as in the recent past, smoking remains an integral part of Shandong banquets, especially in areas that have less frequent contact with outside cultures, such as Qixia, Laiyang, and Zibo. Cigarettes are important props found on every banquet table in Shandong Province and are used by hosts as a tool to entertain guests. When I inquired into the purpose of smoking at banquets, one Shandong businessman explained that although he did not particularly enjoy smoking, he felt that smoking is an important means of interaction among men. He went on to explain that offering a cigarette to a stranger is a ritual act that expresses one's desire to open dialogue with that person. Furthermore, if a guest is quiet or appears to be bored, a host can offer a cigarette to fill in the gaps. It is also general practice in Shandong for hosts to offer cigarettes to their guests in the early stages of banquets. Cigarettes are frequently smoked before eating the first bite of food. People who typically do not smoke often "play around, *shuǎ* (耍)," by smoking one or two cigarettes during banquets. If guests do not smoke, hosts still present them with plastic, Bic-like lighters and name-brand cigarettes as gifts, which they can then take home to offer the guests they entertain on other occasions.

First, hosts generally offer cigarettes to guests, and people of lower status offer them to those of higher status. Kipnis (1997, 52) states that in Fengjia village, "Cigarettes were smoked only when offered and lit by someone else." However, more often than not, when someone offers cigarettes to others present at a banquet, it is because he or she wishes to smoke. Smoking without first offering a cigarette to the others present is seen as selfish and a breach of etiquette; therefore, if one wishes to smoke, one must first offer cigarettes to those within reach. This pertains to both guests and hosts.

Additionally, many Shandong men observe a ritual manner when offering a cigarette: They first tap the bottom of the box so that one or two cigarettes extend from the pack. They then offer the box to the receiver with both hands. If more than one cigarette extends from the box, the receiver always takes the lower one to display deference to the offering party. As soon as the person accepts, both parties rush to light the cigarette. I have witnessed people, who later turned out not to have a lighter with them, refuse a light from others they perceived to be of high social or political status. If a person did accept a light, he would first place the cigarette in his mouth and then surround the lighter along with the offerer's hand with both of his hands before lowering the cigarette to the flame. Once the cigarette was lit, he would then tap the back of the offerer's hand lightly in a display of gratitude. If someone offers cigarettes to more than two people, the offering party lights each cigarette in the same fashion. However, once two cigarettes have been lit, the lighter must be extinguished and then relit for additional people; this stems from the homonyms "three fires, *sān huǒ* (三火)" and "dissolve or disband (referring to the group present), *sànhuǒ* (散伙)." In the local dialect, the two have the same pronunciation, and "fire, *huǒ* (火)," is another term for a light (of a cigarette).

At one banquet in Weihai, my host expressed the significance both smoking and drinking held for him. At the beginning of the banquet, two American members of our party refused to drink or smoke with our host for personal reasons: one said that he did not drink, and the other explained that it was against his religion to drink. Both also said they did not smoke. Near the end of the banquet, our host began discussing what his notion of a friend involves by saying that a friend is willing to hurt himself for you. The analogy he used was a friend is someone who is willing to cut out both of his ribs for a friend. He went on to express veiled criticisms of the two guests who did not partake of smoke or spirit. He said that because he had made himself uncomfortable on their account by not smoking around them, they should be willing to make themselves uncomfortable on his account by drinking with him. This particular host's response was a commonly seen reflexive reaction invoked by his sense of a loss of face. His discussion of friendship was consistent with many others that I heard while in Shandong.

The idea is that each culture has its own valued activities and rules for how those activities take place and for how people are expected to act while participating in them. When interacting in Shandong, Shandong rules apply. Most Shandong people make conscious or subconscious adjustments when dealing with foreigners and people from other areas of China, but not all people are cognizant that there are multiple ways of interpreting and partaking of reality. Thus, to be successful in professional interactions that take place in Shandong, nonnatives must make behavioral and interpretive calibrations; they must do things in ways recognizable to Shandong people. If someone does not smoke, he or she must decline in manner that is acceptable to locals, which involves acknowledging the overture made by the offering person and must take action to make up for not engaging in this particular mode. Declining to smoke because of religious beliefs is not effective in Shandong because religion is not an officially accepted type of belief system. If someone does not drink, he or she still must play the game; they must partake in the verbal play and ritual toasting using a nonalcoholic drink. If unable or unwilling to engage in one or more modes of play, participants must use other modes to compensate. By telling stories, complimenting, singing, dancing, or eating in prescribed ways, people can still be recognized as participants in Shandong banquets even if they do not drink or smoke.

CHAPTER THREE

Eating and Drinking

Shandong banquets are social events that revolve around the consumption of good food and fine spirits. Thus, many of the most frequently encountered and readily observable behaviors found in any banquet are connected to the eating and drinking modes of play. When combined with the local cultural emphasis on the correct performance of ritual etiquette, this high rate of occurrence makes effective eating and drinking basic skills necessary for all banquet goers in Shandong. This chapter explores some of the ritual behaviors associated with eating and drinking that I have observed as a participant-observer in banquets.

Lu Cuisine

Regional cuisines in China vary widely, with each locale having its own characteristic style, foods, and customs. In fact, places are commonly associated with regional specialties or foods produced; examples include Beijing duck, Sichuan hot pot, Laiyang pears, Yantai apples, and Qingdao seafood. The types of regional cuisine are colloquially categorized into eight major systems, *bā dà càixì* (八大菜系). Shandong cuisine falls into the northern category referred to as *Lǔcài* (鲁菜), which is named for the Kingdom of Lu that controlled western Shandong during the Warring States Period (476–221 B.C.) and was the home of Confucius. Lu cuisine, which became widely popular after the Song Dynasty because many of the court chefs were from Shandong, is often described as saltier and oilier than the foods of other regions and can be further divided into Jinan and Jiaodong subtypes reflecting the inland and coastal cultures characteristic of Shandong. What Shandong people generally consider the best of Lu cuisines consists of fresh seafood. Most restaurants have tanks with a wide variety of live seafood for guests to select from, the reason being that if seafood is not alive, *huó* (活), just before cooking, it is not considered to be fresh.

Important guests are treated to the most exotic delicacies, which include live scorpions, snakes, snake eggs and blood, bird brains, any of the thousands of gastropods found in the Bohai Gulf, and various insect larvae. Hosts allow guests to select the particular fish, shellfish, pangolin, civet, or scorpions that they desire to eat during the ordering ritual, which sometimes involves the host and a representative of the primary guest taking a tour of the potential foods that are placed on display in a central location in most restaurants.

Eating as a Mode of Play

Culinary discourses fill large amounts of time during banquets. Hosts frequently regale banquet goers with stories about the lore of Chinese food. These may include explanations of the nutritional value of certain foods, the details of preparation, ways of eating particular dishes, or folk beliefs about how foods are to be handled during a meal. One tale that I frequently encountered in the Jiaodong region stemmed from coastal fishing cultures where the local fishermen have elaborate repertoires of food rituals and taboos: when turning over a fish with chopsticks, which is served whole during banquets, the action must be described as "sliding, *huá* (滑)," rather the typical "flipping, *fān* (翻)," because it would be inviting the inauspicious event of capsizing on their next trip out to sea because of the homonym in Chinese, *fān chuán* (翻船).

By sampling all dishes presented and engaging in the dialogue of food, banqueters can make themselves part of the interaction even if they do not play the game in other available modes such as drinking. The script available for guests to draw from while operating in the eating mode involves repeated comments on the quality and quantity of food. Effectively timed and delivered praise about the dishes served plays a major role in one's attempt to be a "good" guest. Guests' flattering remarks that I have witnessed include: "So rich and sumptuous, what an undeserved reward, *zhème fēngshèng, wǒ zhēnshi wúgōng-shòulù* (这么丰盛，我真是无功受禄)"; "Look at all of this great food. There's no way we can eat it all, *zhème duō hǎo chī de cài, juéduì chī bù liǎo* (这么多好吃的菜, 绝对吃不了)"; "The food here is really a unique treat, *hěn yǒu tèsè* (很有特色)"; and "The chef's skill is superb, *chúyì zhēn jīngzhàn* (厨艺真精湛)."

On the other hand, the script for hosts that accompanies eating performances includes key self-deprecating remarks such as "our simple and crude conditions, *tiáojiàn jiǎnlòu* (条件简陋)"; "There is no good food, *méi-yǒu shénmo hǎo cài* (没有什么好菜)"; "It's only a simple meal, *jiācháng biànfàn* (家常便饭)"; and "paltry food and watery wine, not suitable for entertaining guests, *báocài shuǐjiǔ, bù chéng zhāodài* (薄菜水酒, 不成招待)." Timely responses to such disclaimers of performance give the host face and include the speaker in the action of the game. *What* is said is not as important as the act of engaging in the back-and-forth dialogue during which feelings are enhanced. Engaging in food-oriented complimenting and taking part in discourses about food are ways to be recognized at banquets. That is, although *when* participants eat is dictated by the host and *how* they go about the physical act of eating is dictated by cultural expectations, *effective eating* is one mode that allows performers to be a part of the interaction that does not have to involve drinking alcoholic beverages.

Drinking

In his monogram on Shandong culture, Liu Dezeng (1997, 30) proclaims, "When discussing the entertainment of guests, one can not avoid discussing alcohol. In Shandong, drinking is the theme of the entertainment of guests." In other words, drinking is the most common and readily observable cultural medium adopted by players in banquet games and thus forms the core of the game of professional banqueting in Shandong. By drinking with someone, one demonstrates a willingness to do anything for a particular relationship, including harm oneself. In Shandong, drinking also reveals to the audience that one has nothing to hide, affords others face, and shows respect. Drinking, as I have observed the mode of play, serves four main purposes: (1) building face; (2) creating or enhancing feelings; (3) displaying that one is honest and straightforward; and (4) creating a positive atmosphere.

Drinking to Build Face

According to Yang (1994, 140-1), "The Chinese notion of 'face' is an important mechanism through which obligation and reciprocity operate." She defines it as "a combination of a sense of moral imperatives, social honor, and self-respect." Quoting Hu Hsienchin, she adds that face "is gained or lost in the jockeying for social prestige and social advantage. One accumulates face by showing oneself to be capable, wealthy, generous, and possessed of a wide network of social relationships." However, Ambrose King's (1986) notion of face is a more succinct way of capturing the concept: he describes face as a sense of social status that includes what a person thinks of him- or herself in relation to all other people.

The following incident reveals the importance of drinking as a form of face building in Shandong as well as the importance of performing for the group. While I was in Qingdao, a government official intended to invite me to serve as a *péikè* for a banquet that she was hosting. However, she phrased her invitation in this way:

"We have an activity tonight, if you don't have anything to do, come over and hang out, *jīnwǎn yǒu gè huódòng, méishì guòlái wánr* (今晚有个活动, 没事过来玩儿)," and did not explicitly state that I would be a *péikè*. She went on to inform me that she had invited a number of guests and she had told them that a young foreign friend who could speak Chinese would participate. For someone familiar with Shandong banquet culture, the invitation itself would have signaled either that the host wished to request assistance, wanted to reciprocate for something the person had done for her, or needed someone to entertain her guests. Once cued in such a manner, an informed listener would have easily understood his or her role when the host then provided the additional details about who was attending and why. Unfortunately, I interpreted the host's invitation as a gesture of friendship and an expression of her desire to develop our friendship rather than as a request for my assistance in entertaining her guests.

That night, she picked me up on her way to the restaurant, and we arrived before the guests to inspect the banquet room. When, it came out in the course of small talk that I had been too busy to have lunch that afternoon, my host friend immediately became excited and reprimanded me for not eating. At first, I thought my friend's reaction was a display of concern for my well-being; then she asked me how I expected to be able to drink on an empty stomach. I replied that I would be careful to drink only a glass or two. To that, my friend adamantly replied that I had no choice—I must drink and I must "show off, *biǎoxiàn biǎoxiàn* (表现表现)." Again, the phrase "show off" would have immediately cued a native to his or her role in the event. My host friend assumed that I too had understood my role but never explicitly stated that I had been invited to serve as a *péikè*. The urgency in her voice signaled to me that my role was one other than guest. Not knowing what to do in such a situation, I told my host friend that I would just have to drink on an empty stomach. She proceeded to order a plate of dumplings, *shuǐjiǎo* (水饺), for me to eat before the guests arrived. When I told her that I would not be able to eat dinner if I ate *shuǐjiǎo*, she responded that it did not matter if I ate during the meal as long as I could drink. So, I sat at a table for ten by myself, eating *shuǐjiǎo*, while my host friend and her other *péikè* entertained the guests outside the door. When I had finished, the guests were brought in and introductions were made. It is now obvious that my friend would have lost face had I not been able to perform for her guests, and that there were unstated cultural expectations attached to my role as *péikè*. This incident served as story fodder at later banquets and as evidence of my willingness to sacrifice for the relationship.

Drinking to Create Feelings

In Shandong, banquets provide a forum for building *gǎnqíng;* drinking is a vehicle for doing so as well as a means for bridging the gap between two people. One never drinks alone at Shandong banquets even when one is thirsty. Drinking is an inherently social behavior and is a unique shared experience that can serve as the foundation for future exchanges. Most players either first make eye contact with others before raising their glasses in a nonverbal salute prior to simultaneously taking a drink, or they wait for the opportunity to take the stage to toast one person, a group, or all of the participants. This is the case even when everyone knows one another.

Urging

This interpersonal function attached to drinking is the representative characteristic and the most important aspect of banqueting. The goal for players is to engage in the shared experience of drinking and the back-and-forth ritual play associated with the process; it is in this interplay that feelings are developed and enhanced. Host responsibilities include urging guests to drink and eat as much as possible, *quàn jiǔ cài* (劝酒菜). Shandong people have elaborate repertoires for pressuring guests to drink: Players may invoke face issues, class or status, manhood, feelings, friendship, violations of local etiquette, waste or economy, local customs, patriotism, or peer pressure. Following is a list of the verbal scripts used to urge guests to partake; these phrases have different meanings in other situations, but under the right contextual and felicity conditions, they are moves to exert pressure on people to either drink or return the volley.

"Show me a little respect/give me face, *gěi wǒ miànzi ba* (给我面子吧)."

"Are you too good to drink with me, *nǐ kàn bù qǐ wǒ ma* (你看不起我吗)?"

"If you don't drink, you're not a real man, *bù hē bú shì hǎohàn* (不喝不是好汉)."

"When feelings are deep, it's down the hatch in one gulp; when feelings are shallow, drink more to show your sincerity; when feelings are solid as steel, drink until you spit up blood, *gǎnqíng shēn, yì kǒu mēn; gǎnqíng qiǎn, tiǎn yi tiǎn; gǎnqíng tiě, hē tù xiě* (感情深, 一口闷; 感情浅, 舔一舔; 感情铁, 喝吐血)."

"Cut two ribs out for a friend, *wèi péngyou liǎnglèi-chādāo* (为朋友两肋插刀)."

"I'll drink first as a salute to you, *xiān hē wéi jìng* (先喝为敬)."

"You arrived late so we'll fine you three glasses, *lái wǎn le fá nǐ sān bēi* (来晚了罚你三杯)."

"Don't let it go to waste, *bié làngfèi* (别浪费)."

"Good things come in pairs, *hǎoshì chéngshuāng* (好事成双)."

"Three glasses if you sit down, *rù zuò sān bēi* (入座三杯)."

"We're all drinking so you have to too, *nǐ zhān le* (你沾了)."

"Let's drink to the Fatherland, *wèi zǔguó gānbēi* (为祖国干杯)."

"One look and I knew you were above board, *yī kàn jiùshi gè shízài rén* (一看就是个实在人)."

"Today I've really drunk a lot/I'm having a good time, *jīntiān hē de shízài tòngkuài* (今天喝得实在痛快)."

"Break a rule today, *jīntiān pòlì* (今天破例)."

"One look and I knew you could drink an ocean, *yī kàn jiù zhīdào nǐ shì hǎiliàng* (一看就知道你是海量)."

"We were destined to meet, *yǒu yuánfèn* (有缘分)."

"Unsolvable problems become solvable at the banquet table, *jiǔzhuō shàng shǎ dōu hǎo shuō le* (酒桌上啥都好说了)."

"When drinking, if you can't drink, it's best not to speak too much, *yǐnjiǔliàng bú dà, zuìhǎo shǎo fāhuà* (饮酒量不大, 最好少发话)."

"Feelings are still not there yet, *háishì gǎnqíng méi dào wèi* (还是感情没到位)."

"Drinking can spur economic development, *hē jiǔ néng gǎo huó jīngjì* (喝酒能搞活经济)."

"If you want to develop business, you must lift bowls when drinking, *shēngyì yào fāzhǎn, hē jiǔ yào duān wǎn* (生意要发展, 喝酒要端碗)."

"Drinking while standing doesn't count, *zhànzhe hē bú suàn* (站着喝不算)."

"Leaders can drink as they please, *lǐngdǎo kěyǐ suíyì* (领导可以随意)."

"When drinking with intimate friends, a thousand glasses is not enough, *jiǔ féng zhījǐ qiān bēi shǎo* (酒逢知己千杯少)."

"If the fish head stops at you, it's three glasses. If the tail stops at you, it's four glasses, *tóu sān wěi sì* (头三尾四)."

"Let's drink one, *wǒmen hē yí gè/wǒmen gān yí gè* (我们喝一个/我们干一个)."

"It's (our feelings/the words are) all in the wine, *dōu zài jiǔ lǐtou* (都在酒里头)."

Deflecting

Although it is the guest's responsibility to partake of the repast provided by the host, guests do not have to drink every time hosts suggest that they do. As the Chinese proverb states, "The drinker's mind is not in the wine, *zuìwēng zhī yì bú zài jiǔ* (醉翁之意不在

酒)." That is, while playing this game, the importance of drinking is secondary to the interplay with others present. While hosts are toasting and urging guests to drink, guests are thinking of and offering reasons why they should not have to drink. When a player urges another to drink, there is no requirement to drink but rather to make a corresponding move—and the more creative the move, the better the atmosphere becomes. Thus, successful deflections often employ traditional sayings, proverbs, and quotations of famous people in innovative ways, and others have been turned into witty rhymes. A successful return prolongs the round by requiring an additional countermove by the initiator. I have been witness to volleys that ranged from one response to several minutes. It is believed that the keys to banquets—feelings and atmosphere—emerge and develop during these exchanges.

As a result, the verbal script for deflecting urges to drink is just as elaborate as the one for urging. Guests can refuse to drink on the grounds they are ill or hung over, are taking medicine or have a toothache, have work to do, do not drink at all or are allergic to alcohol, or lack the ability to drink. Likewise, they may evoke face, status, friendship, local customs, or the opinions of important third parties. Here are a few of the reasons I have heard for not drinking; some of them were standards used by numerous players, and others were patented by individuals to be used whenever necessary.

"Too much liquor influences work, *jiǔ duō wùshì* (酒多误事)."

"My stomach is bad, *wǒ wèi bù hǎo* (我胃不好)."

"My tolerance is limited, *wǒ jiǔliàng yǒu xiàn* (我酒量有限)."

"We are all old friends, is there any need, *wǒmen doū shì lǎo péngyou, hébì ne* (我们都是老朋友, 何必呢)."

"My wife won't be happy, *lǎopo huì bù gāoxìng* (老婆会不高兴)."

"One more drink and I'll fall over, *zài hē yào dǎo* (再喝要倒)."

"I'm done/I can't drink anymore, *wǒ bù xíng le* (我不行了)."

"If you drink it all, I'll drink it all, *nǐ gān wǒ jiù gān* (你干我就干)."

"My tolerance is small, so I'll use a small glass, *wǒ jiǔliàng xiǎo, wǒ yòng xiǎo bēizi* (我酒量小, 我用小杯子)."

"I don't touch a drop of alcohol, *wǒ shì dī jiǔ bù zhān* (我是滴酒不沾)."

"It's too hard on the body, *tài shāng shēntǐ le* (太伤身体了)."

"I drank too much yesterday, *zuótiān hē dà le* (昨天喝大了)."

"When friends are piled together, they don't push alcohol, *péngyou yì duī, hē jiǔ bù tuī* (朋友一堆, 喝酒不推)."

"I have a toothache, *wǒ yá téng* (我牙疼)."

"I'm allergic to alcohol, *wǒ hē jiǔ guòmǐn* (我喝酒过敏)."

"I'm on medication, *wǒ chī yào le* (我吃药了)."

"I can't control myself any longer, *wǒ cǐ bú zhù le* (我跐不住了)."

"I will drink only a little, *wǒ shǎo hē yìdiǎnr* (我少喝一点儿)."

Even when it appears that players are not coercing others to drink, they may actually be applying pressure. For example, I have been in situations in which both "leaders can drink as they please" and "there's no need to force (someone to do something he doesn't want to), *nà jiù búbì miǎnqiǎng le* (那就不必勉强了)" were delivered with the opposite effect—they increased the pressure to drink with only a subtle shift in intonation or facial expression.

Drinking to Display Candidness

One of the characteristics Shandong people value most is being *shízài* (实在), a notion that cannot be likened to one word in English. Additional terms that can be found in Shandong that refer to this same concept include "forthright," *shuàizhēn* (率真), a more literary term, and "upright," *zhígāng* (直刚), a term used in the Zibo dialect. People who are *shízài* are candid in their relationships, straightforward about their motives and intentions, and honest in their speech and actions. If one is willing to sacrifice oneself for a friend, one is perceived as being committed to the friendship and as not having any ulterior motives. Thus, the person is deemed *shízài*.

Shízài also involves the notion of one's true nature or character. Drinking provides a means for both displaying that one is *shízài* and for assessing if others are *shízài* because alcohol tends to break down fronts so that our true colors show through. As a local saying puts it, "After drinking, we spit out the truth, *jiǔhòu tù zhēnyán* (酒后吐真言)." In a public setting, the weight of display is added because of the presence of face. Drinking with someone affords him or her face, and such a performance in front of a group, if effective, can prove that you are *shízài*, thus deepening feelings by closing the gap between players. Because drinking is viewed as a way to determine if a player can be trusted and depended upon, to abstain, under certain conditions, would be a statement of one's unwillingness to reveal something to the group, which would leave doubt in the minds of the other players about that person's trustworthiness and dependability.

More often than not, Americans in China were not viewed as *shízài* by our hosts, but were often considered *shăhūhūde* (傻乎乎的), a term that can be rendered as "simple-minded." This is a drastically different concept that described the drinking patterns of people who, because they did not understand the purposes underlying the drinking ritual or the rules of the game, continually overdrank. They focused on the outward behavior, in this case drinking, as an act on its own detached from the interpersonal play and atmosphere of the event. One friend explained to me that drinking to excess in a sincere display of friendship under the right conditions, and without ulterior motive, was a display of true *shízài*. On the other hand, drinking to excess without knowing why one was doing so was considered *shăhūhūde*. Often players derived pleasure out of getting foreign guests drunk by continually telling them that they were *shízài* in their drinking, which encouraged them to drink more. This deceptive act itself was deemed to be anything but *shízài* by many other Shandong people, but entertaining nonetheless.

Drinking to Test Manhood

The phenomenon of face sometimes turns banquets into competitive situations, referred to colloquially as "drinking challenges, *hē dŭqì jiŭ* (喝赌气酒)," in which players challenge one another's drinking capacities. Because the ability to drink large amounts of alcohol is seen as a symbol of being a man, those who can drink without getting drunk, or at least who can appear not to be affected by large amounts of spirits, earn a certain amount of face and status. References to folk figures such as Wu Song and Liu Ling, who reportedly had unrivaled capacities to drink, are often used to describe such people. Also, *báijiǔ* is perceived to be the most potent of all alcoholic beverages and is accorded a special place in the minds of Shandong people. Therefore, men who can consume large quantities of *báijiǔ* without appearing to be drunk are looked upon as "real men, *hǎohàn* (好汉)." Kipnis (1997) points out that men often size up their competitors by the number of ounces of *báijiǔ* they can consume.

Men who cannot drink are seen as having less face and, therefore, as less capable. The ramifications are that in the social setting, there is extreme pressure on Shandong men to drink in order to display their capabilities and protect their face. On several occasions, I witnessed superiors, such as managers and teachers, repeatedly pressuring their subordinates and students to drink. In each case, the superior ridiculed the subordinate for not being up to standards and stated that by forcing him to drink, the superior was helping the subordinate develop the ability to drink through practice, *duànliàn* (锻炼), which he also claimed would make the subordinate a better person. The added element of performing up to their superior's standards and giving face to superiors often led to over-consumption and drunkenness on the part of the subordinate.

The Art of Drinking

As a result of the elaborate interplay and drinking wars that occur during banquets, drinking has developed into an art form. Tactics for when to drink, when not to drink, when to toast, when not to toast, how to respond to toasts, how to make others drink, and how to keep from drinking too much all are indispensable. On numerous occasions, banqueters suggested that I read *Romance of the Three*

Kingdoms and *The Art of War* for strategies and tactics that could be applied to the banquet setting. The combination of face and the notion that hosts feel it is their responsibility to ensure that their guests drink sufficient amounts of alcohol makes it easy to see how someone not well versed in the Shandong-style art of drinking could become drunk very rapidly. This is especially the case when there are tactics such as the "wagon wheel tactic, *chēlún zhànshù* (车轮战术)," adopted for dealing with outsiders and adversaries. In this strategy, several people take turns attacking one individual in order to defeat him or to achieve the ultimate goal of ensuring all guests, even those who have large drinking capacities, drink to their fill. In the banquet setting, this tactic involves several players working together, taking turns toasting someone one by one, usually the honored guest, until he is drunk. They each drink once for the target's numerous drinks, generally without his realizing what is happening until it is too late.

Although some know only how to participate in this single mode of play, drinking is merely one mode among many available to banquet participants. Perhaps because drinking takes such a devastating toll on the body, there are also numerous modes of performance that don't involve alcohol, including toasting, singing, smoking, storytelling, dancing, and joke telling. Each of the modes—with the exception of toasting, which often intensifies drinking situations—can be used as a means of engaging others present in recognized and acceptable ways diverting attention from drinking. Singing, storytelling, dancing, and joke telling typically occur in the latter stages of banquets after participants have had sufficient time to eat and drink. Moreover, these activities can be going on at the same time. For instance, I have been present at banquets in which some participants were engaged in drinking wars, while others were singing karaoke, and still others were dancing along with the music. However, when most performances such as dancing, singing, or storytelling are completed, participants typically applaud and toast the performer.

Toasting

Toasting, *jìngjiǔ* (敬酒) or *zhùjiǔ* (祝酒), is an integral but extremely complex skill associated with the drinking mode. Many of the moves involved in the art of drinking are implemented through some form of toasting: how to toast, when to toast, and when not to toast are all types of knowledge vital to banquet survival. The importance of toasting is also noted by Kipnis (1997, 53-4), who sees refusing a toast as tantamount to refusing to give face, which is the "starting point for relationships." There are three distinct periods of toasting in Shandong banquets. First, activities generally open with six ritual toasts—three each—delivered by the principal and assistant hosts. Up to the point of the sixth toast, guests do not initiate any toasting, and all interaction is directed by either the principal host or the assistant host. The rhythm of interaction is fixed with a toast followed by short intervals of eating and small talk before another toast is offered. Second, there is a period of open toasting in which all players freely toast one another, although the higher status participants toast first and lower status individuals wait for an appropriate time to offer their toasts. During numerous banquets, when an individual broke ranks by toasting out of turn, comments that acknowledge the recognized order were offered by other participants. This type of error is described as "destroying order, *pòhuài zhìxù* (破坏秩序)." Finally, drinking and the banquet are brought to a close with a ritual toast lead by the principal host.

Although in performance, this opening ritual occurs in many variations, local tradition insists that at least three ritual toasts are conducted to open banquets. Some banqueters claim that omitting one of the three ritual toasts would be symbolic of violating the fraternal pact made famous by the novel *Romance of the Three Kingdoms,* and thus the participants would not be considered fraternally loyal, *yìqi* (义气). In the famous scene, "the peach garden pact, *táoyuán sān jiéyì* (桃园三结义)," the three heroes Liu Bei, Zhang Fei, and Guan Yu swore allegiance and brotherhood. Others associate the tradition of three drinks to open a banquet with other events recorded in the literary tradition. Many banqueters allude to the folk hero Wu Song, who in the novel *The Water Margin* killed a tiger with his bare hands after having gotten drunk at an inn at the foot of Jingyang Mountain. A sign posted at the inn stated that those who drank three or more bowls of wine could not cross the mountain, "*sān wǎn bú guò gǎng* (三碗不过岗)." Whatever its origin, most players in Shandong observe this tradition of three ritual toasts regardless of whether they strictly adhere to other rules of banquet etiquette.

The Opening Ceremony

The principal host signals that the event is about to begin with a ceremonial first toast in which he welcomes his guests, invites them to partake of the repast, and delivers disclaimers of performance in the form of self-deprecating remarks. All players are expected to participate in this inclusive toast, even those not drinking alcohol, who are expected to raise glasses of tea or water in symbolic acts of participation. These nondrinking participants always offer performance disclaimers such as those mentioned earlier to excuse themselves from the consumption of alcohol. If a player is to abstain during a banquet, this is the period in which it is possible to do so. It is virtually impossible to stop drinking once you have started to do so without offending someone at the banquet. With that in mind, one effective strategy that I have seen players (this seems to be more commonly employed by women than men) adopt is to start the banquet off by stating that one does not drink. Then, once many rounds of toasts have gone by and most other participants have consumed large amounts of alcohol, players using this tactic state that because they are having such a wonderful time that they will break their habit of not drinking as a display of their sincerity towards those present.

While offering his toast, the principal host raises his glass, with all present following his lead. When the host has finished delivering the verbal portion of the toast, all players continue with a ritual touching of the glasses. On formal occasions, hosts move around the table touching glasses with each participant. During banquets when a large number of people are meeting for the first time, players tap glasses with each participant one by one. During more casual events, players may tap glasses only with those seated next to them but still attempt to make eye contact with each participant. Once eye contact is made, both parties raise their glasses and lower their heads slightly in a symbolic act that takes the place of actually touching glasses. After the ritual touching of glasses has been completed, participants often tap the Lazy Susan to allow the feelings to flow among participants and the toast is completed with the phrase "dry glasses, *gān bēi* (干杯)." Here are several examples of opening toasts that I observed:

1) Everyone please open your minds and drink and eat to your fill. Weak liquor and paltry food, not worthy of entertaining guests, I hope everyone has it in them to forgive me.

   Qǐng dàjiā kāihuái-chàngyǐn, chī hǎo hē hǎo, shuǐjiǔ báocài, bù chéng zhāodài, wàng dàjiā hǎihán.

   请大家开怀畅饮, 吃好喝好,水酒薄菜, 不成招待, 望大家海涵。

2) Everyone please eat until you are satisfied, drink until you are merry and play to your heart's content.

92

Qǐng gèwèi chī de mǎnyì, hē de kāixīn, wán de jìnxìng.

请各位吃得满意,喝得开心,玩得尽兴。

3)   Everyone please eat well, drink well, play well and delight well.

Qǐng dàjiā chī hǎo, hē hǎo, wán hǎo, lè hǎo.

请大家吃好,喝好, 玩好, 乐好。

4)   Everyone please fill your glasses full of wine, open your minds and drink freely…I hope everyone forgives me (for any insufficiencies).

Qǐng dàjiā zhēn mǎn jiǔ kāihuái-chàngyǐn….wàng dàjiā duōduō bāohán.

请大家斟满酒开怀畅饮…..望大家多多包涵。

5)   First, I would like to express a warm welcome and my sincere thanks that everyone was able to come and participate in (today's/tonight's) party.

Shǒuxiān, wǒ duì dàjiā néng lái cānjiā wǎnhuì biǎoshì rèliè de huānyíng he zhōngxīn de gǎnxiè.

首先,我对大家能来参加晚会表示热烈的欢迎和衷心的感谢。

The various ritual mannerisms associated with the act of toasting should be addressed here. First, one purpose that such inclusive toasts serve is to create a positive atmosphere and get all present involved in the action. Next, the size of banquet tables is often too large to allow players to reach any other participants besides those to their immediate right and left. As a result, the custom of tapping the glasses on the glass Lazy Susan, that is, "conducting electricity" mentioned earlier, has emerged to prevent everyone from having to get up and circle the room to bump glasses. When glasses are tapped, *pèngbēi* (碰杯), the expectation is that all of the contents in the glass will be emptied in one drink regardless of what it is; to do otherwise is deemed not being *shízài*. That is, when players desire to down their entire glass in one gulp, they bump glasses and when they want to take a sip, they make eye contact and raise their glass in a symbolic gesture without actually allowing their glasses to touch. It is possible to add a half-glass disclaimer, but it must be delivered before touching glasses.

Additionally, when touching glasses, players hold their glasses with *two* hands and attempt to lower the rim of their glass below that of their counterpart in acts of deference. I have observed this carried out to the extreme with some players lowering their glasses below the edge of the table and almost touching the floor. When both delivering and receiving toasts, the phrase *gānbēi* (干杯) is said by all parties involved in the toast. *Gānbēi* literally means "dry glass" and carries the sense of "bottoms up" and "cheers." Finally, after a player empties his glass, he normally tilts it toward the person who has toasted him, allowing him to see the dry bottom of the glass. This ritual, called "revealing your glass, *liàng bēi* (亮杯)," symbolizes the actors' attempt to be *shízài* and is occasionally recognized with a verbal acknowledgment, "thank you, *xièxie* (谢谢),"a nod, or by raising one hand—open palm facing the person who has revealed his or her glass—and a smile.

After drinking the first glass, the principal host then invites all guests to partake of whatever food is on the table. While the guests are eating, their glasses are immediately refilled. Normally this is performed by waitresses; however, if a waitress has left the room to get the next dish, one of the lower-ranking *péikè* will take it upon him- or herself to refill all glasses beginning with the most important guest. A guest's glass must never be allowed to remain empty, which keeps waitresses extremely busy at large banquets.

Following a brief period of small talk, the host then carries out his second inclusive toast, the content of which is normally very broad in nature. In business situations in which two parties are in the midst of negotiations or where two organizations have been working on a joint project, the principal host takes the opportunity to deliver a statement of his desire for overall success. The second toast is performed in the same manner as the first and again is followed by the host inviting the guests to partake of food and glasses being immediately refilled. This toast is also followed by a period of small talk in which the hosts obtain information about their guests that may be useful in subsequent toasts later in the banquet. This is also the period in which players begin sizing each other up for potential drinking contests. Examples of this form of toast include "Wishing our cooperation is smooth, bottoms up, *zhù wǒmen hézuò shùnlì, gānbēi* (祝我们合作顺利，干杯)," "To our smooth cooperation, bottoms up, *wèi wǒmen de hézuò shùnlì, gānbēi* (为我们的合作顺利, 干杯)," and "Wishing our cooperation is successful, *zhù wǒmen hézuò chénggōng* (祝我们合作成功)."

Finally, the principal host's part in the opening ceremony comes to a close with his third group toast. The content of the third toast varies widely, but always attempts to make a connection with all of the participants. Examples of this type of toast are "To our friendship, bottoms up, *wèi wǒmen de yǒuyì, gānbēi* (为我们的友谊, 干杯)" and "To today's get-together, bottoms up, *wèi wǒmen jīntiān de xiāngjù, gānbēi* (为我们今天的相聚，干杯)."

If a banquet involves multiple tables, both the principal and assistant hosts are expected to perform a ritual toast at every table. This is performed sometime after the end of the opening ceremony, first by the principal host and then by the assistant host. So that guests at the main table are never left unattended, the two hosts switch seats, even if that includes gathering up their chopsticks and glasses and moving to a different table. Some hosts who wish to display their hospitality and to strictly observe local etiquette toast each guest at every table, but most avoid forcing themselves to drink any more than is absolutely necessary at this early stage in the festivities as all participants are expected to drink everything in their glass during the first toast. Once the principal host has performed his ceremonial three toasts, control of the interaction will shift to the assistant host, who has the responsibility of delivering the next three toasts. One friend commented that the assistant host must be more creative and flexible than the principal host for at least two reasons. First, the principal host's toasts come first and are normally restricted to welcome toasts that have prescribed formats. Second, the host usually does not need to worry that what he says will offend anyone in the hosting party. The assistant host, on the contrary, must be sure not to encroach on the principal host's face.

Because of this second fact, the assistant host generally opens his first toast by building up the principal host's face before delivering his own version of a welcome toast. This type of toast might begin with a statement such as *wǒ dàibiǎo Wáng júzhǎng* (我代表王局长…), which can be translated as either "On behalf of Director Wang..." or "I represent Director Wang," and concludes by repeating the act of welcoming guests. Another variant involves the assistant host's use of the phrase "borrow flowers to present to Buddha, *jièhuā-xiànfó* (借花献佛)." (Referring to the intended target of the toast as "Buddha" is a way of showing respect to them while "borrowing flowers" offers acknowledgment to the host for providing the opportunity.) Once the formality of giving the principal host his due has been disposed of, the fifth toast allows the assistant host to display his verbal creativity. For the most part, assistant hosts utilize this second toast to build the atmosphere and draw everyone into the festivities. A banquet's opening ceremony comes to a close with the delivery of the assistant host's third toast, which normally expresses his and his host's desire to have many more opportunities to host the guests present at the event.

On one occasion while being hosted by the local government of Shidao, a small fishing town located on the southeastern tip of the Jiaodong Peninsula, one of our US/China Links colleagues, who was aware of the importance of toasting but not the importance of timing, attempted to offer a toast of appreciation to the principal host at his table before the sixth toast had been delivered. What followed was an elaborate explanation of the toasting procedures and rules that must be observed in Shandong Province, a sure signal that this man had violated the rules of etiquette. In nearly every instance in which I observed a foreign guest violate rules of banquet etiquette, the act was immediately followed not by direct correction, but by explanations of how Shandong people conduct themselves in like situations. "Reprimands" of this sort clearly show that there are recognized rules that constrain and guide participation and are important sources of information about etiquette in Shandong. These "reprimands" also indicate that there is the understood assumption that all participants should comply with the established rules of banquet etiquette.

When hosts deliver toasts, guests typically respond with one or more of the phrases to avoid drinking listed earlier (the phrases can be very creative and can build on one another), which prompts hosts to employ one of the phrases used to urge guests to drink. This verbal jousting associated with drinking can be an interaction mode in and of itself. Many women, men who have low tolerance for alcohol, and older participants play the game with tea or soft drinks in place of alcoholic beverages. Other times, the phrase *suíyì* (随意) meaning "drink and eat as you please," signals to participants that the drinking mode will take a back seat to other interaction modes. In such instances, toasting is carried out as a ritual means to show respect or gratitude without or with minimal drinking involved. This further suggests that the pleasure and significance in the drinking ritual lies not in the drinking itself but in the verbal jousting and human interaction associated with it. One highly skilled veteran player stated that she found herself in banquets nearly every day but rarely had to drink because of her verbal prowess. She claimed to talk other players drunk, *bǎ tāmen shuō zuì le* (把他们说醉了).

Free-Flow Toasting

Once the opening six toasts have been delivered, the drinking wars begin in earnest. This stage is frequently initiated with the phrase *suíyì*. During this extended period, hosts and guests alternate toasting one another in a much less ordered fashion while dialogue becomes more free-flowing than in the early stages of a banquet. A concurrent shift in conversation patterns also occurs moving from a more formal, much slower form of interaction in which one player speaks at a time to a multiparty interaction in which players must process significant amounts of information from different sources simultaneously. Toasting, during this phase of the game, serves one of four functions: (1) bridging the gap; (2) exchanging feelings; (3) building the atmosphere; and (4) displaying mutual respect or giving face. Although the function is left unstated, participants recognize which is being invoked by the wording used to deliver the toast.

Toasting to Bridge the Gap

As stated earlier, one important goal of banqueting is to bridge the gap that exists between strangers. Through toasting, both hosts and guests appeal to shared identities in order to bring others into their inner circles. Yang (1994) notes that people from the same place, colleagues, and classmates possess the types of relationships considered most intimate and valued. Thus, banquet goers often attempt to bring other players into their circles by using intimate terms of address or by acknowledging a fictitious intimacy with them during toasting.

In Shandong, I observed two distinct strategies for attempting to bridge the gap with me that involved using intimate terms of address. First, hosts, who were in every instance older, would often adopt the term *xiǎo* (小), meaning "young," as a prefix to my surname when toasting me, in an attempt to place us on familiar terms. The second strategy adopted the opposite and more honorific *lǎo* (老), meaning "old," for the same purpose. When I inquired about the logic behind fifty-year-old officials calling a thirty-year-old guest old, the reply was that it should be interpreted in the sense of old friend, and is employed because it sounds more intimate, *qīnqiè* (亲切).

Another move I encountered was elevating me to the status of a local. On numerous occasions, hosts and *péikè* employed statements such as "You are half a Shandongnese, *bàn gè Shāndōngrén* (半个山东人)," or "You are half a home-townsman, *bàn gè lǎoxiāng* (半个老乡)." These statements were intended to bring me into the user's inner circle and bridge the gap that existed between us. These were strategies consciously adopted by the user and were more often than not adopted by players not already on intimate terms with me; players who were intimate displayed similar feelings in their actions rather than verbally.

An effective strategy for successfully performing in a banquet that experienced Shandong players rely on can be viewed as making oneself less of an outsider. One use of this tactic involves employing the inclusive form of the pronoun *zán* (咱), or "we," rather than the more commonly used noninclusive *wǒ* (我) when referring to the host unit. For example, when addressing the host, Director Wang, guests would include themselves as one of Mr. Wang's subordinates by saying "Our Director Wang..., *zámen Wáng zhǔrèn* (咱们王主任)..." rather than "Director Wang." Or, when referring to the hosting unit Yantai Port Authorities, a guest wishing to sound more intimate would use "Our Port Authorities, *zámen gǎngwùjú* (咱们港务局)." It is important to note that when foreigners adopt this strategy of using inclusive terms, there are sometimes different negative results. Although people from Shandong frequently make statements indicating that they accept outsiders as members of the group or as participants in an activity, many are sensitive to outsiders making those claims themselves. I have heard negative behind-the-scenes comments about such claims by nonnatives and have been advised by friends on several occasions to avoid making them myself.

Toasting to Exchange Feelings

Toasting is also an effective means of acknowledging friendships through the exchange of feelings. This use of toasting is employed by players who have banqueted together previously or who are familiar with one other in some other capacity. Toasts in this category often refer to the length of time players have been friends and are personal in nature. By the third time I drank with an individual, I was often honored with a toast that included some version of the statement "We are already old friends, *wǒmen yǐjīng shì lǎo péngyou le* (我们已经是老朋友了)." Another phrase frequently used to express the same idea is, "The first time we drink together we are strangers, the second time we know one another, *yī huí shēng èr huí shóu*(一回生二回熟)." It is in this capacity that players are expected to display *shízài*. Friends are well aware of each other's drinking capacities and expect each other to be *shízài* in their drinking and toasting. As noted earlier, the expectations of the group place tremendous pressure on individual players, in this case, to drink. Drinking as an activity is used to create bonds among individuals, alcohol is often viewed as a conduit for the flow of feelings, and toasting is the mechanism that sets this process in action.

Toasting to Build the Atmosphere

A third function of toasting is to build the atmosphere of the occasion. If hosts feel that the occasion is not festive enough or is too tense, or if they sense that their guests might be bored, they immediately propose a toast to liven things up. Kipnis (1997, 54) also observed a similar phenomenon in western Shandong: "skillful host reps coaxed their guests to drink and relax." Examples of such toasts are typically inclusive, characterized by terms such as "Liven up, *rènào rènào*, (热闹热闹),"and employ appeals to feelings. For this reason, it is important for guests to appear to be enjoying themselves whether or not they actually are. Otherwise, hosts will continue to toast them until they are "happy, *gāoxìng* (高兴),"which, as Kipnis (1997) notes, carries the connotations of consuming large quantities of alcohol and food.

Toasting to Give Face

Showing respect for a player is another goal of toasts. Kipnis (1997, 54) observes that "toasts materialize respect" among participants at banquets. It is expected that guests, at a minimum, show their respect and appreciation to the principal host with one toast of gratitude during the course of the event. An example of a typical toast of gratitude is "Thank you for your gracious hospitality and cordial treatment, *xièxie nín de shèngqíng kuǎndài* (谢谢您的盛情款待)." Most guests feel it necessary to toast everyone present at least once so as not to offend any particular player by not giving him or her the face a toast affords. Although skillful declines are appreciated, players must be aware of the implications of not drinking or not participating in the toasting ritual. The face gained and given and the feelings built through participation far outweigh the discomfort of drinking a few glasses of *báijiǔ*. Moreover, experienced players consciously manipulate their toasting strategies so that they take advantage of such attitudes.

One example of how players manipulate toasting can be seen in the female host friend mentioned earlier. Women hold an advantageous position in the drinking game because they are not expected to drink. Additionally, because of male attitudes about their superiority in drinking, men in Shandong feel that they cannot refuse when toasted by a woman. If they refuse to drink with a woman, they lose face and are shamed, *diūliǎn* (丢脸), in front of the group for being less manly. This female host mentioned before was well aware of this fact and deftly used it to her advantage. She was able to make men drink whenever she felt it necessary, but did not have the same set of expectations placed upon her by her male counterparts to drink. As soon as she wanted to stop drinking, she merely needed to say that she had consumed too much. For women, there were no repercussions for stopping in the middle of battle, a fact that caused men to avoid getting into drinking contests with women because of the obvious lose-lose situation. A local proverb reflects the powerful advantage women hold in the banquet setting: "If you are a skilled drinker, you still have to defend yourself from women, *hē jiǔ yǒu shuǐpíng, yě yào fǎng nǚrén* (喝酒有水平，也要防女人)."

A second tactic critical to survival in Shandong drinking wars as revealed by an experienced native can be seen as a type of bluffing. First, one must size up the competition while determining the purpose and importance of the banquet. If, in the early stages of the interaction, another player reveals some weakness in his drinking abilities, it may be safe to use the "big talk, *shuō dàhuà* (说大话)" approach in which one brags about the amount of alcohol one can consume in an attempt to scare one's opponent out of a direct confrontation or at least place a seed of doubt in the minds of unfamiliar players. However, the player adopting this strategy must be prepared to suffer the consequences in the event the opposition calls his bluff.

A third tactic that some players adopt when their reconnaissance reveals that the opponent might be a formidable drinker is the reverse psychology method; this involves continually stating that one's capacity to drink is minimal, but delivering such self-effacing statements in a manner that causes the opposition to interpret them as displays of modesty and attempts to draw them into a drinking competition. The goal again is to avoid drinking by insinuating that one is a wily and seasoned veteran.

On many occasions, it is during the free-flow toasting segment of a banquet that the purpose for the banquet becomes clear to the participants. Because the stage is open for all participants to make toasts or raise topics of conversation, propositions and requests are made, future plans are laid out, and players' desires and intentions are revealed. However, this is also the stage in which banquets often become competitions involving players each trying to out perform or one-up the other in both drinking and verbal jousting. One of the most successful players I observed in the banqueting game of Shandong commented that all participants in a banquet are thinking all the time of what to say, always trying to build on what others have said, and waiting for their opportunity to make the requisite statements and toasts. He further stated that participants are not thinking of eating during a banquet, but rather are spending every ounce of energy trying to outperform other participants.

Performing Toasts

As has already been shown, the verbal component of toasting can be quite creative and is event specific. However, the fundamental structure of toasts includes a preface with the phrases "I toast/salute you, *wǒ jìng nǐ* (我敬你)," "I wish, *zhù* (祝…)," "For the sake of…, *wèi* (为…)," or "I propose, *wǒ tíyì* (我提议)," and an ending of "dry glasses, *gānbēi* (干杯)." Titles and names typically precede such phrases, and the deliverer always stands, raising his or her glass with two hands in a display of respect toward the target of the salute. More important, the toaster must toast with a full glass and down all of the contents to display sincerity and *shízài*. In every banquet I have attended in which a player has attempted to toast with a partial glass, other players have insisted that he first fill the glass completely before they would acknowledge the toast. Some players used the act of filling an empty or partially filled glass after getting everyone's attention as an overt display of their sincerity. Toasters who did not empty their glasses after delivering toasts invited verbal attacks from other players that not only ensured that they finished what was in the glass but also required additional "penalty drinks, *fájiǔ* (罚酒)."

I close this chapter with a list of common toasts that I encountered while banqueting in Shandong:

"This glass is to you, *wǒ jìng nǐ yì bēi* (我敬你一杯)."

"Wishing you thriving business, *zhù nín shēngyì xīnglóng* (祝您生意兴隆)."

"Wishing you career success, *zhù nín shìyè yǒuchéng* (祝您事业有成)."

"Wishing you a healthy body and success at work, *zhù nín shēntǐ jiànkāng, gōngzuò shùnlì* (祝您身体健康，工作顺利)."

"Wishing you all that you desire, *zhù nín wànshì-rúyì* (祝您万事如意)."

"Wishing you success in your studies and daily improvement, *zhù nǐ hǎohāo xuéxí tiāntiān xiàngshàng* (祝你好好学习，天天向上)."

"Wishing your heart's desires become reality, *zhù nín xīnxiǎng-shìchéng* (祝您心想事成)."

"Wishing your good dreams come true, *zhù nín hǎo mèng chéng zhēn* (祝您好梦成真)."

"Wishing you a happy family life and continual riches, *zhù nín jiātíng méimǎn xìngfú, tiāntiān fācái* (祝您家庭美满幸福, 天天发财)."

CHAPTER FOUR

The Language of Banquets

The language used at banquets is particularly rich and varied. Banquet goers draw from their entire inventory of classicisms, proverbs, rhymes, jokes, metaphors, allusions, stories, and crosstalk, *xiēhòuyǔ* (歇后语). Moreover, verbal exchanges at banquets accomplish a variety of ends including information exchange, construction of *gǎnqíng*, social and business transactions, humor, management of face, and the performance of rituals associated with the banquet context. Much of Shandong banquet language is either associated with ritual complimenting and etiquette or is some form of what folklorist John McDowell (1992, 139) refers to as speech play; that is, "the creative disposition of language resources or the manipulation of formal features and processes of language to achieve a striking restructuring of familiar discourse alignments." The speech play found at banquets is most often used to establish or enhance social bonding among participants, which, as already stated, is the primary goal of banquet play.

McDowell (1992, 140-4) divides speech play into wordplay, verbal games, special linguistic codes, and poetic forms. Wordplay refers to isolated, discrete moments of speech play such as puns, speech metaphor, antistasis, hyperbation, synecdoche, wellerisms, conundrums, spoonerisms, and malapropism. Verbal games refer to situations in which speech play is harnessed to gaming structures such as jokes, riddles, catches, and verbal dueling. Special linguistic codes are speech play carried out systematically over an entire discourse segment to produce distinctive ways of speaking for special social purposes. Finally, poetic forms are speech play harnessed to artistic expression in traditional genres such as proverbs, ballads, and limericks. All of McDowell's examples of wordplay can be found in the various verbal activities, toasting rituals, and general discourse of banquets including puns, proverbs, *yànyǔ* (谚语), *chéngyǔ* (成语), and *súyǔ* (俗语), which can be similar to wellerisms in use.

Accommodation and Banquet Language

As in any communicative situation, the forms of rhetoric adopted and topics of discourse broached are determined by the players present, their relationships, and the goals of the event. Young (1994), among others, has shown that people make choices about language use based on characteristics of other participants in the speech event. She adds that "individuals choose unconsciously (without having to think about it) which communicative features are most appropriate given the person(s) to whom they are speaking." This means that banquet players need to know not only the discourse types and patterns but also what to say and how to say it when different combinations of players are present. The result is that Shandong players' choices of what to talk about when Americans are present are inherently different from when only Chinese are present. In banquets I have attended that involved other foreign participants, what normally developed were discussions about the United States, US-China relations, or differences in American and Chinese culture, especially those concerning dining, drinking, and banqueting.

When dealing with foreigners who are not viewed as players, the register in which Shandong players speak can be called "foreigner Chinese" (Duranti 1981; Ochs and Schieffelin 1990): this is a modified Chinese, or metalanguage, adopted to facilitate communication and comprehension. Native players consciously and subconsciously alter their speech in terms of speed, vocabulary, register, discourse strategies, references, structures, and topics when dealing with foreign interlocutors. They also make adjustments in terms of cultural expectations, ways of establishing and interpreting intentions, and the goals of interaction when dealing with foreigners. Such a shift facilitates communication in the cases where the speaker knows very well what the foreign listener knows and understands. Banquets conducted in "foreigner Chinese" are inherently different from those that are played by the normal rules of the game. In banquets in which I was the only foreign player, which were more than likely conducted in a mode somewhere between "foreigner Chinese" and the normal game mode, a number of such distinctions became discernable. In an environment of less accommodation, the number and use of classic quotes, proverbs, and idioms increased dramatically as well as the number and types of speech play.

In banquets involving only locals, the amount and importance of verbal play are more pronounced. When foreigners or Chinese not from Shandong are present, other forms of participation may come to the forefront because of barriers caused by use of the local dialect and locally specific background knowledge, which supports McDowell's notion that speech play is inherently ecological (McDowell 1992). When outsiders do participate, the context shifts to a slightly more formal one reserved for outsiders. The presence of foreigners brings about the use of English words and foreignisms, and the presence of nonlocal Chinese restricts speech play to the standard national dialect and local culture and in-group-based humor is often eliminated from these banquets as a result (Apte 1992, 73).

Complimenting

As alluded to earlier in connection with guesting, because of the cultural themes of modesty, reciprocity, and face, complimenting is an important verbal component of that particular mode of play. Guests use flattery, *pěng* (捧), and compliments, *gōngwéihuà* (恭维话), to ingratiate themselves with the host as well as to divert attention away from drinking. Hosts use flattery to make guests feel comfortable and to include them in the interaction. Guests compliment hosts on their ability to select dishes appropriate for the guests and the occasion, to assemble interesting groups of people, and to select fine restaurants. Hosts compliment guests on their appearance, abilities, and any valued traits, including physical appearance and other uncontrollable attributes such as intelligence. Moreover, it is particularly valued and thus a useful strategy to compliment others on their accomplishments, abilities, and character in front of their superiors, friends, and close relatives because this affords them an additional boost in face with members of their inner circles. One common strategy involves complimenting a man's wife and children rather than complimenting the man directly.

Speech Play in Banquets

Artistic speaking is an integral facet of Shandong banquets that when altered, such as when nonplayers are present, changes the entire atmosphere of such performances. Each participant tries to outperform others not only in terms of content of speech, but also in creative style and artistic delivery; players with superior rhetorical skills enjoy significant amounts of prestige and rate extremely high in the group. Thus, verbal skills, like drinking, can be employed to enhance one's position in society. One common form of banquet wordplay that is conspicuously absent from banquets involving nonnatives is the creative use of set phrases, *tàoyǔ* (套语), for aesthetic effect. For instance, a government official might adapt a portion of the official discourse to the situation to show his ability to manipulate the discourse. An example of such a technique can be seen in the following two phrases.

1)   Let's drink half a glass.
       Hē dào dāng zhōngyāng (喝到当中央).
2)   Let's drink to the Party Leadership.

Hē dào dǎng zhōngyāng (喝到党中央).

The two phrases are a play on the homonyms *dǎng* (党), "Communist Party" and *dāng* (当), "just to a certain point," which differ only in tones. Although usually employed with *dāng* (当) and meaning a toast roughly equivalent to "Let's drink half a glass" or to the point on the glass where the speaker points, it evokes images of the Communist Party because the homonym *dǎng* (党) changes the phrase to "Let's drink to the Party center."

A second type of wordplay found at banquets revolves around political slogans and their associated images. This wordplay is sometimes done just for aesthetic effect, but can also be used as an urging technique to apply pressure on another player to drink.

1)   It is not a problem of size; the key is in your attitude.
   Wèntí bú zài dàxiǎo, guānjiàn zài yú tàidu.
   问题不在大小，关键在于态度。

2)   Whether a person does something well (or not) is a question of ability, whether he does it (or not) is a question of attitude.
   Gàn hǎo gàn huài shì shuǐpíng wèntí, gàn yǔ bú gàn shì tàidu wèntí.
   干好干坏是水平问题，干与不干是态度问题。

Both phrases were political phrases formerly used to call into question a person's political attitude; now they are used to question one's attitude toward and sincerity in drinking at banquets.

Players venture into more than the political realm during wordplay; literary and historical references also abound, especially in the *xiēhòuyǔ* genre, which, as already noted, involves stating a phrase that has a set response based on a cultural story. *Xiēhòuyǔ* is frequently used by the veterans of Shandong banquets to show their verbal prowess. An example of crosstalk is "(General) Zhang Fei eats bean sprouts-just a small dish, *Zhāng Fēi chī dòuyá--xiǎo cài yì dié* (张飞吃豆芽--小菜一碟)." This particular example works on the notion that Zhang Fei is one of the most feared and powerful generals in Chinese history; therefore, eating bean sprouts to him is very simple. Crosstalk phrases are forms of speech play with set responses. After the first part is delivered, it may be followed by a pause and then the speaker's response. The pause may or may not also be followed by a response from the audience. Because highly educated members of the culture know each of these phrases as a semantic whole, mentioning the first half of the set, triggers the whole in the minds of the listeners, which allows them to access the meaning regardless of whether the second half of the phrase is stated verbally. Depending on speaker preferences and listener reactions, the entire phrase may or may not be stated verbally. For instance, if a speaker uses a particularly rare cross talk phrase, he or she would most likely deliver both halves together. If all participants in the event are highly educated and the phrase being used is quite common, the speaker may only state one half of the phrase assuming that the listeners understand the entire meaning. If a speaker states the first half of a cross talk pair and his listener(s) appear to not understand, then the speaker delivers the punch line. When listeners want to indicate to the speaker that they are following what they are saying and understand completely, they sometimes respond with the second half of crosstalk phrases. This may be done in place of the speaker or in unison with him or her. Following are a few additional examples:

1)   Zhu Bajie teaching *The Analects*--A phony saint
      Zhū Bājiè jiǎng Lúnyǔ--jiǎ shèngrén
      猪八戒讲论语--假圣人

This particular reference plays on the characteristics of Zhu Bajie, a key character in the classic Chinese novel *Journey to the West*. The phrase can be used to criticize another player's logic because Zhu

Bajie was a bungling idiot.

2)   Zhuge Liang takes an ugly wife--He's thinking
        about his career
        Zhūgé Liàng qǔ chǒu qī--wèi shìyè zháoxiǎng
        诸葛亮娶丑妻--为事业着想

Example two is used to describe a man who has married an ugly woman because she is connected and thus capable of advancing his career. The reference is to Zhuge Liang, the renowned strategist in the classic novel *Romance of the Three Kingdoms*.

3)   An old lady counting eggs--Slowly/one by one
        Lǎo tàitai shǔ jīdàn--mànmàn lái
        老太太数鸡蛋--慢慢来

This particular example uses vivid imagery-an old lady examining and counting eggs one by one-and is a humorous strategy for deflecting pressure to drink.

Singing
Aside from eating, complimenting, drinking, and toasting, Shandong banquet goers also frequently utilize singing as a mode of participation. Karaoke is by far the most common version of the singing mode; all participants are urged to try their hand at numerous types and genres of songs during and after meals. The shared experience of karaoke brings participants together and, as Geremie Barmé (1999) suggests, "initiates liaisons that might never otherwise have occurred." Popular songs from Taiwan and Hong Kong, folk songs, revolutionary songs, Western pop songs, and songs associated with traditional theatrical forms such as Beijing Opera can all be heard. One performer I witnessed at a banquet in Yantai who had learned a lengthy piece from Beijing Opera used the same piece on several occasions, singing different lines each time. Occasionally, participants also improvise for the specific audience by altering the source of songs; at one banquet I attended in Weihai that involved

participants from China, America, Norway and Japan, each group had to select a representative to sing their respective national anthem.

Storytelling

Another variation on the speaking mode is storytelling. Experienced banquet goers develop elaborate repertoires of multiple genres of stories, *duànzi* (段子), for all audiences and occasions. To be effective, banquet *duànzi* have to be interesting, entertaining, and relatively short. *Duànzi* involve a wide variety of topics and styles ranging from personal anecdotes to satirical rhymes to dirty jokes but nearly always are either informative or humorous. Some banqueters have revealed to me that they prepare for banquets by reading extensively so that they have content readily available for storytelling opportunities; less talented storytellers repeat different versions of the same story over and over again. For example, I witnessed one host who used the same story of his trip to the United States on seven occasions; each time, he made subtle adjustments to suit the particular audience.

I have also observed extremely accurate imitations of political leaders Deng Xiaoping and Liu Shaoqi as well as numerous renditions of the myriad local dialects found throughout China. At one banquet, a particularly talented banqueter delivered an impromptu performance of a traditional genre of folk storytelling called the Shandong fast tales, *Shāndōng kuàishū* (山东快书). Afterward, he commented that the other players had been so captivated by his performance that they forgot that he had not been drinking. Because *kuàishū* and other folk performance genres are particularly effective in creating mirthful atmospheres, professional and avocational performers are frequently invited to serve as *péikè*.

Shāndōng Kuàishū

One genre that I have witnessed in multiple banquets is *Shāndōng kuàishū*. The genre involves a single performer rhythmically narrating short humorous tales to the accompaniment of two brass plates. If one looks carefully, it is possible to find cultural scripts (See chapter 7) of typical banquets embedded in the stories members of the local culture tell; while listening to *Shāndōng kuàishū* storytellers, I came across a short story that was entirely based on just such a script. The story was pointed out to me by my instructor Wu Yanguo during the China Shandong Fast Tales Research Association annual meeting. The story is entitled "The Banquet," and although it is a fictional account of a banquet involving county-level government officials in an imaginary Shandong county, the story provides an excellent example of the general script Shandong people use to make sense of banquets. The text presented here is found in *Short Humorous Selections of Shandong Rhythmic Tales, Shandong kuaishu youmo xiao duan xuan* (山东快书幽默小段选) (Liu Hongbin and Liu Xuezhi 1995, 138-142). The story unfolds in a sarcastic tone that is critical of banquets and of local government officials, which is not my intention. It is impossible to find an example of a story that is not written from someone's perspective so I present this example--even though I do not agree with the criticisms of banquet or official culture--because it contains many of the key elements that make up banquet events and because it is an example of the type of story told in banquet settings.

The Banquet
Zhao Lianjia

(In) Dongkui County, Party Commission,
was busy entertaining reporter Chen Yumei.
The Propaganda Department Director broke a leg,
inviting Commissioner Zhang, Commissioner Wang, Commissioner Li, Commissioner Zhao as well as two commissioners named Lei.
The Director said, "A reporter's pen, an anchorwoman's mouth,
can exaggerate (so) come to the banquet and put on a display.

If happy, she can make a barren hill more beautiful than a park,
a little pig sound as if it were fatter than an elephant.
This kind of person, if she doesn't get her way,
will describe Mount Tai as a pile of dirty clay.
Let's have extra food and the best spirits today,
to ask her to send a little boasting our county's way.
All together the commissioners said, "Yeah, yeah, yeah,
we'll enthusiastically accompany her at play."
As they were talking, in walked the young lady reporter,
the commissioners enthusiastically greeted her offering their seats.
Pushing and declining they took their places,
a round table surrounded by ten ready to accompany,
and there was still a fat guy without a place,
(So) they moved over a stool, (and) chuckling he squeezed into the fray.
The Propaganda Department Director made introductions:
"At our Provincial Paper Reporter Chen is an authority.
In order to welcome you, we especially arranged a lunch buffet,
eating while we're talking is the most efficient way.
Banquets are imported from abroad,
this format can raise your weight and can help you cut the fat away."
The reporter thought: "I was supposed to come listen to a report,
Oh! They are using this as an excuse to put on a display."
Looking on the table, delicacies from the mountains and sea filled the plates,
every type of famous spirit filled the glasses all the way.
The Director said, "Come, let the banquet begin!
These are all our local specialties, just a family style meal,
warmly welcome Reporter Chen on her first trip to Dongkui."
The reporter said, "Huh? Your place here is not close to the sea?"
"Doesn't rest on the sea, (it's) a mountain region."
"Where did you grow this seafood in a mountain promenade?"
"This…the local products I spoke of are the wines!"

"Luzhou special barley originates in Dongkui?"

"No, it's Sichuan. Just now, what I said was…"

"What was it?"

"It's this cabbage, eggplant, carrots."

The director quickly raised his wine,

"Come, let's first drink to our guest from far away."

The reporter said, "I have never drank before,

sorry, forgive me, I'll have to abstain."

"Drink just a little!" "There's really no way."

"Ok then, if you don't drink, eat some more,

otherwise, waitress hurry up, bring some tea, serve some coffee (ay)!"

"No need."

"Then, we'll drink wine, you drink water, okay,

let's drink one all in company.

Come, put one away!"

Whoa, the banquet got livelier and livelier,

the commissioners urging and declining away.

They used every excuse to make toasts,

really knowing how to borrow an opportunity to put on a display.

This one said, "Commissioner Zhang, managing agriculture you've really made the grade,

I toast you three big glasses today.

Drink!" "Gulp, down it flowed!"

That one said: "Commissioner Wang, you've got a handle on county industry,

today you should really drink away.

Drink!" "Gulp, down it flowed!"

"Commissioner Li, your handling of family planning has been superb,

if you don't drink a lot who's getting in your way?

Drink!" "Gulp, down it flowed!"

"Commissioner Zhao, at large-scale cooperation you've been splendid,

without you, where would our county get all of this coal!

117

Drink!" "Gulp, down it flowed!"
"This one drank until his body swayed,
that one, grinned from ear to ear hey, hey, hey;
this one, laughed until tears began to cascade,
that one, rambled nonsense, bragging away,
droplets of spittle flew above the table astray!
Only that fat guy didn't say a word,
he just sat there, little by little piling it away,
Those commissioners toasted back and forth not paying attention:
"Hey, where did fatso go?"
Oh, from under the table the sound of snoring, like thunder began to
brey!
The lady reporter was tossed to the side with no one to play,
everyone forgot that at the table there was a Chen Yumei.
She sat at the side watching the melee,
when suddenly, one of them confronted her his hand a sway:
"Hey, what are you sitting there staring at?
Didn't you see there's no wine left on the table?
Hurry up and go get more wine!"
"Hey!" The reporter thought: I, the guest, have become a bus girl,
I'm just going to leave, at this kind of scene I can no longer stay.
She walked to the door, turned around for a look,
what kind of feeling she felt, it's hard to say,
(but) her camera, with a quick shutter, a click and a flash,
captured this chaotic melee.
Before long, she had returned to her hotel,
where with a surge of emotion that was difficult to suppress she lifted
her pen and got underway.
She reported, pictures and all, on the buffet,
the headline read: "Who's entertaining who anyway!"

Wūcǎnhuì
Zhào Liánjiǎ

(The transcription is based on the language used in Shandong Kuàishū.)

Dǒngkuì xiàn, xiànwēihuì,

zhèng màng zhe zhǎodài jìzhē Chèn Yùmèi.

Xuǎnchuàn bùzhāng pāo duàn le tuī,

qīng lài le Zhǎng chàngwēi, Wàng chàngwēi, Lī chàngwēi, Zhào chàngwēi, hài yōu liāng gè chàngwēi dǒu xìng Lèi.

Bùzhāng shuǒ: "Jìzhē de bī, guāngbǒyuàn de zuī,

nèng kuázhǎng lài huì fǎhuì.

Yì gǎoxìng, huángshǎn xiē de bī gǒngyuàn mēi,

xiāo zhǔ shuǒ de bī dàxiàng fèi.

Zhè lèi rèn yàoshi yí dèzuì,

Tàishǎn nèng xiē chèng zǎng tū duǐ.

Zàn jíntiǎn cài yē dǔo lài jiū mēi,

qīng tǎ gēi zàn xiàn chuǐ yi chuǐ."

Chàngwēi liàn shuǒ: "duí, duí, duí,

zàn yào rèqíng lài fèngpèi."

Shǔohuàjiǎn, zōu jìn lài niànqǐng de nǚ jìzhē,

chàngwēimen rèqíng zhǎohu ràng zuówèi.

Tuǐ tuǐ ràng ràng luò le zuò,

yìzhǎng yuàn zhǔo shì rèn wèi,

hài yōu gè pàngzi mèi zuówèi,

bǎn le gè dèngr, tǎ xǐ pì lài liān wàng lī sēi.

Xuǎnchuàn bùzhāng zuò jièshào:

"Chèn jìzhē zài zàmen shēngbào shì quànwěi.

Wèi huǎnyìng nèn, zhuǎnmèn gāo le gè wūcǎnhuì,

biàn chǐ biàn tàn zuì shìhuì.

Wūcǎnhuì yē shì còng guōwài lài yīnjìn,

zhèzhōng xìngshì nèng zhāng tīzhòng nèng jiān fèi."

Jìzhē xiāng: Yuàn shuǒ ràng wō lài tǐng huìbào,

Ǒ! Tǎmen shì jiètì lài fǎhuì."

Zhuǒshàng kàn, bāi mān le shánzhěn hè hāiwèi,

Gēzhōng mìngjiū zhěn mān le běi.
Bùzhāng shuǒ: "lài ba, wūcǎnhuì kǎishī la!
Zhè dǒu shì zàn dǎngdì tùchān jiǎchàng fàn,
rèliè huǎnyìng Chèn jìzhē tòucì lài Dǒngkuì."
Jìzhē shuǒ: "Yì, nīmen zhè dìfǎng bù kào hāi ya?"
"Bù kào hāi, shǎnqǔ."
"Zhèxiě hāiwèi, shǎnqǔ lī zài nār lài zǎipèi?"
"Zhè...wō shuǒ de dǎngdì tùchān shì zhèxiě jiū!"
"Lùzhǒu tè qǔ chāndì yuànlài shì Dǒngkuì?"
"Bù, shì Sìchuǎn. Wō gǎngcài, shuǒ de shì...."
"Shì shènme ya?"
"Shì zhèxiě bàicài, qièzi, hùluòbēi."
Bùzhāng gānkuài duǎn qī jiū:
"Lài, zàn xiǎn xiàng yuān dào de kèrèn jìng yì běi!"
Jìzhē shuǒ: "Cònglài wō mèi hě guò jiū,
duìbuqī, shù wō bù nèng lài fèngpèi."
"Shāo hě diān!" "Zhěn bù huì."
"Nà hāo, bù hě jiū duǒ chī cài,
yàobùràn, fùwùyuàn gānkuài shàng chà shàng kǎfěi!"
"Bù yòng la."
"Nà...wōmen hě jiū nèn hě shuī,
zàmen gòngtòng gǎn yì běi.
Lài, gǎn!"
Huò, wūcǎnhuì yuè kǎi yuè rènào,
Chàngwēimen hùxiǎng ràng lài hùxiǎng cuǐ.
Yòng gēzhōng mìngmù lài zhù jiū,
zhěn nèng jiè tì lài fǎhuì.
Zhègè shuǒ: "Zhǎng chàngwēi, nèn guān nòngyè yōu chèngjì,
Jíntiǎn wō jìng nèn sàn dà běi.
Hě!" "Zīliū!"
Nègè shuǒ: "Wàng chàngwēi, xiànbàn gōngyè zhuǎ de hāo,
nèn jíntiǎn hāohāo hě yíhuì.
Hě!" "Zīliū!"

"Lī chàngwēi, nèn jìhuà shěngyù zhuǎ juè liāo,
nèn bù duǒ hě hài ràng shèi?
Hě!" "Zīliū!"
"Zhào chàngwēi, dà xièzuò gāo de zhěn chǔsè,
mèi yōu nèn, zàn xiàn nā yōu zhème duǒ mèi!
Hě!" "Zīliū!"
Zhèyígè zhī hě de shènzi zhì dā huāng,
nèiyígè, liè zhe gè dà zuī guǎnghěihěi;
zhèyígè, hǎha dà xiào liù yānlèi,
nèiyígè hùshuǒbǎdào dà chuǐ dà lèi,
tuòmo xǐngzi mān zhuǒ fěi!
Jiù nèige pàngzi bù shuǒhuà,
zuó zài nàr, yìdiānr yìdiānr wàng xià duǐ,
nà jīwèi hùxiǎng jìng jiū mèi zhùyì:
"Ài, pàngzi nār qù la?"
Huò! Zhuǒ dīxià, dāhǔ de shèngyǐn xiàng chènlèi!
Nǜ jìzhē bèi shuāi zài yìbiǎn mèi rèn guān le,
dǒu wàng le zhuǒ shàng hài yōu gè Chèn Yùmèi.
Tà zuó zài yìpàng kàn rènào,
Hǔrànjiǎn, yōu rèn chòng tǎ bā shōu huǐ:
"Ài! Nèn hài zuó nàr lèng shènme?
Mèi kànjiàn zhuǒ shàng jiū hě mèi?
Kuài nà jiū qù!"
"Hèi!" Jìzhē xiāng: Wǒ zhè kèrèn chèng le pāotàngdi,
gǎncuì zōu ba, zhè chāngmiàn bù nèng zài fèngpèi.
Tà zōu dào mènkōu huìtòu kàn,
nàn shuǒ xǐn lī shà zǐwèir.
Tà de zhàoxiàngjǐ, kuài mèn yī àn děng yì shān,
shè xià lài zhè luànqìbǎzǎo yī dà duǐr.
Zhuānyǎn huì dào zhǎodàisuō,
Xǐn chào nàn pìng bā bī huǐ.
Bàodào gè dài chǎtù de wūcǎnhuì,
biāotì shì: "dàodī zhè shì zhǎodài shèi!"

121

午餐会
赵连甲

东奎县，县委会，
正忙着招待记者陈玉梅。
宣传部长跑断了腿，
请来了张常委，王常委，李常委，赵常委，还有两个常委都姓雷。
部长说："记者的笔，广播员的嘴，
能夸张来会发挥。
一高兴，荒山写得比公园美，
小猪说得比大象肥。
这类人要是一得罪，
泰山能写成脏土堆。
咱今天菜也多来酒美，
请她给咱县吹一吹。"
常委连说："对对对，
咱要热情来奉陪。"
说话间，走进来年轻的女记者，
常委们热情招呼让座位。
推推让让落了座，
一张圆桌十人围，
还有个胖子没座位，
搬了个凳儿，他嘻皮赖脸往里塞。
宣传部长作介绍：
"陈记者在咱们省报是权威。
为欢迎你，专门搞了个午餐会，
边吃边谈最实惠。
午餐会也是从国外来引进，
这种形势能长体重能减肥。"
记者想：原说让我来听汇报，
噢！他们是借题来发挥。"
桌上看，摆满了山珍和海味，
各种名酒斟满了杯。

部长说: "来吧, 午餐会开始啦!
这都是咱当地土产家常饭,
热烈欢迎陈记者头次来东奎."
记者说: "咦! 你们这地方不靠海呀?"
"不靠海, 山区."
"这些海味, 山区里在哪来栽培?"
"这....我说的当地土产是这些酒!"
"泸州特曲产地原来是东奎?"
"不, 是四川. 我刚才, 说的是....."
"是什么呀?"
"是这些白菜, 茄子, 胡萝卜."
部长赶快端起酒:
"来, 咱先向远道的客人敬一杯!"
记者说: "从来我没喝过酒,
对不起, 恕我不能来奉陪."
"少喝点!" "真不会."
"那好, 不喝酒就多吃菜,
要不然, 服务员赶快上茶上咖啡! "
"不用啦."
"那。。。我们喝酒你喝水,
咱们共同干一杯.
来， 干! "
噢, 午餐会越开越热闹,
常委们互相让来互相催.
用各种名目来祝酒,
真能借题来发挥.
这个说: "张常委， 你管农业有成绩,
今天我敬你三大杯.
喝! ""吱溜! "
那个说: "王常委， 县办工业抓得好,
你今天好好喝一回.
喝! " "吱溜!"
"李常委, 你计划生育抓绝了,

123

你不多喝还让谁?
喝!" "吱溜!"
"赵常委,大协作搞得真出色,
没有你,咱县哪有这么多煤!
喝!" "吱溜!"
这一个只喝得身子直打晃,
那一个,咧着个大嘴光嘿嘿;
这一个,哈哈大笑流眼泪,
那一个胡说八道大吹大擂,
唾沫星子满桌飞!
就那个胖子不说话,
坐在那,一点一点往下堆,
那几位互相敬酒没注意:
"哎,胖子哪去啦?"
嗖!桌底下,打呼的声音像沉雷!
女记者被甩在一边没人管了,
都忘了桌上还有个陈玉梅.
她坐在一旁看热闹,
忽然间,有人冲她把手挥:
"哎!你还坐那愣什么?
没看见桌上酒喝没?
快拿酒去!"
"嘿!"记者想:我这客人成了跑堂的,
干脆走吧,这场面不能再奉陪.
她走到门口回头看,
难说心理啥滋味.
她的照相机,快门一按灯一闪,
摄下来这乱七八糟一大堆.
转眼回到招待所,
心潮难平把笔挥.
报道个带插图的午餐会,
标题是: "到底这是招待谁!"

The event related in the story is a version of a professional banquet involving the local officials of a fictional Dongkui County who are entertaining a reporter from the provincial newspaper. There are approximately ten participants whose roles follow those described in chapter 1: the Director of the Propaganda Department is the principal host; Commissioners Zhang, Wang, Li, and Zhao, the two Commissioners named Lei, and the fat guy are invited to serve as *péikè*. The female reporter from the provincial paper is the primary guest, and waitresses are also referred to. The purpose of the banquet is to request assistance, specifically to ask the reporter to promote the county and to prevent her report from reflecting poorly on the county. The props involved are those frequently found in banquets as described in earlier chapters; they include copious amounts of food and the best spirits, a round table, wine glasses, and tea.

The sequence of events in the story also follows the order described in chapter 2. The Director, as host, issues prebanquet instructions to his *péikè*, stating that the occasion is an important banquet so the commissioners as *péikè* must be warm and hospitable to the guest reporter to ensure that she is "happy," and that they should arrange for extra food and the best of wines to be available. The banquet begins with greetings and is followed immediately by a seating ritual similar to the one described in chapter 2 in which pushing and declining are involved to get each participant in the proper position. As the banquet begins, the principal host controls the interaction beginning by making opening remarks that include introductions, a welcome to the honored guest, a clear statement of the reason for the banquet, and an indication of their sincerity and hospitality through the presentation of local delicacies. Participants' glasses are filled to the brim with numerous famous liquors. The Director/principal host announces the beginning of festivities, offers self-deprecating remarks, stating that the meal is only a typical family meal, and at the same time states that they have arranged for the best of local specialties to be served for the honored guest. The Director/principal host then welcomes the honored guest again during a toast to open the festivities that resembles those described in chapter 3. This urge to drink is deflected by the guest leading immediately to another urge to drink and an additional deflection in a verbal volley as described in chapter 3. Because the guest is a woman, the volley ends when tea and coffee are offered as replacements for liquor; the male participants toast with liquor, and the female reporter uses tea. This initial toast is also an example of the inclusive toasts described earlier.

As the banquet in the story proceeds, the participants engage in urging and deflecting, using "every excuse" to toast one another. The story presents a series of specific toasts that are examples of what was described as "toasting to build face" at the end of chapter 3. The toasts, because they are intended to give face, also provide examples of the complimenting described in this chapter. As the story unfolds, the one participant who did not partake in the verbal interplay, the fat guy, was forgotten, which reinforces the suggestion offered earlier that to become part of the occasion, participants must engage in one of the recognized modes of play. When this particular participant was remembered later, he was not remembered by name, only as "fatso." The reporter also was forgotten and pushed aside because she did not participate in the verbal interplay beyond the initial exchange.

This story sets up the basic schema that people in Shandong share about what takes place during a typical banquet event, and these frames of meaning involve expectations about what should or should not happen under similar circumstances. The reason this version works as a humorous story for members of the culture is because once those frames of expectations have been established, the storyteller then plays with the script by changing key details such as the hosts' completely forgetting about the principal guest-which is a major blunder for a host according to local cultural norms.

Satirical Rhymes

In addition to storytelling genres, satirical rhymes, *shùnkǒuliū* (顺口溜), are commonly performed during banquets. Literally "smooth mouth flow," *shùnkǒuliū* are brief *duànzi* that range in length from a single couplet to sixty or seventy lines. *Shùnkǒuliū* typically involve humorous, satirical comments about Chinese society and function the way jokes do in that the goal is to create humor and to make people laugh. They are highly structured verbal forms that are characterized by grammatical parallelism, end rhyme, and prosody. They may give pleasure, create playful moods, create an atmosphere of conviviality, induce feelings of social solidarity, permit venting of aggression, relieve tension, criticize, or ridicule, all of which are functions of humor (Apte 1992).

The humor of *shùnkǒuliū* hinges on rhyme, plays on words, puns, metaphor, and veiled criticisms of the system. They are sometimes told at banquets by businesspeople and government officials as a way to express disapproval about the corruption or other social phenomena found around them. *Shùnkǒuliū* are ways to vent in a humorous manner that involve less risk than direct statements do. They are also told in groups as a way of drawing boundaries, either setting off "the other" or creating solidarity within in-groups. The appearance of spontaneity and improvisation is also important for *shùnkǒuliū* to have their full, intended effect. Following are a few examples of satirical rhymes that were taught to me in the banquet context.

1)
(As for) Eating basically have someone invite (you)
(As for) Drinking basically have someone toast (you)
(As for) Salary basically don't use (it)
(As for) Old lady basically don't touch (her)

Chī fàn jībĕn yŏu rén qĭng,
Hē jiŭ jībĕn yŏu rén jìng,
Gōngzī jībĕn bú yòng,
Lăopo jībĕn bú dòng.

吃饭基本有人请,
喝酒基本有人敬,
工资基本不用,
老婆基本不动.

2)
Drink but don't get drunk,
Take gifts but don't take bribes,
Dance but don't fix your partner,
A little later (yet) then go home to sleep.
Boldly eat,
Carefully take,
Prudently travel,
Secretly play.
Sing two old songs,
Rub two saggy tits,
Pay the bill (and it's) in the thousands,
Go back home (and you) still have to listen to the old lady bitch

Hē jiŭ bù hē zuì,
Shōulĭ bú shòuhuì,
Tiàowŭ bú dìngwèi,
Zài wăn huíjiā shuì.
Dàdăn de chī,
Xiăoxīn de ná,
Jĭnshèn de yóu,
Mìyáo de wán.
Chàng liăng shōu jiù gē,

Dǎ liǎng gè làn bō,
Yī jiézhàng jǐ qiān duō,
Huíjiā hái yào tīng lǎopo luōsuo.

喝酒不喝醉,
收礼不受贿,
跳舞不定位,
再晚回家睡.
大胆地吃,
小心地拿,
谨慎地游,
秘窑地玩.
唱两首旧歌,
打两个烂波,
一结帐几千多,
回家还要听老婆罗嗦.

Ending the Game

As any game, Shandong banquets are bound events with a distinct opening and closing. After the fish and soup have been served, the goals of the banquet have been achieved, and the host senses that guests have had their fill of food and drink, he or she inquires about what staple food will be eaten as the final course and a ritual toast is conducted to signal the end of drinking festivities. Examples of such a toast include "Finally, to our long lasting friendship, one last glass, *zuìhòu, wèi wǒmen de yǒuyì chángcún, zài gān yì bēi* (最后, 为我们的友谊长存, 再干一杯)," and "Finally, thank everyone for coming, *zuìhòu, gǎnxiè gèwèi de guānglín* (最后, 感谢各位的光临)."

After the staple food has been served and eaten, the principal host will signal that the curtain is about to close by asking whether the guests have had enough to eat and drink and if they have enjoyed themselves. The questions themselves are ritualistic acts that have only one valid response associated with them-yes. Guests always offer affirmations of how much food and drink they have eaten and how happy they are because of the host's ability to throw a gala event. All players know that regardless of the circumstances, no guest would ever answer in the negative. Thus, such a question brings the performance to an end on a high note and indicates to the players that the festivities have come to a close. On occasion, principal hosts make closing remarks or verbally indicate that the banquet is over.

After the closing remarks, players begin making their way to the exit, which itself is the site of further performances. All players attempt to allow others to pass through the door before them in displays of deference and modesty; what results is that players become entangled in disputes of etiquette to determine who should go last. Although deferring to another person is deemed to be a positive characteristic in Shandong society, in the end, it does not matter who leaves first as long as each participant performs sufficient acts of resistance to establish that he or she is modest and understands etiquette.

Once outside the banquet room, principal hosts have the responsibility to see guests at least to an elevator, where they will be sure to push the button for their guests. When I inquired about this point, an experienced player explained that pushing the elevator button for a guest makes him or her feel as though you have thought of everything, down to the most minor of details. Most Shandong principal hosts also see their guests out to their transportation or provide it for them in the case of foreign and important guests. Hosts not only have the obligation to walk their guests to their transportation, but also must wait patiently until they drive off, at which time they raise both hands in a ritualized wave. In the Shandong wave, hosts extend both hands, palms open, just above head level in a ritual wave, and the host's responsibilities end as the last guest drives off.

CHAPTER FIVE

The Need for a Pedagogy of Culture

As a result of the events on and since the September 11 terrorist attacks, the U.S. government and many institutions of higher learning have realized that there is an urgent and strategic need for advanced-level (ILR/FSI Level 3-4; ACTFL superior) skills in all languages, as well as an even greater need for these skills in difficult and less commonly taught languages such as Chinese. This sudden realization that under current pedagogical approaches, most language learners tend to plateau with high-intermediate skills (ILR/FSI Level 2; ACTFL advanced), regardless of the language (Leaver and Shekhtman 2002; Mitchell and Myles 1998), has resulted in significant time and resources being invested and/or earmarked for the development of materials and programs that assist language learners in going beyond the high-intermediate level. Although a majority of people working in language-related positions have attained high-intermediate proficiency, their current abilities neither meet the new standards being set by governmental agencies nor adequately equip them for the demands of professional interaction in their target languages. The direct experience of creating and operating US/China Links (a language and culture training program that nationally recruits participants with a variety of language backgrounds) that my colleagues and I have gained suggests that the Chinese case is not an exception to this pattern. That is, few Americans are operating at advanced levels of Chinese language and culture skills, even taking into account those who have both received four years of college-level instruction and spent time studying abroad in China or Taiwan.

Our experiences in US/China Links have proven that the typical Chinese knows a great deal more about American culture than the average American knows about Chinese culture. Moreover, for the relatively small number of Americans who do know something about Chinese culture, that knowledge usually lies in domains associated with achievement or grand culture such as the Chinese philosophical or literary traditions. Americans know very little, however, about Chinese behavioral culture or cognitive orientations. Add to this equation the notion that knowing *about* a culture and knowing what to expect while in a culture are completely different levels of engagement than knowing *how to do things* in that culture. Most real work in government, business, and academia is conducted in English and/or in relation to American cultural orientations, with American participants limited to what Chinese allow them to understand about the situation. The result is that although the number of Chinese who have actually developed "how to" knowledge about American culture also is quite small, Americans are at a distinct disadvantage when dealing with Chinese in professional settings. Moreover, if American learners of Chinese continue to be exposed to declarative knowledge, most government agencies, companies, and academic institutions must invest significant time and resources for additional training before new hires can assume professional responsibilities. American learners must learn *how to do things* in Chinese culture even after they know *about* Chinese culture; otherwise, few will be able to interact successfully with Chinese on their terms.

The additional adaptation period during which learners add procedural and intuitive cultural knowledge to their skills sets is not only costly but also typically haphazard; the default assumption for most people is that they will "just get it by living in the target culture." However, by shifting our pedagogical approach to include behavioral culture and by systematically emphasizing procedural and intuitive knowledge, we can better prepare our learners for professional careers involving China. By focusing before learners enter the target culture on the behaviors they need to be able to perform while interacting in the target culture, we reduce the amount of time necessary to become competent participants in target culture activities.

Included among the multitude of reasons for our failure to achieve advanced proficiency levels in foreign languages is the irrational structure of language learning in the United States: Students are exposed to the most difficult foreign languages during their college experience, when they ought to begin their study at early ages. Simply stated, learning foreign languages and cultures requires vast amounts of time and energy. Consequently, one hour of class time per day for four years of college is simply not sufficient exposure for students to attain advanced level skills. We are at a disadvantage when compared to other countries because we do not begin language training in earnest until learners enter college and are already adults. In countries such as China, foreign language training typically begins when learners are in elementary school and sometimes earlier than that. More fundamentally, few American learners have access to or training in the localized discourses, situated meanings, and particular meaning-making methods found in foreign cultural domains other than the few mainstream academic and achievement culture domains found in most language programs. American ineptitude in foreign languages stems from both long-standing folk beliefs about language and culture learning and inadequate existing pedagogical approaches.

Because the immigrant experience of many Americans influences our beliefs about language learning, we tend to associate learning the expressive means and cultural behaviors of foreign groups with assimilation or acculturation. Acculturation, in turn, is often equated with giving up our base culture and losing our own identity. As acculturation theorists state it, "It seems clear nevertheless that the two constructs are closely linked. Accompanying the acculturative changes that occur over time in a new culture are related changes in identity" (Phinney 2003, 78). Scholarship on acculturation further maintains and fosters this linear, zero-sum concept of identity (that is, gains in one area entail a corresponding loss in another) and other changes associated with learning new cultures, which constrains what it means to learn a new culture:

> The traditional view of acculturation is the assimilation of minority ethnic people into the majority context; that is, in the United States, they become "Americanized." In this view, which suggests a linear adjustment, there seems to be a series of phases that the foreigner experiences: The phases begin with preparation and entry into the new culture, at which point the feelings are normal to high; a second phase, in which the foreigner is a spectator, wherein emotions vary from mostly high to very low; a third phase, in which increased participation makes the foreigner realize the magnitude of the differences between the host culture and home culture, which in turn starts a downward trend in emotional well-being; a fourth phase of shock, wherein the emotions are very negative. Then the adaptation (fifth) phase begins, in which the emotions return closer to normal as the foreigner learns to function in the host country. The end of the process is characterized by the minority person or group giving up its traditions, values, and language and replacing them with those of the majority culture. (Clayton 1996, 5)

Rather than disputing the idea that immigrants who are successful in their attempts to integrate into mainstream society have corresponding changes in personal identity, the contention here is that it is problematic to apply such logic to the process of learning foreign language and culture in general without considering specific circumstances. For the learner who approaches foreign language learning from the acculturation perspective, uneasiness tends to develop about losing part of one's identity. Sociologist Erving Goffman (1974, 28–9) hints at the difficulty of cultural adjustment in stating, "Individuals exhibit considerable resistance to changing their framework of frameworks." This explains in part why people— especially in the initial stages of contact—tend to resist accepting or trying out the values of the group of study; that is, because learning new cultural values is equated with giving up one's own, many Americans are consciously or subconsciously reluctant to experiment with ways of conceptualizing the world: we believe that identity exists in the individual and ignore the social and cultural influences that Goffman suggests.

Further exacerbating the problem, foreign language teachers, especially native speakers of noncognate cultures such as Chinese, cater to the zero-sum notion through their approaches: they tend to relate content to what they deem familiar because they fear the learners will not understand or because they feel it will be more interesting. Another common approach adopted by native speakers of Chinese is to teach American students to say what they want to say and be who they want to be because "that's what Americans are like." Although these approaches typically are utilized to retain student interest and to alleviate some of the uneasiness associated with learning language, the result is that Americans typically learn to "be American" in a second linguistic code. In reality, such approaches can actually hinder learners' progress when they deal with cultures and values that differ significantly from mainstream American ones. Instead, viewing what it means to learn a foreign language as the process of learning the cultural behaviors of the group of study and viewing that process as developing a set of new skills to add to one's existing cognitive repertoire, rather than as losing one's identity, will facilitate the process and lead ultimately to more successful outcomes.

Experts in acculturation and English as a foreign language education have only recently begun to become aware of the limitations inherent in viewing language and culture learning as a zero-sum affair:

> Because the end goal of this unidirectional model is assimilation, there is not room for variation in response, only greater and lesser degrees of assimilation. A more recent view of acculturation is a multidimensional pattern, which suggests a variety of end-states. Assimilation may be one of the responses, but another may also be one of integration, separation, or marginalization...
>
> In assimilation, the newcomer becomes one with the new culture, taking on the values, language, and traditions of the new culture; in integration, the newcomer is able to integrate both cultures into his or her life, to make a contribution to the host community as well as to be affected by it. Marginalization refers to the opposite of integration, wherein the newcomer no longer feels comfortable in either culture. Separation occurs when, for any number of reasons, the person withdraws and strengthens ties with the old culture. (Clayton 1996, 5)

Nonetheless, folk ideas tend to be tenacious and quite often persist long after academic revelations debunk them. Language learners may be reluctant to change behaviors or may feel uneasy about studying foreign languages because they are unable to control interaction as readily as in their base culture. This phenomenon is quite distinct in the case of learners of truly foreign languages such as Chinese, where the behaviors required to be successful in interactions are so radically different for the American learner. This may suggest that a large number of American learners of foreign languages still view foreign language learning as a zero-sum affair. The resulting reluctance to experiment with and adopt aspects of various target culture worldviews ultimately holds learners back.

Aside from this zero-sum problem, an acculturation paradigm typically considers cultural changes in terms of *groups* of people rather than individuals and, more specifically, *immigrant groups*. Although astute is the notion that there is a multiplicity of possible responses to continued interaction within new cultural surroundings, this view emerged from contexts in which there are clear intragroup social hierarchies and clear benefits for immigrants to assimilate into the mainstream. Moreover, in such paradigms, the subjects are immigrants who will remain permanently in the country of study. Thus, acculturation studies tend not to be focused on how people go about learning the new culture but rather on the stages through which foreigners pass on their way to "becoming American."

The conditions characteristic of the acculturation situation and those of American foreign language learners are fundamentally different. Most American learners of Chinese will never find themselves in the immigrant situation—other than heritage learners immigrating to the United States, a situation in which the target culture is American culture rather than Chinese culture. American learners, rather, study Chinese for various other reasons: they have an affinity for Chinese culture, they harbor romantic images of an exotic other, they want to be "different," they are fulfilling a foreign language requirement, they have Chinese (girl/boy) friends, or they have bounced around from major to major before finding one of interest. More recently, with the sustained surge in Chinese economic development and China's concurrent rise in the international community, a large number of learners have also begun their study of Chinese with utilitarian purposes: finding a job, starting a business, entering a diplomatic career, and the like.

Unfortunately, rarely, if ever, does a new student of Chinese give as the reason for studying Chinese "learning a new set of skills that will allow me to participate in Chinese realities."

Complicating matters further is the troubling fact that many Americans are surprisingly unaware that there is a multiplicity of ways of viewing the world and/or of organizing reality. True, some who have come in contact with foreigners living in the United States understand that they are different and that they need to adapt to their new surroundings, but when those same Americans go about learning foreign languages, they do not automatically apply the same logic to their own situation. That is, they carry a default assumption that there is a single reality of which we all partake and that learning a foreign language merely involves learning and mapping out the corresponding labels the target group uses for that reality. Whenever incongruencies arise, they—as do all of us—have the natural tendency to rely on their own base culture interpretations and explanations of events. The knee-jerk reaction is to determine that whatever does not conform to our own cultural framework is wrong or flawed.

US/China Links experience in training learners from various programs around the country has confirmed that most American learners of Chinese are not tuned in to subtle, culturally defined ways of meaning making, techniques for establishing culturally appropriate intentions, or nuances of behavioral culture that are distinct from their own. Participants have exhibited clear difficulties in identifying Chinese roles and situations, interpreting interlocutor intentions and motivations, effectively managing superior-subordinate-peer relations in professional contexts, recognizing and understanding Chinese worldviews, and developing healthy, long-term relationships with Chinese counterparts who do not already possess the predisposition for interaction with Americans. These deficiencies, primarily in the areas of behavioral culture and interpersonal interaction, put American learners at a distinct disadvantage in professional interactions—competitive situations, strategic negotiations, and cooperative ventures—involving Chinese counterparts who generally are more familiar with American culture and cultural norms. This pattern holds true even when dealing with learners who have progressed to high-level programs or who have gone through advanced language programs and study-abroad programs, which suggests that methodologies currently employed by Chinese-language programs[1] rarely *effectively* take such cultural and interpersonal phenomena into consideration during curriculum design or implementation. Many aim at a much lower level of linguistic code and have low expectations for learner achievement. I suggest that it is precisely these cultural skills that are critical for successful interactions in professional contexts and thus for the advanced levels of language performance we seek to develop. Our failure to account for such phenomena in curriculum design and teaching methodology is another reason for our students' failure to go beyond high-intermediate levels of proficiency.

The approach advocated here addresses ways in which American learners of Chinese can level the playing field and reduce the amount of accommodative work that Chinese professionals must engage in while dealing with Americans. This type of accommodative behavior happens in most situations when Chinese interact with foreigners: sometimes it is conscious, intentional behavior, but sometimes Chinese adjust their behavior without actually realizing that they are doing so. Chinese professionals who frequently deal with foreigners in China describe this accommodative burden with a range of terms including "tiring, *lèi* (累)," "annoying, *fán* (烦)," and "outright dissatisfaction, *tǎoyàn* (讨厌)." The presence of a metadiscourse supports the notion that Chinese are the ones adapting rather than the American learners. The first step is to rethink what it means to *know* a culture to include

---

[1] I refer here to language programs both in China and in the United States; some use Chinese as the language of instruction, and others use English.

performative knowledge, or the "how-to" knowledge situated in everyday behaviors, and to ensure that performance is informed by the underlying cognitive orientation that organizes and drives the everyday behaviors of the members of the target culture.

Performance Theory

Performance is a complex term that remains a contested concept—there are at least three different but interrelated notions of performance generally recognized in scholarship on the subject (Carlson 1996):

1. A display of skills, as in a martial arts exhibition or an ice skating competition
2. Success of activity in light of some standard of achievement, as in the sense of academic or work performance
3. A display of a recognized and culturally coded pattern of behavior

These characteristics of performance exist in all human activities because of the social nature of those activities (Carlson 1996). Dell Hymes (1975, 13 and quoted in Carlson 1996) maps out the place of performance in human social interaction by pointing out a hierarchy that has behavior—anything and everything that happens—at the top; conduct—behavior that conforms to cultural rules and norms—is a subset of behavior, and performance—behavior for which a person assumes responsibility to an audience or tradition—is a further subset of conduct (Carlson 1996; Cole 1996).

The work on performance done in psychology and sociology by Erving Goffman and others demonstrates convincingly that all social behavior is staged to some degree in that it involves distinct frames of meaning that define the situation at hand, roles involved, and the behavior of participants (Goffman 1959, 1963a, 1963b, 1967,

1969, 1974). Goffman's work elaborates a key element of performance by showing that social relationships are often viewed as *roles* in performance and that people engage in significant backstage preparatory work even in their native cultures. He also highlights the second fundamental criterion of performance by pointing out the relationship between a specified space—what he labels the floor— and the sharing of meaning.

It is also certain that no performance, in the sense of the notion employed here, can occur without an audience in cooperation with the performer(s) sharing attentional focus and simultaneously serving as critic for the performer (Carlson 1996; Bauman 1977). Richard Bauman (1977) advocates the notion that performance is always "for" some audience that validates it as performance. That is, for a performance to occur, performers are always subject to someone for evaluation. Performances require not only isolated actors related in no other way to their audiences than by their observations, but also active engagement between the two. Goffman points out this dialogic nature of performance by asserting that the essential quality of performance is that it is "based on the relationship between the performer and the audience" (quoted in Carlson 1996, 38).

Performance for scholars such as Goffman, Bauman, and Hymes is a unit of analysis that shifts our focus to the context surrounding speech and behavior. This view defines performance in terms of five basic elements: (1) specified place, (2) time, (3) roles, (4) script, and (5) audience (Carlson, 1996). For an event to be a performance, all five criteria must be satisfied. Performance in this sense suggests doing things: completing a process (or series of acts) in a recognized role(s), in a prescribed way (script). This *doing*— whether verbal, kinesic, or some combination of the two—is situated in a particular setting, occurs at a specific time, and is done for a particular audience (Bauman 1977). Anthropologists since the early 1960's have achieved such an orientation to culture and performance as ways of doing things (Schegloff 1996). By applying this view of performance, eating, meeting, and parting can be performances, as can larger-scale cultural events such as rock concerts, storytelling sessions, and football games. The idea is that looking at culture in terms of performances provides students of culture with a convenient heuristic metaphor with which to segment culture.

Teleological Agents

Performance as seen here also involves the notion of intentionality: Both performer and audience should be viewed as teleological, or intentional, agents (Cole 1996). In any performance in which performers have the same background, actors and audiences interact based on shared interpretive frameworks to generate meaning (Bateson 1972; Goffman 1974). Performers and audiences alike have intentions that affect the outcome of the performance itself. Shandong banquets can be viewed as performances on a number of levels. They are cultural productions that involve participants assuming responsibility to an audience (which could be certain participants, all participants, servers, or onlookers). Banquets also take place in specified places—*dānjiān*—at designated times—lunch and dinner—and there are clearly defined roles for participants— guests, hosts, and escorts. Banquet events involve cultural scripts in that banquets unfold in a patterned manner that involves prescribed speech and behaviors.

Moreover, banquet participants have access to a range of intended goals for participation (new goals may also arise during the course of banquet activity as well), there are recognized modes of participation, and there are means—appropriate and inappropriate— for achieving intentions within the banquet context. Host goals may include getting an official to agree to assist his or her company, repairing a damaged relationship, and reciprocating for previous assistance. Guest goals may include having a good time, meeting important people, and seeing old friends. Escort goals may include following orders, looking good in front of a superior, repaying owed debts, and placing someone in social debt.

It is culture that provides the cognitive framework shared by a group that informs, enables, guides, and constrains the behavior of members of the group (Goffman 1974; Tyler 1978; Bruner 1986, 1990; Shweder 1991; Cole 1996; Walker 2000; Walker and Noda 2000). Culture is both the forum in which meanings are negotiated and hold salience and the framework for communicative interaction for its members in that it informs its members' interpretations, choices, and decisions (Bruner 1990; Cole 1996). Culture, as a shared framework, creates joint attentional contexts (Tomasello 1999), which, in turn, provide available meanings, intentions, goals, and roles for members of the group. It is through the negotiation of shared cultural meanings that we construct and participate in the reality of the group (Schutz 1945; Goffman 1974; Goodman 1978; Bruner 1986; Shweder 1991; Walker 2000).

Janet Dougherty and James Fernandez (1981, 415) argue that culture is a constitutive process that involves "a series of productive and individual acts aimed toward the construction of meaning for the acting individuals whose behavior is guided by an integration of cultural symbolization/classification and personal experience." That is, for meaning to be generated by the participants of a speech event, establishing and interpreting recognized intentions are critical (Grice 1971, 1975; Tyler 1978; Searle 1969). Intentions, accurately interpreted or not, affect the meanings generated and assigned to any utterance of speech or act of behavior performed by participants in the event. As members of a cultural community, we hold certain presuppositions about which intentions are possible in any given context. For example, I misread my interlocutor's intention in the example provided earlier in which a government official invited me to serve as a *péíkè* at a banquet because I was applying an American cultural framework in which this particular intention is less likely to occur. Because of the norms guiding guest-host relationships in

American culture, I assumed that an invitation had been extended, when in fact it was a request for assistance. (An additional example is described later, in which an American has the intention of assisting a female friend in putting on her coat at dinner. As is discussed in chapter 6, such an intention is not typically an option in Shandong culture.) As H. P. Grice noted, for meaning to be achieved, an intention must be associated with the act and intentions must be consistent with their felicity conditions—"just the set of circumstances in which an intention is feasible or justifiable" (Grice 1975).

In first-culture performances, we are generally aware of the participants involved in those performances and actively attempt to fulfill our obligations in a particular role, whether it be performer, audience, or some combination of both. Cultural performances also present intentions to the group for evaluation, interpretation, and recognition. Performance, thus, is an overture to others, an explicit display of the desire to share intentions. Thus, cultural performances are not linked to artistic performances conducted solely for aesthetic value, but are also a common means for participating within a group. In this way, performance is a recognized and culturally coded pattern of behavior.

Performed Culture

Performed culture is an emerging pedagogical approach to language in culture. The term itself carries with it inherent assumptions about learning, language, culture, and the operations of mind and memory. The intellectual genealogy of the notion of performance as applied here can be traced to the performance theory detailed earlier (Bauman 1977; Turner 1987; Schechner and Appel 1990; Carlson 1996). Drawing inspiration from anthropologist Victor Turner (1986), Galal Walker (2000) has applied this notion to foreign language pedagogy: Walker advocates the idea that to perform is to complete an involved process rather than merely a single deed or act. Viewing performance from this perspective permits us to consider both the local and global aspects of individual agents' intentions. Tuen Van Dijk also succinctly phrases a similar notion "an immediate speech act can be best understood as a single operation in a whole series of actions directed toward a general goal" (quoted in Carlson 1996). Actors' intentions are not bound to the narrow confines of a single performance, but rather encompass a much broader spectrum of interconnected performances. Motivations for actions in an isolated performance may not be fully understood without analyzing them in terms of other related performances. The idea of interconnectedness of events is particularly important in the Shandong context, where every event is understood to be connected to every other event and every person interconnected in a web of relationships. If something happens in one banquet event, it affects the participants in the event and as well as other events and people because of this interconnectedness. One local described the situation to me using a "throwing a stone into water" metaphor: when the stone breaks the surface (an event takes place), there are outward ripples that result (affects on other events and people). In the banquet setting, strategies adopted for participation are affected by repeated engagements with the same people. For instance, a banqueter who adopts the strategy of stating that he or she does not drink because of health reasons must be consistent in his or her behavior. Also, if a person drinks at one banquet but declines at a subsequent banquet with the same participants, he or she will be seen either as insincere or as not giving the participants face in the latter engagement. Moreover, what is said is affected by repeated banquets with the same people: toasts used to build relationships and to bridge the gap between participants shift toward ones that are designed to reaffirm ties; polite language tends to be used less with familiar parties because it puts unnecessary boundaries between people; stories may also be repeated in subsequent banquets precisely because they are an effective means of reaffirming existing relationships. Thus, after having banqueted with a particular group of people on several occasions, I witnessed experienced banqueters begin to tell one another "the story of what happened to us on 'x' occasion" or "the story of how we met." Behavior at banquets may also be a direct reaction to what happened at previous banquets. For example, one banqueter who had had too much to drink at a banquet I attended stated that he was drinking so much because the guest had treated on a previous occasion and had drunk a large amount then. Banquets affect other banquets also in that participants discuss what takes place during the event and may recount behavior at one event in order to apply pressure to drink at another event ("I heard you drank ten beers at one banquet. Don't you think I am worth drinking ten beers for?"). Furthermore, how participants approach and interpret performances constantly shifts over time and with the information gained during the process of performance: as new information is incorporated and evaluated, participants' decisions are adjusted, which affects outcomes as well as future performances.

Performance further suggests that there are distinct, analyzable—and, thus, learnable—segments of the flow of human social activity (Walker 2000). That is, performances are spatially and temporally bounded events that set up distinct frames of reference for the interpretation and construction of meanings, intentions, goals, and actions negotiated by and shared among the participants (Bauman 1977; Goffman 1974). A shared reality emerges from participation in performances because they are activities of joint purpose and attention. Performances also provide the participants the personal experience of doing things in a specific context, which allows them to construct knowledge schemas of the events that can be drawn on and elaborated in future encounters with similar contexts (Walker 2000).

Marvin Carlson (1996, 52) sees performance as a mode of understanding, claiming that performance refers to "doing, re-doing, and self-consciousness about doing and re-doing on the part of both the performers and spectators". Likewise, Walker (2000) indicates that "repetition" is an element of performance. Thus, there exists the potential for re-creating and remembering performances or, at minimum, segments of performances. This view enables a foreign language/culture learner to focus on these repeatable aspects of performance as a source for stored cultural praxes. The repeatable nature of cultural performance also provides for a means of grouping information for later storage in memory. The performance metaphor also offers the notion of evaluation for the way the acts involved are completed, which implies differing levels of competence depending on the experiences and knowledge of the individual performers (Bauman 1977, 1986; Bender 1989, 1995). So performance suggests situated behaviors that can be staged by an individual (or group) for an audience, which provides experiential knowledge upon which memories can be constructed (Walker 2000).

Finally, as noted by Gregory Bateson (1972), Goffman (1974), Hymes (1975), and Bauman (1977), performance sets up, or represents, an interpretive frame within which the messages being communicated are to be understood. In this view, cultural performances inform actors and audiences about what type of situated event they are engaged in, which allows them to adopt behaviors appropriate for that category of event. Performance sets up culturally patterned frameworks that, as Goffman (1974, 8) states, answer "What is it that's going on here?" for the participants. Based on these ideas, a performance can be viewed as an event in a process, which involves teleological agents—a performer and a symbiotically linked audience—accomplishing the repetition of dialogic segments of a shared culture.

The difficulty for language instructors is twofold: they not only need to get students to realize that "something is going on here," but they also must ensure that the learners recognize that the "something" is different from what happens in their base culture. We have approached this problem in the US/China Links program by supplementing the performed culture approach with an element of training that provides direct cultural and behavioral contrast: We have designed mirror programs for Chinese students learning English and have integrated their culture learning with that of our American students' learning of Chinese culture. Program participants—both Chinese and American—attend classes together, and the focus of instruction is divided between the two groups. The core course of the training program focuses on interpersonal interaction and consists of two hours of class—one in Chinese focused on teaching American students to interact with Chinese and one in English focused on teaching Chinese students to interact with Americans. Course curriculum is coordinated so that each class allows students of both cultures to perform in identical contexts (e.g., meetings, eating situations, greetings, expressing opinions) in both their own culture and in their target learning culture in back-to-back hours. The direct contrast highlights the differences in ways the two cultures handle particular contexts. Performing in both cultures also aids in internalizing the knowledge and behavior used in such contexts.

In addition to contrasting the two cultures in training, we place learners in "live" target contexts by arranging for program participants to live as roommates and for American students to work as interns in Chinese organizations. With guided instruction that continually focuses learner attention on cultural behaviors, the participants begin to develop a mode of thinking that forefronts behavioral culture. Once their attention is shifted to "what it is that is going on here," participants are required to repeatedly perform (for native audiences—their classmates, instructors, and coworkers) appropriate behaviors (including speech) necessary to navigate the given contexts. Repeated rehearsal fosters internalization— transferring this type of behavior from the conscious to the subconscious realm and from short-term to long-term memory.

Culture in Performed Culture

The second component of the performed culture approach is culture, which, based on notions found in cultural psychology, cognitive science, and anthropology, is understood as the cognitive framework shared by a group that enables, guides, and constrains the behavior of members of the group (Bruner 1986, 1990; Cole 1996; Walker 2000; Walker and Noda 2000). That is, culture is the forum in which meanings are negotiated and hold salience as well as the framework for communicative interaction for its members in that it informs its members' choices and decisions (Bruner 1990; Cole 1996). Culture as a shared framework creates joint attentional contexts (Tomasello 1999), which in turn provide meanings, intentions, goals, and roles for the members of the group. It is through the negotiation of shared cultural meanings that we construct and participate in the reality of the group (Bruner 1986; Walker 2000).

According to a performed culture approach, a group's culture includes both the behaviors (cognitive, linguistic, and kinesic) typical of the members of the group and the accompanying cognitive orientation that informs those behaviors. Knowledge *of* a culture provides the basis for interpretation and analysis of the culture; knowledge of *how to do* a culture provides the basis for participation in the culture. It is assumed that culture can be segmented differently depending on one's focus of attention. That is, there are different aspects of culture—revealed, ignored, suppressed—as well as different types of culture—material culture, information culture, popular culture, folk culture, achievement culture, and behavioral culture, among others—upon which we can focus our attention (Hammerly 1982; Walker 2000). Rather than the products of cultural activity (linguistic or material), the primary concern of a performed culture approach is the culture of everyday life, or that of the sociobehavioral realm (Walker and Noda 2000; Walker 2000).

Finally, culture as understood here also implies that each cultural group has unique ways of organizing the world. That is, culture is not static: it varies across time and space, and each group of people has its own unique cultural traits and ways of organizing the world that accumulate and evolve over time (Geertz 1983; Turner 2001). What's more, variation exists within cultures, and specific domains of knowledge provide varying ways of viewing and describing the world within seemingly homogeneous groups (Geertz 1983; Bruner 1986). Goffman (1974, 27) describes the situation in a country such as the United States as an "incomplete sharing of cognitive resources"; as a result, people must calibrate behaviorally when interpreting things in and from different places (especially within broad, diverse cultural groupings such as American or Chinese culture. Walker uses the game analogy to express the same concept, suggesting that as soon as one dribbles the ball while playing volleyball, one is no longer playing the same game. If we are familiar with the rules of volleyball, we clearly understand that dribbling in volleyball is not a useful skill, but we do not always think this same way about learning culture. Performed culture calls for learners to make adjustments in their manner of approach when learning language. That is, they must interpret actions and compose meanings in a different web of conventions in order to "make sense" when dealing with cultures other than their own. And, more important, they must adjust their behaviors to fit the appropriate medium or game.

Performed culture, then, is segments of consciously staged culture of everyday life, and performing culture is *doing* everyday culture of a particular group of people (Walker and Noda 2000). It involves the staging of behaviors or groups of behaviors (events) typical of a particular group of people in ways that are recognizable to them. In other words, these behaviors conform to target culture expectations. A unit of performed culture could be as simple as greeting a person in a culturally appropriate way for that occasion or as complex as an elaborate comedy show on a stage. In any case, performed culture involves at least two levels of knowledge: the declarative-level content of the event and the procedural knowledge of how to stage that particular type of event (Walker 2000). It involves observable behavior as well as the underlying cognitive frameworks that inform and shape that observable behavior. Learners must have a personal experience in which they encounter the differences that result from underlying notions so that they realize there is a difference. The most memorable experiences are usually situations in which communication breaks down or in which learners fail to achieve their intended goals. Although they may not understand exactly "what it is that is going on," they become aware that "something is going on" and it may be different from the "something" they had assumed was going on. With repeated exposure to similar situations or with appropriate coaching—from mentors, peers, or instructors—learners gradually develop ever deeper understandings of the cognitive framework at work. Units of performed culture as learnable segments of larger cultural events can be models of actual behavior used to rehearse future stagings of that type of event (Walker 2000).

Because it arms learners with modes for establishing and interpreting intentions in target cultural ways, performed culture as a pedagogical approach, then, can be a means of participating in the shared realities of any given group. As I have stated elsewhere in reference to American learners of Chinese:

> The significance of the "performed culture" approach for Chinese language pedagogues is that by taking into account behavioral culture, American learners will ultimately be capable of more deeply penetrating cultural events and thus of gaining access to deeper understandings of Chinese people and culture. Moreover, learning to establish intentions in distinctly Chinese ways, understanding how to generate desired meanings in forms recognizable to Chinese people, and knowing how to behave in ways familiar to Chinese people will

facilitate the learner's movement in the culture. Greater ease of movement will allow American learners to cultivate networks of deeper human relationships with peers, mentors and patrons, which, in turn, will open more avenues to learning. Knowing how to build and maintain interpersonal networks will provide the social setting in which further cognitive development (linguistic, behavioral, and cultural) can take place. (Jian and Shepherd, forthcoming)

In the banquet context, by performing culture—delivering a timely compliment to a host, dipping one's glass when toasting an elder or a person of status—American participants reduce the accommodative load that Shandong people must bear to make communication successful; this lightened workload when dealing with foreigners (and with Chinese from other regions of China) makes natives feel closer to the performer. Shandong natives are often afraid to interact with Americans because they know there may be communication barriers. They are also much less likely to interact with strangers (out-group people) than with those people with whom they have *gănqíng* (in-group people), regardless of whether they are foreign. When people from Shandong discover (as a result of a successful performance) that there may not be as much difficulty communicating as they had originally assumed, they typically become more interested in interacting and tend to open up more. Performances also indicate to natives one's willingness to make the effort to learn about them as people (it is perceived that most Americans are too self-centered to do so) and that one has taken the time to learn difficult behaviors—how to deliver a complicated toast, how to tell a story in the local language, how to accept a business card, how to pour tea or beer. Performing in culturally appropriate ways indicates to natives that one deems them (and interaction with them) important, which is key to developing deeper relationships. In sum, paying attention to the details and doing the little things during banquets both makes one seem less foreign to locals (and thus easier to approach) and reveals that one is sincere in one's attempts to develop friendships, which opens the doors to move beyond surface-level interactions.

Performed culture is based on a view of language learning that assumes learning language is part of the larger process of developing culturally defined cognitive behaviors; this process involves adding new skills to one's repertoire. Thus, linguistic code is merely one of a wide array of expressive modes and cognitive behaviors available to any cultural group. The culture-specific meanings generated through these various modes arise in the joint activity of multiple people engaged in communication. Participants in such joint cognitive activity rely upon multiple cognitive processes that work in simultaneous coordination to successfully construct shared meanings. Different languages involve different skill sets. This is true not only for motor skills but also for cognitive orientation and ways of organizing reality. The best example in the banquet context is the differing fundamental views of the guest-host relationship in China and in the United States. For Chinese—and particularly Shandong people—guests do as the host pleases, whereas for Americans, hosts do as guests please. That is, when a guest comes to dinner in China, the host does everything for the guest, including making most decisions about what will be eaten and what will be done in order to take care of the guest. But when a guest comes to dinner in the United States, the host allows the guest to make all decisions about what he or she wants to eat, drink, and do in order to make him or her "feel at home." Another example is how the body, illness, and remedies for illness are viewed in Chinese and American cultures. The first time I caught a cold while living in China, I had a sore throat, so I followed my mother's (a nurse for more than thirty years) home remedy of extra fluids and Popsicles to soothe the inflamed throat. When I told my Chinese friends that I had eaten cold food while sick, they were shocked and rushed to get me as much warm food as they possibly could. They acted as if I had violated a basic, commonsense idea that everyone should know: when one has a cold, the body is out of balance, and warm foods are required to regain that balance; cold foods only exacerbate the imbalance. In this particular situation, Chinese and American "commonsense" ideas are quite different. Richard Nisbett (2003, 189) also has pointed out that "Easterners and Westerners differ in fundamental assumptions about the nature of the world, in the focus of attention, in the skills necessary to perceive relationships and to discern objects in a complex environment, in the character of causal attribution, in the tendency to organize the world categorically or relationally, and in the inclination to use rules, including the rules of formal logic." Moreover, these cognitive modes are not mutually exclusive: learners are capable of developing multiple sets of cognitive and behavioral skills that can be called upon when in different cultural environments and in varying contexts within those environments. In such an approach, the goal for students of Chinese becomes not merely to learn one of the many linguistic codes used by Chinese people but also to develop the cognitive and behavioral skills—including the linguistic code—necessary to participate in the shared meaning-making events—the realities—with any particular group of Chinese people (Jian and Shepherd, forthcoming).

Performances as Games
Performance theory has shown that performances are a useful way to analyze cultural behavior because they provide the cultural framework within which words and actions are interpreted. One question that arises, then, concerns how to segment and categorize different types of performances. The performance approach does not equip us adequately to distinguish between performances that are more or less common in a given culture and those performances that are more or less valued by that particular culture. Theatrical or staged performances are clearly distinct from everyday performances,

and some performances are valued more than others by each cultural group. As a result how participants subjectively perceive and approach a given performance differs depending on the perceived cultural emphasis or the potential social gain or loss associated with that type of activity. For example, in China and in most cultures, one approaches a dinner that takes place in the family home or among intimate friends differently from a dinner among professional colleagues. Both dinners are performances, but they involve distinct types of goals and approaches on the part of participants.

In every culture, there are certain focal performances that are key to becoming part of a social group, are integral in accumulating valued resources, or affect members' status, movement, or ultimate success within the group. In American work culture, there are many types of performances—meetings, company picnics, power lunches—but in the end, the game of getting promoted (or getting a raise) is the one that is most important to the participants. For American academics who conduct classes, hold seminars, participate in conferences, and hold meetings the game is tenure. For Shandong professionals, it is gaining status in the hierarchical social network. I argue that game is a useful metaphor to describe and understand such contexts. Goffman also (1974, 5) implies such an approach:

> A game of chess generates a habitable universe for those who can follow it, a plane of being, a cast of characters with a seemingly unlimited number of different situations and acts through which to realize their natures and destinies. Yet much of this is reducible to a small set of interdependent rules and practices. If the meaningfulness of everyday activity is similarly dependent of a closed, finite set of rules, then explication of them would give one a powerful means of analyzing social life.

My suggestion is that the flow of everyday life *is* organized into just such habitable universes: games. All social activities involve culturally defined purposes and sets of interdependent rules and practices an understanding of which informs the actions of participants; thus these activities can be considered to be games.

Philosopher Bernard Suits (1967a) argues that games are activities that contain a number of elements that make those activities not only intelligible but also distinct from other kinds of actions. To him, games are stable, orderly, rule-governed, and goal-directed activities (discussed in Torres 2002). Suits's (1990, 34) formal definition states:

> To play a game is to attempt to achieve a specific state of affairs, using only means permitted by rules, where the rules prohibit use of more efficient in favor of less efficient means, and where the rules are accepted just because they make possible such activity.

This definition is a useful starting point in applying the notion of games to the analysis of cultural activity that Goffman suggests, but because play and activities we deem more meaningful differ inherently, it needs subtle tweaking. As the definition is applied here, games are social endeavors that are frequently associated with a given field of play. That is, there is a recognized space or location for carrying out game activities. Games are also frequently engaged-in, culturally emphasized activities that have become institutionalized over time, which merely implies that traditions associated with them have been compiled by the group over generations. In addition, games are performances that involve participants in various recognized roles playing by established rules within recognized frames of meaning.

Having dinner with the family, rehearsing a speech before going on stage, driving on the freeway, shooting baskets with friends are all examples of performances that are not games because the participants do not approach them as games—there is no scoring system. Each of these activities could be component (subgame-level) segments of game activity that when combined with other activities could become games. They could also become games if the participants agree to a set of rules about how participation should occur, what the goals for participation are, and criteria for who wins and loses. Thus, a simple statement such as "I'll play you to twenty-one" can change a shoot around into a game, driving can be part of work associated games, rehearsing could be pregame practice, and for some families important progress games take place at dinner. Shopping is an activity that is not necessarily a game for everyone but buying things at a market where bargaining in possible involves the game of negotiation. Moreover, some people view shopping as a game of getting the best deal while for others it takes on less importance. The idea is that a game involves the participants taking a particular approach to an event—placing added significance on the outcomes—and agreeing upon a set of rules for participation.

Culture games are activities that are distinct from other segments of reality in that there are established sets of rules, behavior, language, frames, etc. associated with that particular activity and field of play (Spradley 1972). In a game, an understood agreement by the players to play by the rules of that game underlies the activity and frames the interaction. Furthermore, sets of institutionalized conventions and recognized parameters constrain and guide behavior within that particular type of activity. There are also consequences for not following those conventions—that is, for not playing by the rules. Finally, culture games involve established shared means of participation, exhibit recognized means for generating particular intentions and achieving the desired goals associated with that type of activity, and are typically characterized by the presence of a culturally accepted mechanism for evaluating successful and unsuccessful performances—a scoring system.

Play and Games

Participation in cultural games generates a shared sense of purpose, attention, activity, and reality for the participants. In fact, because games are the primary means with which we create shared social reality, we tend to organize the world in terms of games. The rules of the games we are playing ground us by providing an interpretive framework and by providing the means to and reasons for maintaining social relations. We know we are "gaining social status" or "getting a promotion but do not always think of the situation abstractly as playing a game. As Goffman (1974, 1) states, "Presumably, a definition of the situation is almost always to be found, but those who are in the situation ordinarily do not *create* this definition, even though their society can be said to do so; ordinarily, all they do is to assess correctly what the situation ought to be for them and then act accordingly." We are engaged in the activity and concerned with the immediate requirements and aspects of the activity, so we tend not to analyze it. Following Goffman, I would argue that we do know we are playing games; we just don't conceptualize what we are doing as a game per se but rather as an instance of "x." Here, it is necessary to include a caveat about the difference between games and play. Our common tendency to associate games with *organized play* leads us to avoid connecting games with what we consider *real life* or serious matters. Suits (1967b, 1978), however, has clearly shown that games are not always merely for amusement and can be very serious matters.

Both Goffman (1969) and Eric Berne (1964) and have extended the game analogy to social encounters, but their analyses have focused primarily on the ludic and strategic aspects of social behavior. My argument is that playing in cultural games is what gives our lives significance: We win. We reach goals and desired states. Or, if we lose, we redefine goals so that we have something to work for. Knowing the game and the rules focuses our perspective and provides us with meaning by delimiting the frameworks possible in a particular event. Moreover, playing in games, as Cesar Torres (2002, 2) suggests, is both "a subjective and meaningful way of relating, experiencing or unfolding in the world" and "an objective process capable of being isolated, measured and manipulated." Through game play, we generate and regenerate culture (Huizinga 1980; Torres 2002). Games as such provide us with an organizing concept and with activities that allow us to generate shared space. They also allow us to share focused attention, time, and reality. In short, cultural games are the contexts with which we construct and partake of reality.

For language learners, the importance of the game metaphor lies in the fact that it allows us to view interacting in different cultures as involving distinct sets of skills that do not necessarily overlap or transfer. That is, people must change the way they are doing things when the game shifts, whether it be in their own culture or going from one culture to another. Different games involve distinct sets of rules and ways of participation. Just as a baseball swing on the golf course will not produce desired outcomes, American moves and rules do not apply in Chinese games even when the game is the same general category of game. For example, participating as a guest in an eating engagement in China while following American rules of dining and social etiquette will generate an undesirable interpretation of your intentions; typical American dining behaviors tend to foster impressions of arrogance, self-centeredness, lack of cleanliness, and a general lack of consideration. The event is an eating game but a Chinese one, so American moves do not work and American rules and scoring systems do not apply. Walker and Noda (2000, 195) argue that "different cultures and different games are played according to different sets of shared rules and expectations." They also caution: "Different games share features, but shared features may have contrasting, even conflicting meanings and outcomes. Competence in one game often does not translate into competence in another." To be able to play, one must know what game one is playing and the rules and possible moves. For language learners, the caution is that they must calibrate their behaviors, the equipment they use, and the discourse strategies they apply according to the immediate field of play.

Playing in Games

As understood here, playing in a game simply refers to participation in the activities in a role recognized by the other participants in the event in which scoring is possible. It is only in the role of player that goals deemed desirable by members of the target culture can be achieved, and it is through games that groups construct reality and generate meaning. It is in these shared attentional events that cognitive activity, development, and learning take place, and it is in culture games that we are able to engage members of a culture in a personal way. Through participation in games, we partake in the same reality and become recognized as belonging to the same group. Thus, the experience of playing in cultural games, which requires personal investment and an acceptance of the rules of the game, is key to having meaningful learning experiences.

Moreover, because the act of playing involves an element of risk, it goes beyond the mere role-playing that much pedagogical material was based upon in the past: players must invest themselves in the event and can gain or lose depending on the quality of their performance. Finally, the shared experience that emerges from joint participation in cultural games not only ensures that intentions are being generated and understood according to the same set of rules, but also is key in being recognized as members of a larger whole, which facilitates access to idiomatic, suppressed, hidden, and ignored meanings associated with that particular activity. The experiential knowledge of playing also builds long-term memory of the event, and the ability to shift roles within games facilitates cognitive development and understanding. From this perspective, becoming a competent player in at least one culture game is the desired goal for language learners, and participation in game activities is vital to the success of language learners.

Levels of Participation

A game analogy implies participation on varying levels by the actors. As the level of participation becomes more involved, higher degrees of competency are required for success. This supports the idea of increasingly complex levels of participation that culminate in a sophisticated level of participation in which the group does not accommodate the foreign player. Accommodation refers to the phenomenon of players consciously or subconsciously making adjustments in game styles, rules, or expectations because they are interacting with a nonnative of the group. To discuss these levels of participation in greater detail, the game analogy can also be extended to a sports analogy.

Walker has categorized six basic levels of participation: (1) Observers; (2) Spectators; (3) Fans; (4) Commentators; (5) Players; and (6) Shareholders. Students of any language may be operating at one or more of these levels, or their goals may be to reach one of these levels. The notion suggested here is that depending on the type of performance and their experience with that performance, learners are able to participate with varying degrees of effectiveness. Learners pass through one or more of these six stages each time they encounter a new type of performance, and they can return to stages through which they have already passed. In the section "Eating in Chinese," I provide examples of people at these different levels performing or interacting in the banquet context.

Observers

The first stage of participation is the observer stage. This is the level at which a performer knows something exists. A person at this level of competency is capable of observing cultural phenomena and cultural performances, but does not know the intricacies of what he

161

or she is witness to. For example, after seeing the news or attending a required class on world history, he or she knows there is a country called China and that Chinese people eat with chopsticks. However, observers know little more than what can be inferred through surface-level behaviors. Because learners remain the most detached from the target culture at this level of engagement, it is also the shallowest level of involvement and thus requires the least emotional investment. Consequently, there is little or no risk. Any interpretation done at this stage involves using previously stored information to assess the situation.

The observer stage is the level most students are operating at when they arrive in China even though many have had one, two, or even three or four years of language training. As a result, initial observations often begin with unproductive comments such as, "Chinese don't stand in lines at bus stations," "Chinese frequently spit on the ground in public areas," and "Chinese bump into people without saying excuse me."

Spectators

When the learner-performer makes some sort of low-risk initial investment in the target culture, he or she becomes a spectator and moves closer to the field of play, so to speak. The diner going to a Chinese restaurant and the tourist taking a trip to China are both examples of people performing at the spectator level. Although they are closer to the action, learners at this level still do not penetrate the surface level of the target culture. As a result, they are not privy to insider information or to all of the rules of the game. It is possible for learners to remain at this level of participation even while living and working in the target culture if they do not take risks and engage those around them.

Fans

Through repeated engagement with a particular game, learners may move into the next stage of participation. This stage, analogous to the sports fan, involves people who frequently engage the same game in some capacity, usually as an interested observer. Walker (2000) refers to fans as collectors because they often amass things from and knowledge *about* a culture. Fans are people who, after gaining experience with a particular type of performance, come to like some aspect of it. Through repeated engagements, fans develop a level of understanding of the game culture without actively participating in the game as recognized players. They also may be deeply emotionally invested but remain at a low level of risk because they are not subject to losing. As a result, deeper cultural meanings are still hidden from the fan's view. Fans tend to make quick generalizations based on prior knowledge and often categorize the target culture in terms of their own worldview or base culture. The culture that fans are familiar with usually reflects traditional notions of culture in that they tend to collect things related to high culture rather than elements of hidden or behavioral culture.[2] Fans engage games but are not willing or able to put themselves in a situation where they may ultimately be declared a loser. Thus, they deal mainly with declared types of knowledge, and their worldview is not called into question. Because fans don't rethink their values in terms of the information the new culture provides, they are unable to access deep levels of knowledge gained through participation. A collector of Chinese paintings and someone who enjoys going to Chinese restaurants in the United States both fall into this category of participation.

---

[2] My meaning is that because when most people—especially in China—refer to culture, they do not include aspects of behavior and interaction. They merely think of art, literature, and other tangible elements of what is valued by the culture. The *products* of the behavior and interaction rather than what leads to those products.

Commentators

Once fans become familiar enough with the knowledge associated with a particular game to be able to comment on and manipulate that knowledge on a declarative level, they have moved to the level of commentator. Commentators, or analysts, as Walker (2000) describes them, are able to make educated guesses about, extrapolate patterns from, and make inferences about the target culture for purposes of comparison, analysis, or discussion. Commentators are often perceived to be authorities because they possess knowledge *about* the target culture. The analyst is often familiar with reified, or public, aspects of a culture and may have participated in games as a player (see the next section). They are distinguished from fans and players in that they attempt to analyze and comment on game phenomena; however, many remain detached from interaction within the target culture in order to be reflexive and objective. An example of someone operating at this stage is an American businessman I encountered who has lived in China for more than seven years but who does not interact with his coworkers outside the Americanized work environment of his company. He knows a great deal about China but very little about how to interact with Chinese people on Chinese cultural terms.

Although they claim to do the opposite, many anthropologists and pedagogues deal with performances in this mode: they present declarative knowledge about the target culture to the learner. The problem with presenting cultural knowledge in this manner is that the way learners process and use this type of knowledge differs greatly from the way they would engage behavioral and procedural knowledge. The issue is the way teachers present knowledge to students not the way anthropologists and pedagogues operate themselves (although often times the two are both problematic, sometimes the anth./ped. operates in a procedural mode when in the culture but teaches about the culture when presenting it to students. Sometimes they only know and teach about culture). Many analysts do not have the necessary skills to be successful players, or they were once players and are now no longer active. Because they remain relatively detached, commentators are not at risk of losing in the target culture (according to target culture norms). What is risked depends on the particular culture and the game involved. In the case of Shandong banquets, status, position, friendships, and resources are all at stake.

Players

Players are people who put themselves directly on the line in scored situations and are recognized as full-fledged participants by other players. That is, they are invested emotionally, physically, and socially in the outcome of the game and have chosen to be subject to the game's rules and scoring system. Players put their skills and knowledge of the game on display while interacting with other players under game conditions. Thus, a player is willing to take the risks associated with playing and has attained a sufficient level of understanding of the knowledge necessary to successfully negotiate at least one game according to a group's set of rules. Players are not necessarily members of a group but are able to participate in performances of the group without significant problems. Players also may not possess all of the knowledge about the target culture that commentators possess but they are equipped with the knowledge and skills of how to do things associated with that game.

The player level is what we should target for learners of foreign languages. The argument is that by playing the game by its established local rules, nonnatives can reduce the degree to which they "stick out" culturally. By adjusting behaviors to suit the field of play, learners reduce the burden of accommodation they force on natives, which increases the odds that natives will wish to continue to interact with them. Moreover, becoming the accepted foreign player is an attainable goal for our learners; it does not require them to attempt the unrealistic goal of becoming a native. (see chapter 8)

The key is becoming a player in a meaningful role recognizable in the target culture. Because foreigners speaking good Chinese were rare for a period in recent history and because of the Chinese folk notion that Chinese is the most complex language, foreigners who can speak a few words of Chinese, regardless of accuracy or smoothness of delivery, attract attention and draw compliments. Moreover, foreigners are invited to participate in activities such as banquets, trade fairs, and festivals to add an international flavor or to afford "legitimacy" in the case of economic-related activities. Unfortunately, they are typically invited for their white faces, and when they speak Chinese, they provide entertainment for Chinese audiences rather than being recognized as legitimate, capable players in the interaction. They attract attention but serve little serious function, which Galal Walker (2000) has described as the "performing monkey" phenomenon: when the audience applauds, it is not because it is a good dance, but because a monkey is doing it. The goal of a performed culture approach is to create players in roles other than that of the performing monkey.

Shareholders
Shareholders are those people who have or who attain a level of membership in the group that the player does not have; they have the largest investment—that is, they are married to a native or their parents are natives who emigrated out of the area—and therefore the largest risk—that is, they can cause relatives to gain or lose face, status, or resources— in the target culture. Ethnic Chinese who are learning Chinese culture and language fit into this group. They also must become players but more is at stake for them, and the way they engage Chinese culture is certainly different from that of other foreign players.

Game Competence and Expertise

It should be noted that the player category involves a continuum of experience beginning with rookies, who find themselves in game situations but have not refined their game skills or stored enough game knowledge to perform successfully on a consistent basis. It is unlikely that a rookie can step into a game and immediately perform at a high level of effectiveness. It is more likely that as the rookie participates in a given game more frequently, he or she will compile information that can be used to increase his or her ability to perform in that game should it be encountered again. Veterans, on the other hand, are players who have developed a feel for the game. They have compiled elaborate stories of the game that allow more options in terms of moves within the game. They have acquired sufficient information and have made sufficient moves so that their participation is smooth and automatic.

The notion of player should also include ideas of good and bad players. There are people in every culture who understand the rules of specific games but are not competent at playing by the rules of those games. Cole (1996) defines cultural competency as the ability to function in and be accepted by a cultural group. Players operating at a low level of competence force other players to either accommodate or reject them. As one moves up the scale of competency, the burden of accommodation placed on other players decreases and the level of play gradually becomes more sophisticated and natural. It should be noted that because of the complexity of culture, the number of games in any given culture is too large to allow for an individual to reach veteran competency in all of them. Thus, if competence in a culture is viewed as the number of games one can participate in, it is conceivable for someone to be a competent veteran in one game but an incompetent rookie in another.

As already noted, there are different types of players: There are more experienced and less experienced players. Some are better than others, and even at the player level, there are different ways of engaging Chinese culture. Some players are participants in the expatriate communities in China but never leave those narrow circles. An American teaching English in a university in China who does not speak Chinese or who interacts with Chinese mostly in English may become a player in the university community, but obviously this person's scope of activity is limited, and interlocutors bear a heavy burden of adjusting to his or her behavior and culture. Going on a study-abroad program where students live in a foreign students' dormitory and are grouped with other foreigners involves one type of player. The problem is that because such players speak with Americans and Chinese who are experienced at interacting with and accommodating foreigners, they are engaging in performances that do not provide them access to deeply situated cultural meanings. This situation is also very different from an experience in which the participant is required to become an accepted member of a community completely in Chinese and on Chinese cultural terms.

Eating in Chinese

Here, we look at an example that better illustrates these various levels participation in culture games. I use eating because it is the area in which I have the most personal experience. The observer could tell you that there are a large number of Chinese restaurants and maybe even that Chinese food is good. The spectator would know that Chinese meals are sometimes elaborate, festive affairs with tremendous amounts of food and drink. The spectator may even know that Chinese are very hospitable and like to make sure their guests are satisfied and happy, which, in Shandong, involves forcing large amounts of food and alcohol on them to ensure that they are satisfied. The commentator would be able to tell you that there are many types of meal occasions, including banquets. He or she would also be able to tell you when and where the various types of banquets are seen, who participates in them, what foods are eaten, the toasting and seating rituals that are part of the festivities, and that drinking at

Chinese meals involves calculated moves and countermoves. The commentator might even be able to inform you that during a meal, guests should periodically deliver praise for the host's hosting ability and the quality of food.

The player, on the other hand, is able to praise hosts at the appropriate time and in the appropriate manner. The player also possesses the knowledge and skills that allow him or her to be a good guest at a Chinese meal or successfully host one him- or herself. A player would know both what to say and what to do to maintain the smooth flow of interaction. Players in banquets make toasts and deflect or redirect requests for them to drink. Moreover, players may see the drinking involved as a burden and not the focus of the meal; they understand that the most important aspects of banquets are the overall atmosphere and the maintenance of the relationships among those involved. A shareholder, on the other hand, may have to go to dinner with in-laws, an event that would involve greater expectations and have much higher stakes than any of the other levels of performance.

Playing Second-Culture Games

When actors in a performance come from different cultural backgrounds, a host of other factors come into play, the most obvious and frequently cited of which is the contrast in praxis. When two people come from different cultural orientations, their fundamental frameworks of meaning (cognitive orientations) may differ. Before addressing cross-cultural performance, however, it is necessary to revisit the concept of culture.

Culture as a Concept

The concept of culture in scholarly discourse has a history of disputed meanings. Throughout this work, the notion of culture is similar to those espoused by scholars such as Bruner and Cole, which are founded on the framework developed by Lev Vygotsky.

As Cole (1996, 110–14) notes, Vygotsky's "general law of cultural development" states that all means of cultural behavior are social in their essence, origin, and change. Viewing culture as a social phenomenon allows for Cole's (1996, 167) teleological beings. This theoretical foundation also allows for Bruner's and Tomasello's arguments that the emergence and functioning of cognitive processes occur within the social-symbolically mediated encounters of people in the lived events of their everyday lives (Cole 1996, 103; Bruner 1990; Tomasello 1999). That is a key precept for approaching the learning of a culture from a performance-oriented perspective.

Building on these notions, Bruner (1990), in what he coins "folk psychology," has asserted that all human action and experience are shaped by our intentional states. What we do is dictated by the actions of those who surround us and their reaction to what we do. And what we do dictates what those around us do, thus forming a hermeneutic cycle. Bruner also holds that culture is not just a uniform set of characteristics that describes a group; it also creates shared meaning for members of a group through a process of negotiation (Cole 1996, 58–61).

Culture, as the term is applied here, can be explained as a set of learned default values, created through interaction within a group that is used by individuals for interpreting information. This mental framework for processing information continuously adapts over time while maintaining relevance within a particular communal group. The members of this group, whether as diverse a group as an ethnic group or as limited as a nuclear family, are any combination of actors among whom information and meaning are exchanged over time.

It may aid in clarifying such a definition to note that this set of mutual meanings functions as behavioral defaults and is worked out through trial-and-error experience within the group. Group reaction tells a member what is accepted and valued and what is not. Information then is categorized and stored, forming an interpretive framework. Through creating mutual concepts and shared meaning, culture is an indispensable factor in the formation of individual minds. Culture provides the rules for all culture games by spelling out what members do and do not do. What is accepted as the norm and what is considered abnormal forms of behavior are determined by what behaviors and knowledge are collectively chosen to be valued or labeled as taboo (Cole 1996, 301).

Members subconsciously learn group culture by observing and imitating others and by accepting as truths meanings as presented to them by the group. When members mimic successful behaviors performed by other group members, they exhibit consciously or subconsciously absorbed collective culture. Culture informs all decisions, and behaviors as choices are made to accept or reject notions as presented by the group. Through a process of compilation, people construct cognitive frameworks that they then apply in understanding and interpreting all other information they encounter.

F. C. Bartlett (discussed in Cole 1996) describes the cultural influence of mental organization by asserting that culture tells you how you should organize information. Similarly, John Gumperz (in Young 1994), in discussing problems in cross-cultural communication, delineates a number of characteristics of culture including the view that culture is a shared system of cues or contextualization conventions based on different assumptions and with distinct ways of structuring information. Both views support the notion of a set of cultural default values serving as a framework for meaning. Culture as the source for a framework for interactions provides the contexts within which meaning is negotiated by individuals. Meanings then arm an individual with intentions, which, in turn, provide the requisite tools for communication (Walker 2000).

Thus, if we assume the teleological person, communication can be seen as the establishment and acceptance of meaningful intentions, negotiated within the group, within a given context. The dialogic and collaborative nature of communication can then be accounted for. If communication is a social interaction among two or more intentional agents in which meaningful intentions are established and accepted, language learners and pedagogues alike should focus their efforts on the study of how to become an intentional agent in the culture of their study.

As asserted here, the domain of cultural groups varies with overlap and interaction among various subgroups, providing a vehicle for information exchange as well as innovation. According to Cole (1996), a culture comes into being wherever people engage in joint activity over a period of time. Thus, all groups, regardless of their size, negotiate shared culture. Cole's discussion of "microcultures," a term he employs to refer to the "myriad of subcultures that exist in such places as gymnasiums, schools, hospitals, government agencies, markets, companies, circles of friends, and teams" "alludes to this diversity that is present in the size and nature of cultural groups." (1996, 301-2) Microcultures provide the setting for the everyday events in which the negotiation of meaning occurs.

Enculturation

In any cultural group, members learn group culture both consciously and subconsciously. Cultural learning is also a two-directional process of acculturation and enculturation. Members consciously take in group culture when they are indoctrinated in traditions, taught the way to do something, or are informed of accepted behaviors.[3] They also learn through imitation and by assuming roles available in the culture (Bruner 1986, 1990; Tomasello 1999). Cross-cultural investigators also point out that culture is acquired through a process

---

[3] *Enculturation* comes from Cole (1996), which he defines as a process that involves becoming a cultural being and arranging for others to become one. Enculturation and acculturation are intimately linked. I also see the two processes as linked, but operating in different directions. Therefore, I use *enculturation* to describe a process of assimilation carried out by a group on the individual. I use *syncing* to refer to acculturation, or the process of the individual adapting to the group.

of socialization or enculturation by the group. Children, in China or in any culture, are the focal point of a barrage of institutional pressures that operate to ensure their absorption into society, as Margery Wolf (1985) points out in her study of sexism in China. This socialization continues through adulthood in the form of continuous resocialization. Thus, Chinese values such as filial piety are not a random phenomenon, but rather are attributes of those available in the society considered to be desirable characteristics and which have been socialized through education and discipline. If we are to fully understand a society, it therefore is vital to understand how these attributes are established and what factors go into the decision-making process. What makes a group decide that a particular characteristic is appealing becomes equally as important as what that actual characteristic is.

An example of the types of information valued by a society can be seen in Chinese students' general ability to memorize extended excerpts of texts, a skill that stems from a societal emphasis on the ability to quote classics or works of authority. Traditionally, scholars who could memorize lengthy passages were deemed erudite and generally performed well on the official examinations. During the Cultural Revolution, awards were given to those who could recite the most passages from *A Collection of Chairman Mao's Quotations*, *Máo zhŭxí yŭlù* (毛主席语录). Scholars who proved to have the best ability in this area were tasked as Party secretaries to do propaganda work, which entailed the most prestigious and influential positions. Once they realize what form of knowledge is valued by the culture, group members actively seek to obtain mastery of that information through practice, which leads to the development of a high level of proficiency in particular skills. Furthermore, group members seek out ways and opportunities to display their competence in these skills to the group for recognition.

Hidden Culture

Culture proceeds by a selection of specific practices from a large array of those available. Although group members are cognizant of some attributes of their culture, other aspects of the culture are totally unknown to their conscious mind. These essential cultural characteristics underlie the precepts of group members' thoughts and beliefs, thus, limiting them with the yoke of default notions that constitute the meaning in their world or their worldview. These notions, described by folklorist Alan Dundes (1971) as folk ideas, can serve as the root of biases and preconceptions that may alter the way members understand and give meaning to new experiences. The idea of unseen culture, referred to by Edward Hall (1976) as hidden culture, is important because to understand differences in culture, one must first be cognizant of how native culture effects the interpretation of a second culture.

As Hall (1976) also notes, such defaults often become apparent to a group member only upon observation of another group that does not value the same praxis or when a newly introduced nonmember acts in a way deemed abnormal. Hall believes that cultural biases can be described as an organism responding in only one way to a particular situation. He also noted the tendency to destroy or reject "what could not be controlled and what did not perform in a predictable manner (43)."

It should become rapidly apparent to an American visitor to China that he or she is acting on a conceptual framework that greatly differs from those in the new cultural environment, but this is where one of the major problems in cross-cultural interactions lies. People generally do not adjust the way they organize information when interacting in other cultures. Chen Ling (1994, 125), in describing the experiences of Chinese sojourners in America, notes that sojourners "move about as if they knew the ropes, going about their business as if they were still in their native culture. They deal with matters in the way they always do, until that moment when they find themselves in a problematic situation." Although, as already mentioned, the immigrant situation involves an entirely different set of issues and problems, this attitude is not exclusive to Chinese sojourners, but is also characteristic of most people when encountering foreign cultures.

Transcending Your Cultural System

Group members make necessary adjustments by assessing their actions and the corresponding group reactions, a phenomenon Hall (1976) refers to as "syncing." On occasion, for various reasons, individuals do ignore group response. This rejection of the norm usually comes at a cultural price, which may be as reasonable as a simply noting the discrepancy by others or as costly as being ostracized by the group. Normally, the conflict of norms occurs when an individual simultaneously belongs to multiple microcultures, one of which values the novel notion or behavior. It follows, then, that members can adapt to new, outside information by reassigning meanings once they recognize and accept them. Thus, the shackles of subconscious cultural biases can be thrown off after a member becomes aware of the undesired trait, even if the other group members disagree. This is what Hall (1976) refers to as "transcending one's own system."

One example of a learner who had not made this cultural adjustment involved a Chinese American student in our internship program in Qingdao who had good control of the linguistic code. After a few weeks of interacting with Chinese during her first trip to China, she came to me to ask what the term *jiāoào* (骄傲) meant. When I explained to her that it meant "arrogant," she was shocked, stating, "I am not doing anything different than I do in the U.S. Why do they think I am arrogant?" Another example occurred when a student in our Shanghai advanced language program came to me to discuss problems he was having with his new Chinese roommate. He mentioned that his roommate constantly criticized his study habits, organizational abilities (or lack of those abilities), as well as his eating and sleeping habits. The student stated, "In America, we never criticize others unless their behavior affects us." This student was using his base culture to interpret his Chinese counterpart's behavior, which was more than likely driven by the Chinese cultural notion that it is a friend's responsibility to offer constructive criticism in order to show concern and to help a new friend become a better person.

An understanding of the notion of changing one's worldview is critical in any attempt to become an accepted participant in a second culture. The earlier in interactions with an foreign culture that one is able to grasp the concept of cultural registers, or different frameworks for interpreting information, the earlier one will be able to begin constructing a new interpretive framework for interacting in the second culture. It should also be noted that the idea of breaking down existing cognitive frameworks and adjusting one's worldview according to the game at hand also carries with it a sense of overcoming the ego or of humbling oneself. Before cultural learning can occur, individuals must be able to shift from their characteristic egocentric perspectives. These ideas are particularly important for American learners of Chinese whose base culture values the myth of individuality and tends to foster egocentric worldviews. Chinese cultural norms, on the other hand, typically emphasize at least the appearance of tending to the needs of others before those of the self. Michael Harris Bond (1991) has described this other-centered approach to social interaction as "affective behavior."

Here, I return to the theme that began this chapter: Americans rarely achieve truly advanced levels of proficiency in Chinese language. As a result, we are at a competitive disadvantage. We are producing learners who recognize and establish only American intentions. I argue that this failure to achieve high levels of proficiency in Chinese stems from our emphasis as pedagogues and institutions on declarative knowledge as well as from the lack of emphasis on behavioral culture and performance—making our learners do things in the target culture in ways recognizable to the members of that culture. If learners are not able to operate in Chinese culture (or when interacting with Chinese people) according to Chinese cultural norms, they are not likely to be able to establish deep personal relationships with Chinese peers, mentors, and counterparts unless those people are experienced at interacting according to Western norms. Without adequate cultural skills, learners can remain only distant out-groupers with the majority of Chinese people because they force natives to adjust their behavior to interact with them. Furthermore, it is quite difficult to participate in Chinese social realities without Chinese cultural skills—but it is precisely in these social interactions with natives that truly advanced skills are developed.

Culture informs all decisions, behaviors, and choices for its members. Thus, for our learners to understand that "something is going on here" and that the "something" is different, we must focus our attention on Chinese culture. However, knowing about China and knowing "how to" in China are two different levels of knowledge. Knowing "how to" requires learners to understand the cognitive frameworks employed by Chinese people during communication. Moreover, culture is complex: it is more efficient and effective to focus learning on specific events within the culture. The game metaphor allows learners to zero in on the most important events to natives, and it requires them to alter their approach to learning Chinese. In a game-oriented perspective, learners are not students, tourists, missionaries, or performing monkeys; they are striving to be players in Chinese cultural games, which are most easily identified in microculture settings.

Thus, learners who view themselves as players learning to play specific games are not learning about China; rather, they are learning to do specific things with Chinese or learning to do specific things in China—conduct meetings, handle negotiations, participate in banquets, and so on. The goal for such an approach is becoming a member of a community, which requires "syncing," or adapting behaviors and cognitive orientations. To be able to sync, learners must first recognize both their own cultural framework and that of the target culture. They must understand that all behaviors are informed by an underlying culturally conditioned cognitive framework that includes recognized means for establishing and interpreting intentions. They must also be aware that all tools for communication and modes of participation in reality are shaped by this framework and that they need to perform in the target culture to participate in the reality of the target group.

CHAPTER SIX

Language and Communication in Culture

The notions that there is a range of cognitive expressive behaviors including speech (Tyler 1978) and that language is central to but not the determinant factor in human behavior (Pike 1954) are significant for any discussion of foreign language learning. The implication is that because language is situated in the context of behavior and is a part of larger culturally organized cognitive processes, bilingualism should not be our intended goal: biculturalism seems to be a more meaningful target. Based on the view of learning language suggested here, speaking a foreign language is both a form of communication and a mode of participation in social activities (realities) (Tyler 1978).

According to Wilhelm Wundt (discussed in Cole 1996), purposeful human activity is mediated by language and draws on the beliefs and customs of the group. Stating the same axiom another way, ethnolinguists, following Edward Sapir's ideas, hold that all human experience is to some extent mediated through culture and language. Thus, perceiving culture as a framework that provides meaning for individuals has significance when considering the relationship between language and communication. Because meaning is derived from culture, then language without culture is void of meaning. Therefore, to learn how to successfully interact with members of a second culture, one must possess the ability to both interpret *and* manipulate (perform) cultural knowledge. As we have seen, culture provides the framework within which group activity takes place and within which meaning is forged. Language, on the other hand, provides the vehicle for using that meaning in communication as well as for accessing portions of a culture that are recorded and expressed in the language.

If we take the Chinese philosopher Zhuangzi's suggestion that words exist because of meaning (quoted in Young 1994), language can then be viewed as a key for accessing the meaning locked in culture (Young 1994). Or, as Walker (2000) depicts it, we should view language as a code for accessing the contexts a culture provides. This intertwined nature of language and culture has been observed by numerous scholars and has been the source for endless debate on the importance of each. What is relevant here is to note the inseparability of the two: if meaning is not drawn from the second culture, it will be drawn from the first culture, which can cause communicative malfunctions.

The Meaning Beyond the Words

As has already been suggested, there is more to communication than just speech; noises, nonverbal behavior, and the manipulation of silence all contribute to the construction of meaning (Birdwhistell 1954, 1970; Frake 1964, 1968), as does what is left unsaid (Tyler 1978). This point is particularly important when discussing Chinese because norms of interaction dictate that what is *not* said carries as much meaning as what is said, if not more. Chinese proverbs such as "the meaning outside the words, *yán wài zhī yì* (言外之意)" and "writing does not exhaust speech, speech does not exhaust meaning, *shū bú jìn yán, yán bú jìn yì* (书不尽言, 言不尽意)" point to this cultural emphasis on actions rather than on what is explicitly stated.

Although linguistic code and cultural context cannot be separated during communication, it is important to recognize their distinctiveness in any communicative endeavor. The pure linguistic code of a language can be thought of as a public or revealed code with which a user may access surface levels of a given culture. This public code consists of grammar, vocabulary, sentence structure, and observable behaviors. The problem, as anthropologist Michael Agar (1994, 20) puts it, is that "grammar is not enough to communicate and communication can occur without all the grammar." The revealed code, which can be accessed through reified culture found in libraries and other institutions, falls short when it comes to capturing the myriad meanings and behaviors that can be found in any single cultural milieu.

One has to turn to the hidden code found in culture to locate the meaning between the lines. What makes up the hidden code is the vast wealth of shared knowledge recorded by a culture, including accepted routine behaviors, shared meanings, common presuppositions, ways of encoding intentions, and collective expectations. This type of cultural information is not always stored in reified culture: it is created through common experience and is often intuitive and/or procedural in nature. Linda Young (1994, 129) describes it in this way: "The coherence of conversation is based on underlying propositions rather than simply on the surface structure of sentences." The hidden code provides participants in a given group with an additional set of rules—the ones that often determine success or failure—with which to play the games of culture.

When my Chinese friends watch American football, they often comment that it appears to be pure chaos, a bunch of men running around without purpose. However, if they were familiar with the rulebook (written or understood), a version of which all football fans have committed to memory, they would surely be able to see the extremely sophisticated, coordinated movements that have intended results. The difficulty for language learners should be obvious: Such cultural information is not reified knowledge and can be obtained only through shared experiences. What's more, portions of this type of knowledge remain inaccessible unless one obtains some competence in the public code.

Meat and Bones

Communicating effectively in a foreign language involves a wide range of expressive and cognitive behaviors, only one of which is the appropriate linguistic code. As Agar (1994) has shown, it is possible to communicate with members of another culture without possessing the linguistic code, but as he also suggests, the range of options available for accomplishing any desired act would be minimal at best. Conversely, it is also possible, and quite common, for people to obtain certain levels of proficiency with the linguistic code used by a group of people without obtaining the requisite equivalent proficiency in the group's culture. Anyone who has listened to someone tell a joke in a foreign language and just did not get it understands that there is a wealth of information and meaning not explicit in the linguistic code itself; my Chinese friends living in the United States prove this point, when they comment that they know all of the English words Jay Leno uses in his nightly monologues but do not know why the audience laughs.

Lin Yutang provides a descriptive metaphor for the difference between public and private codes in his 1935 book, *My Country My People*. Lin referred to Chinese scholars who had obtained sufficient proficiency with the English public code to produce written texts as "using English meat with Chinese bones" (81) because the "words are English but the intentions are Chinese" (Young 1994, 181). In viewing them as guilty of translating Chinese sentences into English words, Lin demonstrated that sharing a code is not necessarily tantamount to sharing intentions.

Culture Provides the Context

One reason that sharing a linguistic code is not tantamount to sharing intentions and thus communicating effectively is that language is variable and sensitive to context (Tyler 1978; Hymes 1964, 1968, 1974; Gumperz 1968). Various combinations of linguistic code can have different meanings, senses (Tyler 1978), intentions, and goals associated with them depending on what the speaker is doing, the purpose or intention implicit in the situation, the roles of the participants in the event, the time or location of the event, or the location of the utterance in a sequence of events (Goffman 1959, 1974; Gatewood 1985).

My interpretation of a frequently cited example from Chinese suffices to illustrate. The phrase "have you eaten, *chī le ma* (吃了吗)" can be intended as: (1) a greeting—"hello" if two acquaintances pass on the street around mealtime, but their body language suggests that they don't have time to talk; (2) a means of small talk or opening a conversation (a function called *hánxuān* (寒暄) in Chinese) —"what's up?" if two acquaintances meet in a similar situation but stop and through body language, intonation, or other metacommunicative means indicate that they wish to engage in extended dialogue; (3) a question—"I am concerned about your well-being" if a younger person wishes to show concern for the health and state being of an elder person; or (4) an invitation—"let's eat together" if two friends frequently eat together and it is time to eat.

Culture as Framework for Meaning

Language provides accepted and conventional ways of categorizing experience, but culture provides context for the use of language by organizing, limiting, and constraining interpretations of reality and recognized ways of establishing meaning and intentions (Tyler 1978). This suggests that linguistic and cognitive activities are both subclasses of cultural forms (Bock 1968; Bright and Bright 1969). That is, the linguistic code is merely one part of culture. Culture, by ordering experience in shared, conventional formats, provides the contexts within which speech and behavior can be interpreted (Hymes 1968) and thus limits the potential meanings that can be associated with any given event, segment of speech, or behavior (Tyler 1978).

Mark Turner (2001) and Stephen Tyler (1978) have shown how this situating function of culture affects the acquisition and comprehension of language by demonstrating that recognition of the type of situation immediately provides the drastic operational narrowing of alternatives to be considered. This is highlighted in the course of interacting in foreign cultures because nonnatives are not familiar with the discourse types and patterns of behavior associated with various second culture contexts. In other words, they have not developed sufficient cognitive frameworks in the culture to serve as a basis for predicting and constraining the possibilities for what types of information to expect. Not knowing what to expect hinders both nonnatives' comprehension of events and their ability to take action in those events. The language used in banquets is a perfect example. When American learners are first exposed to the banquet environment, compliments, toasts that afford face, jokes, rhymes, and stories are all difficult for them to understand primarily because they are not primed for them. Once learners are informed of what types and formats of information to expect, comprehension and thus ability to take action upon others' speech or behavior increase. One specific example occurred when I hosted a banquet to thank a manager friend who had arranged an internship site for one of my students. The student and I took the manager to dinner, during which he made three overtures to deepen the interpersonal bonds: one a verbal statement to me (in the intern's presence) about their relationship, one a toast to the intern, and one a series of personal questions directed at the intern. The intern did not understand the first two, and although he understood individual questions in the series asked of him, he did not understand that this was an attempt by the manager to move the relationship to a new level. Because the intern did not know to expect such overtures during a banquet outside of the work setting, he did not recognize the manager's intentions and he did not take appropriate action. The result was that the manager made several remarks to me about the intern's lack of ability in Chinese.

Second Culture Intentions

Work on the cognitive development of children has shown that children display the ability to recognize—and thus react to and upon—intentions and that the functions of speech precede the ability to produce speech (Bruner 1990; Tomasello 1999). This suggests that if we are to use a foreign language appropriately, we need to account for culture in meaningful ways. Cultural psychologists and cognitive anthropologists have proposed, as Richard Shweder (1991) states, that "the processes of consciousness (self-maintenance processes, learning processes, reasoning processes, emotional feeling processes) may not be uniform across the cultural regions of the world." In other words, every culture specifies a range of conventional intentions and a range of uses of those intentions that may or may not overlap with those of other groups. Elinor Ochs and Bambi Schieffelin (1990; reprinted in Duranti 2001, 288) noted, "The capacity to express intentions is human but which intentions can be expressed by whom, when and how is subject to local expectations concerning the social behavior of members."

A simple example from my initial experience living in China supports this notion that members of different cultures operate with different sets of felicity conditions in mind when communicating. While working as a language instructor at Yantai University in 1995, I visited the small market area and strip of shops that had developed outside the university's north gate every day after my morning classes. I would eat lunch and visit any number of shops, stopping to chat in Chinese with the proprietors on various topics. Having studied Chinese for two years, I had become relatively proficient in producing grammatically and phonologically correct utterances in a small range of contexts. During the first three months of my stay, my tour of the market included a daily stop at the Liming

Zhaoxiangguan, a privately owned photo shop operated by the Wang family. Upon my arrival, the Wangs would without fail employ the aforementioned *hánxuān* technique *"chī le ma?"* to open up dialogue. Although I knew that *"chī le ma?"* could mean, "Have you eaten?" I had not come to recognize the contextual use so I always provided them with a truthful answer as to whether I had eaten.

On the occasions when I answered negatively, the Wangs would inevitably invite me to their home for lunch. In the early stages, because we were not yet more than mere acquaintances, I refused. Then, after three months of refusing, I accepted what I had interpreted as a repeated invitation to lunch. Mr. Wang, the head of the household, immediately left the store without a word and his wife and son then slowly escorted me to their home, which was about five minutes from the shop. Upon arrival at their home, I was invited inside to sit on their *kàng* (炕)—a traditional Chinese-style bed—to eat melon seeds and drink tea. After about twenty minutes of small talk, Mr. Wang returned with fresh meat and vegetables from the market.

As it turned out, their "invitation" to lunch had not really been an invitation at all: according to Chinese cultural norms, it was proper etiquette for dealing with the situation at hand—interaction with a person with whom you do not have feelings or *gǎnqíng* but with whom you are an acquaintance requires particular polite behaviors. Other Chinese who share this cultural background understand that asking if someone has eaten is a greeting that does not expect any reply, but that if they are extended an invitation, cultural protocol requires at least one polite refusal. That refusal gives the speaker the ability to extend the invitation again, which clarifies it as an invitation rather than as a greeting or small-talk opener. The Wang's intention was to greet me in a manner that maintained the proper social roles of host (Chinese)-guest (foreigner) and insider-outsider (they later explained to me that they did not expect me to accept and why). The intention I interpreted as an invitation to lunch was actually meant to be a polite gesture associated with our social relationships in the context of lunchtime social interactions. I obviously had not achieved cultural competence although I did have some level of linguistic competence.

Domain-Specific Knowledge

Clifford Geertz (1983) and Stephen Tyler (1969) have shown that there is variation in any given culture as well as distinct domain-specific patterns of cultural behavior and cognitive organization. Richard Nisbett, in his *Geography of Thought* (2003), also has demonstrated that human cognition is not the same everywhere and that "Easterners" and "Westerners" differ in fundamental beliefs about the nature of the world as well as in characteristic thought processes. Because each culture provides its members with a shared set of felicity conditions, distinct contextual environments, norms of behavior, and shared fundamental beliefs, a foreign language learner must learn the range of cognitive and expressive behaviors employed by target culture members in order to effectively communicate with them over extended periods of interaction. If, as Sapir astutely observed, there is a multiplicity of social realities (even if they are not determined solely by language as Sapir argued), doing things in a foreign culture becomes participating in a distinctly different psychological reality (Bright and Bright, 1969; Wallace 2003; Shweder 1991; Goodman 1968, 1978, 1984).

The divergent ways of framing and presenting information in professional and business meetings across cultures provide an example. When Chinese professionals make presentations about a company, organization, or city,[1] they tend to give all of what they

---

[1] Because local governments spend significant resources attempting to attract foreign investment to their respective jurisdictions, the manner in which they present information about local companies, organizations, and administrative units (e.g., cities, counties, villages) to outsiders is highly structured. These presentations can be formally conducted in conference rooms or strategically included as part of the casual conversation of banquets. They are designed to systematically present

consider to be the basic facts about their organization as well as any positive indicators about the organization's economic state. Normally, this involves bombarding the audience with raw facts and numbers.

In the Chinese context, this statistical data adds legitimacy to what the presenter is saying as well as to the organization itself; it is a way of establishing the identity and trustworthiness of the organization. Thus, the presenter tends to trace the history of the company in terms of major stages of development or major structural changes, highlighting data that shows the strength or developed state of the company. My experience observing American speakers of Chinese in such contexts suggests that those not familiar with this way of organizing information—large batches of numbers and data—have significant difficulty determining what is relevant and what to focus on. As a result, comprehending what is said becomes problematic. When they understand the context, however, they are able to better predict and comprehend individual segments of the language used and as a result are better equipped to participate in the activities.

Levels of Meaning
Thus far, we have seen that meanings can be found in both linguistic and behavioral realms and that meaning is constrained by the cultural and domain-specific contexts. Variation in meaning can also be found at the cognitive level. Michael Geis (1995) contends there are at least three levels of meaning for every piece of language used in a communicative act:

- *I-meaning*—speaker intentions;
- *L-meaning*—an utterance's literal meaning; and

---

important information about the entity in question to attract the interest of potential investors.

- *S-meaning*—the significance meaning or the meaning assigned by a culture, including all feelings and connotations an utterance evokes.

What is of note here is that when a speaker employs a particular utterance, his or her intentions also need to be taken into consideration if the listener is to appropriately interpret that utterance; this idea was first addressed in the work of H. P. Grice (1975). Because every utterance can be understood on many levels, for a participant in a communicative exchange to accurately assess the interlocutor's intentions, he or she must have access to multiple codes or sources of meaning that allow for extrapolation.

In addition to these types of meaning, receptor and audience meaning should be included. In discussing the role of intentions in communication, the fact that the intention the listener received may differ substantially from the one the speaker intended must be addressed. Cole (1996) accounts for this by pointing out the proleptic nature of speech. Prolepsis, the notion that speakers assume listeners understand what they are saying, is often overlooked by language pedagogues and learners. Young (1994) also points out that meaning grows from a combination of what the speaker intends to say and what the listener understands, but that the two are not always congruent.

Learners, especially at the early stages of learning, focus so heavily on production that they do not stop to check for comprehension by their listeners. This particular problem is exacerbated in Chinese culture, where public correction is deemed impolite. The result is that nonnatives often make unintelligible utterances that they assume are comprehended, but the Chinese interlocutor hesitates to clarify for fear of insulting the speaker or making him or her lose face. On numerous occasions in which multiple foreigners were involved in the interactions, I observed Chinese players act as if they understood what was being said in a conversation with an American only to have them ask me later what the person meant.

In another example that I observed while in Shandong, an American, after dining with some Chinese friends, offered to help a female acquaintance with her coat on the way out of a hotel; this is a gesture that is very American. The American meant to convey the intention that he wished to help her put on her coat. However, in a slip of the tongue, he stated in Chinese, "*wǒ yào tuō nǐ de yīfu* (我要脱你的衣服)," which is actually "I want to take off your clothes." Rather than informing him of this egregious error, the Chinese woman paused for a moment before allowing him to help her put on her coat; her response indicates that she was able to interpret his intentions based on the context. However, when no response follows an action that accompanies one of these unintelligible utterances, misunderstandings arise—the nonnative often blames the Chinese because of the false assumption that his or her intention had been communicated and that the Chinese interlocutor had acknowledged it.

Although what the speaker said was grammatically correct, it was not what he meant to say, which was "May I help you with your coat?" However, had he gotten the grammar right for this intention it still would not have been something a man would say in Shandong. This is an example of something a man in Shandong simply would not say. It is a great example because it is behavior that is culturally driven and because there were multiple layers of meaning involved. The speaker in this case had excellent Chinese language skills. It was simply a case of using Chinese to express an American intention. In Shandong, men do not typically help women—particularly women who are not their mothers or wives—with their coats because of the way male-female relationships work in the area. Local cultural norms dictate that there are clear-cut differences between the way men interact with romantic interests and with women who are not romantic interests. On several occasions, it has been pointed out to me that traditionally men and women who were not related could have only one type of relationship: sexual/romantic; there were no platonic relationships. This is changing but is still an area that is culturally quite different than what is found in the United States. In Shandong, if a man and a woman spend time together alone— regardless of what they are doing, whether it be talking about personal matters or doing things that show concern for one another— a signal is sent to both the parties of the interaction and those who observe the behavior that the two have more than a platonic relationship. Thus, behaviors that are viewed as gentlemanly in the West, such as opening doors for women and helping them with their coats, are avoided when dealing with women in Shandong because they could be perceived as overtures to deepen the relationship in a romantic way. In this case, I am sure that the American speaker did not have a romantic intention because I know him and have talked to him since the incident. However, the behavior struck the native woman both because of the misuse of the linguistic code and because the behavior itself was unexpected. She later explained to me that she interpreted the behavior as "something foreigners do" and so did not attach any significance to it, although she did not know why he was doing what he did at the time or what he meant by the utterance.

Another point about the anecdote about helping the woman with her coat is that none of the five Chinese present informed the American that he had made a mistake. However, if the Chinese interlocutor believes that the information in the utterance might be of import or if his interests are at stake, he *will* clarify unintelligible utterances; I observed this latter characteristic on several occasions during official negotiations in conjunction with US/China Links in 1997.

Additionally, onlookers may produce meanings that differ from those of the speaker and the listener. Returning to the previous example, when the American actor made the statement that he would like to take off his Chinese friend's clothes, both I and another Chinese friend who were present exchanged worried looks. After it was apparent that the Chinese woman accepted the American's intention despite the misuse of the linguistic code, we then exchanged grins. Obviously, there were at least two distinct meanings received by the different players involved.

In the process of what Carlson (1996, 69) refers to as "reconstructing an assumed intention," it quickly becomes obvious that there are multifarious factors that must be considered. Not only does the process involve interpretation of the immediate event, but it also includes assessing an agent's global purposes. Carlson posits that "an immediate speech act is best understood as a single operation in a whole series of actions directed toward a general goal." Additionally, the listener must also evaluate what the other "hearers" involved in the speech act in order to determine whether the utterance was intended solely for his or her hearing or whether it was directed at a number of people for different purposes.

Verifying Reception

As a participant in a performance, the speaker must ensure that interlocutors accurately receive his or her intentions. After speaking, the speaker becomes the listener who must ensure that his or her intention was received as intended. This is especially difficult in cross-cultural communication because of the aforementioned tendency to interpret new information in terms of an already existing worldview. Additionally, a nonnative's repertoire of checking devices is much smaller than the native's.

Establishing Intentions in a Second Culture

Young (1994, 101) suggests that participants in speech acts choose ways of expressing themselves based on their intentions, on what they want hearers to believe, accept, or do. Language "informs listeners by transmitting speakers' knowledge, intentions and attitudes while at the same time providing data for listeners from which to make judgments about speakers." Such a description presents language as a tool or vehicle through which intentions are conveyed and analyzed. It also hints at the cooperative nature of communication: both the speaker and the listener have responsibilities to uphold in order to make a communicative event successful.

However, by stating that the goal of language learning is developing the ability to establish one's intentions in the target culture, we address only half of the equation. Establishing one's intentions is vitally important to success within any culture, but even more important and difficult to the language learner is learning how to interpret the intentions of other cultural players. If one can interpret intentions, one can survive by reacting to those of others. Once learners have the ability to analyze and manipulate a particular intention as established by another interlocutor, they then can draw on such knowledge to establish a similar intention for themselves in other situations. This view also implies that language pedagogues and learners should develop strategies for interpreting and establishing speaker intentions within their target culture framework.

Kinesic Cues

Also salient to mention here is what Hall (1976) refers to as nonverbal clues and Birdwhistell (1954) calls kinesic behaviors. These behaviors are part of the hidden code, which combines with the revealed code to provide the information necessary to interpret a communicative event. Such kinesic cues sometimes carry more meaning than what is being said, and at other times may reveal a speaker's mood or unspoken intentions. Included in this category of communication devices are gestures, facial expressions, and a host of other culturally recognized nonverbal behaviors. A smile may express a speaker's happiness in one culture but reveal nervousness in another. Similarly, gestures, such as a simple nod, employed while speaking may mark an interlocutor's acceptance of a speaker's request or acknowledge reception of presented information.

Being in a Culture

It should be clear now that the main goal of learning to converse in a foreign culture is to gain the ability to establish and interpret intentions in the foreign culture. With such a capacity, the language learner is able to actively participate in larger communicative activities. Or, as Walker describes it, a person is then able to *be* in a culture (Quinn 1994). At first, this concept may seem quite alien to the reader, and as Walker (2000) observes, American foreign language learners often have great difficulty realizing that as individuals in the culture they are studying, they are only whom that culture allows them to be. In other words, the culture is the final judge. Finally, although culture does place restraints on what an individual can do and who he or she can be in that culture, it should be noted that with skillful maneuvering, the keen player can negotiate his or her persona within those constraints. On the first few occasions that I attempted to serve as host for banquets in Shandong, many participants were quite uncomfortable with allowing a foreigner to act as host in their culture. As time went on, I took measures to alleviate this discomfort and to shift the focus away from myself as a foreign host and onto the guests and the activities at hand. I performed hosting duties that conformed to the most traditional (rigid) notions of etiquette, even to a level that many natives no longer conform to unless it is the most formal of occasions. At the same time I was attempting to attend to as much local etiquette as possible, I continually told my guests that I did not know enough about local culture to do things in a Chinese way, so I would host in an American way. That is, I never made claims that I was doing things in the local way.

In many situations, players did not notice when I followed local etiquette , because things were being done the way they were supposed to be done. So, I worked with several mentor banqueters who helped me as assistant hosts and *péikè*. During banquets, they repeatedly pointed out to participants not intimate with me when I had done something that conformed to local etiquette; for example, pouring beer for others, leaving the last few ounces and foam in the bottle as a display of respect, or not filling glasses to the rim with tea because the water is hot and may burn someone. When players realized I was doing such things naturally, they often heaped numerous compliments on me for my hosting skills. When they did not and it was pointed out to them that I was doing things as they should be done locally, there was often a noticeable change in their behavior. These players frequently made positive comments about my hosting skills to my associates rather than directly complimenting me and then would begin paying closer attention to details themselves, such as using two hands when toasting rather than one.

In addition to performing local culture and having locals point this fact out to participants, I made conscious efforts to maintain control of the interaction so that I could focus attention on the guests involved. When attention began shifting to me, I would attempt to redirect the flow of the interaction by asking about the guests, requesting that guests perform in some way—singing, telling a story, telling about experiences—or temporarily giving way to a local who was working with me as assistant host or *péikè*.

An example that shows the restrictions a culture levies on individuals occurred as an ethnically Chinese language instructor and her American-born Chinese student were discussing the term "to permeate or seep, *shèntòu* (渗透)," during a language course taught at Yantai University. The Chinese American made the statement that he was an American who, after living in China for a year, had experienced aspects of Chinese culture beginning to *permeate* his American character. The Chinese instructor corrected the student, saying that it was impossible for aspects of Chinese culture to seep into his American character because he was Chinese. She continued that although he was born and had lived the first twenty-five years of his life in the United States, he was Chinese and that aspects of American culture were beginning to creep their way into his Chinese character. The American student continued to argue his case, but to no avail. In this particular situation, the culture would not allow him to be American because of his Chinese appearance; it would allow him to be only a Chinese who presently lives in America.

Cultural Accommodation

John Gumperz (in Young 1994) asserts that one "cannot assume communication between a competent foreigner and a native is the same as that between two native speakers" because there is an intercultural dimension. Agar (1994) echoes that because natives consciously and subconsciously treat outsiders differently than other natives, the nature of the interactions foreigners face is fundamentally different from that of natives. This is a striking thought when one considers that the goal of many language programs or learners is to speak like a native speaker. The goal of interacting/speaking a foreign culture/language as a native is a misguided one that causes endless frustration for the learner because of its unattainability.

Even if foreigners attain nativelike proficiency in some skill areas, subconsciously, native speakers still adjust their styles of interaction for them; these alterations fundamentally change the rules for communicative interaction. Furthermore, because such a fundamental difference does exist, it would seem that learning and teaching how natives interact should not be the sole area of focus for language learners. Thus, rather than attempting to achieve "nativeness," an activity that wastes time and energy, learners' goals should be to become accepted foreign players in the games of a culture—which, in a role-sensitive society such as China, is the most realizable goal. It is also important for the language learners to realize that they will have to achieve this goal in every game and within every context.

Rising Expectations

As the nonnative's linguistic effectiveness increases, there is a corresponding increase in the expectations of his or her interlocutors; therefore, it becomes much easier to offend others within the group because native speakers begin to assume that nonnative have levels of cultural understanding that they may not necessarily have. Nonnatives then sometimes begin to be seen as somehow having insincere motives, because they should know better. As a result, the person who learns how to interact with the target culture on its terms while maintaining some semblance of his or her individual identity with a trace "foreign-ness," or who is able to forge an accepted identity within the new culture, seems less likely to be rejected by the group.

Cultural Misfiring

It is possible to misfire culturally in one's native culture, but more frequently, faux pas occur cross-culturally because of the natural tendency to interpret new information in terms of previous knowledge. This "interpreting the new in terms of the old" is the root of countless cultural blunders and misunderstandings. One example occurred when my students and I attended a banquet held by a number of local government officials in Shidao. The host fulfilled one of his responsibilities by continually urging everyone present to drink. One of my students did not wish to drink, so when he thought he recognized the situations one in which some people simply wanted to drink, he refused to drink. However, even more problematic than refusing was the manner in which he did so: He said that he did not want to drink because he did not feel like it. He stated that of course he could drink and on a good day could drink quite a lot, but on that day, he simply did not feel like doing so. The result was that he offended our host and appeared to be intentionally refusing to give the host face, which brought heightened pressure to drink upon the other American participants.

Muriel Saville-Troike (1982), among others, notes the existence of culturally determined patterns of communication that are very predictable. Because such patterns affect the way one forms thoughts and establishes intentions within one's first culture, their presence also influences the way one attempts to establish intentions in a nonnative linguistic code. Any native speaker of English who has interacted with nonnative speakers can provide examples in which English words were used without the corresponding cultural code. Here are a few examples I observed while teaching English at Yantai University in Shandong Province.

A. (Chinese student to American teacher when taking leave)
    Teacher, I go first.
B. (President of Chinese University in an opening to a letter written in English)
    When will you return to China? My colleagues and I are all longing for your coming back to Wuhan.
C. (Chinese friend to American in casual conversation over the telephone)
    Do you have enough clothes?

These examples, which were delivered with the English linguistic code, are perfectly acceptable if we interpret them in terms of Chinese patterns of communication; however, they are awkward if interpreted with an American cultural frame of reference. In sentence A, the Chinese student addressed his American teacher with the proper respectful title required by Chinese culture, teacher, *lǎoshī* (老师), and used a common leave-taking phrase to disengage from conversation with his teacher, "I go first, *wǒ xiān zǒule* (我先走了)." Sentence B, which sounds insincere and too dramatic in English, is in accordance with Chinese expectations for correspondence between friends, which emphasizes the "personalness" and intimacy of the relationship. Finally, in terms of Chinese patterns of communication, the question in sentence C is a normal way to show concern for a friend's well-being and generally refers to wearing enough to stay warm rather than whether one owns a certain amount of clothes; however, the latter idea may be the message conveyed when the American cultural code is used.

These examples are all cases where an understanding of revealed code interfered with the communication of an individual's intentions because the revealed codes were connected with the hidden code of the wrong culture. Now consider the following examples of Americans using the Chinese revealed code without an understanding of the Chinese hidden code.

A. (American answering Chinese host's inquiry as to whether he had gotten his fill to eat at dinner)
    (Almost, or Just about.)
    chà bu duō le (差不多了)
B. (American responding to Chinese friend's request for help)
    (I will think it over.)
    Wǒ kǎolù kǎolù (我考虑考虑)

These statements are acceptable according to normal American communication patterns, but they conveyed intentions to the Chinese that differed from what the speakers thought they were conveying. In A, the speaker was my student who made the statement when asked if he had eaten his fill during a banquet we attended together. He answered the host in a very acceptable manner according to his cultural framework. Typical of most American guests, the speaker was straightforward and honest, and he meant that he had eaten enough; however, the intention he conveyed was that he had not quite gotten his fill. In the Chinese context, informing one's host that one has not gotten quite enough to eat indicates that the host has not fulfilled his obligations as host. In this situation, the host's inclination was to order more food so he told the waitress to bring several more dishes. Because I sensed the miscommunication, I spent several minutes talking with the host, explaining to him that all foreigners present had actually had enough to eat. The host continued to suggest that it was not a problem to order additional dishes and insisted that he order several dishes to ensure that we—foreigners who have much larger physical frames and, thus, larger appetites— could eat our fill. The negotiations resulted in the addition of one dish rather than several. Additionally, the directness of the American's statement also may be viewed as a breach of Chinese etiquette, which calls for the guest to praise the taste of the food served while commenting on its overabundance irrespective to reality.

The response in Example B displays a Chinese rhetorical device for denying a request without explicitly stating the refusal. In this situation, a personal experience, I genuinely planned to consider helping this friend, but my response conveyed the exact opposite intention to my interlocutor. What I learned later was that such phrases as *kǎolǜ kǎolǜ* (考虑考虑) translated as "I'll think it over," and *méi wèntí* (没问题), often interpreted as "No problem," are often used by Chinese as conflict-avoidance devices or face-saving mechanisms; they indicate that there may be some difficulty in fulfilling the hearer's request without explicitly denying that request. Such phrases are frequently utilized to put the issue off until a later date. There is no expectation for subsequent action by the speaker in Chinese culture when employed in this manner as would be the case in American culture.

A second function of such devices essentially is dealing with someone by telling that person what he or she wants to hear; Northern Chinese refer to this as "spreading things out, *fūyǎn* (敷衍)," which can also be a device for getting through a situation without disrupting the harmony of the interaction. A native speaker who discussed this issue with me commented that even if her family uses similar terminology with her in response to her requests for assistance, she doesn't know if they were just brushing her off or if the words retain their assigned literal meanings. Thus, she would seek alternative solutions to the problem at hand to ensure that it would be solved. Her description included the proverb "Don't hang yourself on one tree, *bú yào zài yí kè shù shàng diào sǐ* (不要在一棵树上吊死)." Lacking an understanding of a culture's hidden code of meaning may hinder interaction with members of that culture.

Base Culture Interference

When the cultural frameworks informing actors' behavior are not the same and when they act based on different cultural assumptions, performance is hindered. Because of the symbiotic relationship required for meaning to occur, it is vital for actors and audience to be working with the same set of rules. Because actors' worldviews can be incongruent even when they use the same linguistic code, they certainly may encounter such stumbling blocks when negotiating a cross-cultural performance.

An example of such communicative malfunction comes from a discussion of the Chinese phenomenon of *guānxi* (关系), or interpersonal relationships, that I had with an American who had studied Chinese language for five years and who was just finishing a six-month stint working in mainland China. Although possessing the ability to speak Chinese, she continued to use her American interpretive framework to assess what she had observed while participating in intercultural interactions. Her conclusion was that *guānxi* was solely an unethical means to advance one's own cause within Chinese society. She failed to note the value of interpersonal relationships and group ties from any other standpoint and thus cut off the potential for further interaction with all Chinese who used overt relationship-oriented behavioral strategies for interacting with her. Such an interpretation would prevent the full understanding of interpersonal relationships within the Chinese context, thus preventing understanding the intentions of the various actors in such an environment, which resulted in her losing the game. What really matters in the Chinese way of communicating is nurturing bonds and links in human relations. Furthermore, this American failed to note that the same phenomenon exists within her native American culture, the distinction being that American culture does not possess the same established explicit ways of discussing relationships that Chinese culture does.

Misinterpreting Intentions

Because the information one culture holds about another is not always current or accurate, there is the potential for misinterpreted intentions as well as misguided attempts at intention making. An example of a misinterpretation of intentions based on incorrect information can be seen in an incident that occurred in the spring of 1997. At one of the many construction sites in Yantai city, I noticed a number of temporary workers not from the area leaning on their shovels observing my American colleagues and me. I saw a perfect opportunity to simultaneously practice some Chinese and find out what areas supplied Yantai with this type of labor. I approached them and began making small talk with them. I allowed them to dictate the flow of the conversation, which immediately turned to monthly salaries and hometowns. After a few minutes, their manager rushed over, angrily asking who I was and what work unit I was with. Before I could answer, he began explaining that because China was less developed than the United States, they did not have the luxury of machinery to do excavating. He went on to explain that even though the workers had to use shovels, they were treated well. At the time, the interaction did not make sense, because I had not been asking about equipment or working conditions.

While later watching a news story about the Clinton Administration threatening Beijing with sanctions for human rights violations, I realized that the information the culture had stored about Americans had caused the manager to make erroneous assumptions about my intentions. Then, he adopted what he deemed the appropriate strategy to handle an encounter with a meddling American: although we were located in China and were utilizing the Chinese linguistic code, this manager was obviously aware that he was interacting with a member of a different culture. The communicative malfunction occurred as a result of his misinterpretation of my intentions and his desire to save China's collective face.

Establishing an Incorrect Intention

Because an audience judges any performance, and because success in communication is largely dependent upon reception, an actor must be aware of the cultural framework within which he or she is performing. The message is what the audience comprehends and not necessarily what a speaker intends. The following episode illustrates this example. In 1997, I was arranging a banquet for a number of Chinese colleagues who had recently assisted our organization. I consulted a Chinese colleague about an appropriate restaurant, and he introduced me to a local restaurant. When inquiring into prices, I felt that the prices we were quoted were inordinately high and stated so to my Chinese colleague. I then decided to arrange things on my own. My interpretation of the performance, which was conducted entirely in the Chinese linguistic code but without the unspoken cultural code, was that I had politely declined the assistance of my Chinese colleague. However, the Chinese colleague, as well as the restaurant owners, interpreted the performance in a radically different way: they viewed it as an indication that I did not trust my Chinese colleague. The intention was not received as intended. Because of the negative reaction of my colleague, I have discussed this situation on numerous occasions with several locals. Many of them have informed me that they believe my colleague was extremely sensitive and may have overreacted. Nonetheless, they indicated that the way I handled the situation was not tactful. They suggested that I should have first talked things over with my colleague while not in the presence of the restaurant owner; that would have enabled him to make a change in plans without losing face. They also suggested that an effective strategy for handling difficult situations such as this would have been to request a third party—a mutual friend—to serve as the bearer of the news that I was in a difficult financial situation and could not use the recommended restaurant. Again, that would have afforded my colleague the opportunity to handle the situation without losing face, and it would have avoided direct confrontation between the two of us.

Misguided Accommodation

Often, participants in a performance who are aware that cultural differences exist attempt to adopt strategies to accommodate foreign participants and avoid misunderstanding based on the information their worldview holds about members of another culture. However, this type of strategy can be successful only if the information one has about a culture is accurate and if both parties are working on the same assumptions. I observed just such an incident when an American who did not eat beef visited a Chinese home. The Chinese host, in an attempt to adopt an American strategy in order to please her guest, prepared an unusually "American" meal including beef, bread, and milk. When the American did not touch the beef, his Chinese host misinterpreted his actions as a sign that her culinary skills were lacking, because the information she had stored was that "all Americans eat beef"; the information she relied upon as a basis for her interactive strategy turned out to be inaccurate. Interestingly enough, the American obviously was operating based on his American interpretive framework or he would have responded by sampling all dishes and commenting on how delicious they were.

These examples point to difficulties that stem from actors in a performance not operating within the same interpretive framework. The last incident also hints that players should *sync* with their interlocutors, observing and testing to find out which interpretive framework is being applied and then adopting measures appropriate to that framework. However, the emphasis on failures does not insinuate that it is impossible for players from one cultural background to operate in foreign games, but rather accentuates the necessity for an awareness of one's cultural environment and a sensitivity toward participants within that environment. Individuals must be willing to make alterations to their worldview, which requires creating new methods for interpreting information that incorporate elements of the target culture.

CHAPTER SEVEN

Learning Culture

Because cognitive development emerges out of activities in which individuals share attentional focus[1] to negotiate meaning, learning a culture can be viewed not only as creating a more permanent record of the products of shared attention and negotiated meaning but also as constructing a long-term memory of one's experiences in that culture. In this view of learning, memory and the development of memory are crucial to the language-learning process. As Walker and Noda (2000) argue, learning a second culture is tantamount to compiling a memory of that culture. Learning is viewed as the

---

[1] "Attentional focus" is used in psychology and specifically by Michael Tomasello (1999) to refer to two people directing their mental operations toward the same goal simultaneously. Tomasello argues that humans have the ability to identify with other humans' intentional and mental states—what he calls "putting yourself in the mental shoes of someone else" (6). For Tomasello, it is this ability to understand conspecifics (i.e., members of the same species) as intentional beings like one's self that sets humans apart from other species because it allows us to participate in a "cognitive collectivity" (7). He argues that children are able to participate in this cognitive collectivity from about nine months of age, when they first make attempts to share attention with and to imitatively learn from and through their conspecifics. He also suggests that these cognitive activities provide the basis for children's entry into the world of culture. My suggestion is that although children entering the world of their native culture and adults entering the world of a second culture are different processes, there are some instructive aspects in Tomasello's findings for adult learners. If we think of the adult foreign language learner as having to develop the ability to map out and participate in the cognitive collectivity of the target culture—which may differ drastically from that of his or her base culture—we can see that he or she must also learn how to share attention with members of target culture communities as well as understand how to learn from and through conspecifics. The idea is that we cannot learn from target culture members or communicate with them unless we know how to engage in joint cognitive activity (share attention) with them.

continual mental process, conscious or subconscious, through which cultural knowledge is accessed, memorized, analyzed, acquired, internalized, and automatized. It is achieved through repetitions of adapting behaviors while people are engaged in shared experiences. Jerome Bruner (1990) posits that learning is internalizing events into a storage system. He argues that learning occurs when a member participates in culture and that individuals learn responses and forms of habituation by participating in in-group activities. Bruner also notes the negotiation of meaning that occurs between individuals and the group.

In addition to Bruner, Michael Cole (1996) asserts that cognitive tasks do not just happen, but are made to happen in joint activity among people. Tomasello (1999) also describes the importance of what he calls "sharing joint attentional scenes": an individual demonstrates knowledge of a culture by using the knowledge entailed in that culture to participate in interactions with others. Stated another way, there is an ordered sequence to the process of creating and compiling memory in that one first understands cultural knowledge through the process of sharing attention and negotiating meaning before one is capable of employing that knowledge. This sequence, if viewed in terms of Piagetian theory, is tantamount to a preoperational stage followed by both the concrete and the formal operations stages. Becoming able to do something, coming to a realization of something, and acquiring knowledge of something all stem from an individual's negotiations with the culture within which he or she resides. The level of difficulty in such negotiations escalates when one is working in a second culture in which many default values are not available as reference points. Both Bruner and Cole also assert that learning and thinking are always situated in a cultural setting and are always dependent upon the utilization of cultural resources. In Cole's (1996) view, every schema is a mental summary of similar events that serves as an outline that the individual continually revises, filling in the gaps as additional information is collected. Bruner (1990) describes the same notion as adding details to a narrative; Roger Schank (1990) applies the metaphor of compiling and indexing stories. Individuals can then use the information in these structures to make comparisons, contrasts, and intelligent guesses about what to expect in other situations. Thus, because the individual must figure out which schemas, narratives, or stories apply in which circumstances and how to implement them effectively, then language pedagogues ought to emphasize developing these interpretive skills in language learners.

Bruner likens learning to the construction of a map of culture, but the process of learning can also be likened to what occurs in a criminal investigation: the learner can be viewed as an investigator trying to solve a case, and the evidence examined is acquired knowledge. Assembling the evidence and building an account of what has occurred are akin to negotiating within a culture. The case becomes clearer if the investigator is able to locate more clues and interview more witnesses, just as an individual's world becomes clearer as he or she accumulates elements of and experiences with people from a given culture. The type of case an attorney should design becomes clearer as more information is available; once the type of case is clear, the attorney can research all related cases and access all previous experience with that particular type of case. The same process takes place when a person accesses known information categorized in a particular schema.

Because clues are elements of culture and because more clues reveal more about the mystery, the more elements of culture one exposes oneself to, the more knowledge of that culture one can obtain. If an attorney has more case experience, his or her ease at negotiating a certain type of case naturally is increased; repetition promotes ease and fluidity of operations, both in the process of learning and in trying cases. Cole (1996), Schank (1990), and others advance the notion that one's level of psychological development depends on the extent of one's experiences. Thus, the more experiences and types of experiences one has within a culture, the more opportunities one has to acquire cultural knowledge, and, therefore, the greater the likelihood that cultural information will become internalized or recorded in memory—that is, provided those experiences engaged in include sharing attention, the negotiation of meaning and calibration for cultural frameworks, and the learner returns to them again on the mental plane.[2]

Cole's (1996) work supports the notion that if a person already possesses a particular concept, completing related tasks is much easier. People are able to draw more out of a situation if they have had similar experiences because a portion of the available information is internalized during the first encounter, which can then be consciously or subconsciously called upon when a similar situation arises. As Cole (1996, 110) posits, "any function in children's cultural development appears twice, or on two planes. First, it appears on the social plane and then on a psychological plane. It first appears between people as an interpsychological category and then within the individual child as an intrapsychological category." Young (1994, 245) also views the development of language skills in terms of cognitive stages: "children are able to understand before they speak their own words. They respond appropriately to commands and suggestions made by others." Schank (1990) describes this process as *dynamic memory* and argues that we figure out how to behave in new situations by being reminded of old situations that serve as guides of what to or not to do. Walker and Noda (2000) suggest that the same principles apply to adult learners of a second culture. Thus, the more cultural doors an individual knocks on *and* opens up, the more levels of culture he or she will

---

[2] A person can have an experience without learning anything if he or she does not review the experience mentally afterward. The successful learner is one who returns to previous experiences mentally—on a metacognitive level—to review them, evaluate them, and rehearse manipulations or adjustments that could be applied to similar situations in the future.

experience. Repeated experiences in target culture games, then, provide both access to the stories of the culture and opportunities to enhance and solidify the memories of those events.

Learning is opening doors or pathways to a culture's pool of knowledge, which is stored in the form of stories (Schank 1990). A culture's knowledge pool can be likened to a database, the contents of which can be linked through participation in games and connecting the memories of those experiences together with previously existing knowledge. Learners must also be aware that new cultural rules apply when indexing this new knowledge in memory. Simply adding information to old stories is not sufficient if we are to avoid warping the knowledge with our own cultural framework. The stories we learn in a second culture and the memories we create of our experiences in that culture must be indexed separately as a new type of story that applies to a new type of game. Once learners who adjust their approach understand that something different is happening (when interacting in another culture), they can focus their attention differently. Over time, they can consciously construct schemas informed by target-culture events. For example, the first time I ate in a restaurant in Shandong, I noticed that the American script for what occurs in restaurants was different from what I was seeing. There were some similarities, of course, that allowed me to recognize the restaurant situation: the first question asked was "How many (are in your party), *jǐwèi* (几位)," hostesses were seating people, servers were delivering food to tables, the aroma of good food filled the air, and the clinking sound of pots and pans was coming from the kitchen area. However, there also were significant differences: once I was seated, servers didn't ask what I wanted to drink, but simply began pouring tea for me; servers delivered dishes to tables one at a time rather than all at once; the types of foods (and thus aromas) available were quite different; and there was no door separating the kitchen from dining room. After noticing these obvious surface-level differences, I began consciously piecing together what a Shandong restaurant script looks like; each time I go to a restaurant, I add new information about that script to my schema of Shandong restaurants, such as the first time I noticed that paying the bill after dinner was a complex situation in the Shandong context. After watching people pay on numerous occasions, I gradually began to realize that in Shandong, restaurant goers might engage in heated discussions after dinner over who will pay the bill. I also came to understand that sometimes pushing, pulling, and shoving may be involved but that this is not a form of fighting. I added the information that although the participants in such an exchange may have red faces and may be speaking quite loudly, they typically are not angry with one another. As I gathered more information in my schema about restaurant settings, I began to understand that scuffles over who will pay the bill are matters of face in Shandong. Even if a person does not have money and does not plan to pick up the tab, he or she might still resist strongly if someone else makes a move to pay and could even insist several times that he or she wants to pay. I have seen this occur even when it was clear who the host and guest were supposed to be. It is not always necessary to pick up the tab when eating in Shandong— although one must always keep social debts in balance—but for hosts, the American script for paying in restaurants does not work: No one will divide up the bill, no one will accept if you offer to pay your share, and it is not wise to wait for the server to bring the bill. If you are the host, you must make arrangements with the restaurant to pay prior to dinner or you must actively ask for the bill (and get up to get the bill from the server if someone else attempts to intervene). If a participant at the meal says that he or she wants to pay the bill (and you want to pay or should pay based on norms of reciprocity—that person bought last time, so this is your turn), you should still resist no matter how strongly he or she protests. One effective strategy that was suggested to me to avoid bill-paying disputes was to leave the banquet room during the course of a banquet—pretending that I am going to the restroom, but I really am sneaking off to pay the bill.

Hall (1976) promotes the idea that cultures have varying levels of stratification. Accessing these different levels of culture is a skill acquired through modification of behavioral tendencies developed through experimentation and adjustment to the group's reaction. Piaget (1963) also understood human development in terms of adaptation to the environment. Adaptation is made possible through assimilation (using a response already acquired) or through accommodation (modifying a response to meet a new need), what was referred to earlier as *syncing*. Learning, according to this view, is the combination of the processes of enculturation and acculturation, or acquiring the knowledge a particular group deems important by via negotiation with that group.

Ideas underpinning this view include that situating learning in the context of culture and language is central to, but not the determinant factor in, human behavior (Pike 1954) and that learning culture refers to the acquisition of a range of cognitive and expressive behaviors, including speech (Tyler 1978). My position is that we should also be approaching foreign language learning from this perspective, which implies that because language is situated in the context of cultural behaviors and is a part of the larger process of culturally organized cognitive behaviors, bilingualism should not be the intended goal. Biculturalism—a term that as used here includes two distinct sets of linguistic, cognitive, and kinesic behaviors: base culture and target culture—seems to be a more meaningful goal. This conception of learning also suggests that language learners and pedagogues should focus their energies on activities that maintain integrity to cultural situations, allowing individuals to negotiate with the target culture at whatever level they are capable of performing. If, as Cole (1996) suggests, social relations genetically underlie all higher functions, then interpersonal relationships and strategies for negotiating those relationships should be the focal point of these cultural situations.

Syncing

Accounting for unspoken intentions and meanings reveals that a group's culture includes both the behaviors (linguistic and kinesic) typical of the members of the group and the accompanying cognitive orientation that informs those behaviors: knowledge *of* a culture provides the basis for interpretation and analysis of the culture, and knowledge of *how to do* a culture provides the basis for participation in the culture. As previously stated, in addition to spatial and temporal variation across cultures, variation exists within cultures. Specific domains of knowledge[3] provide varying ways of viewing and describing the world within seemingly homogenous groups (Wallace and Atkins 1960; Geertz 1983; Bruner 1986). As a result, participation in nonnative cultures requires behavioral (linguistic, kinesic, and cognitive) adaptation by the learner. This is not to claim that the goal for nonnatives is to "go native" or become natives, an impossible prospect for American learners of Chinese culture because of obvious physiological differences. I suggest, rather, that individuals must *sync* with the target culture—that is, they must condition their actions to conform to group expectations. They need to make subtle calibrations, behaviorally and culturally, when interpreting *and* when performing in games in different cultural locales if they are to effectively communicate.

This notion of integrating oneself into a local culture is not new. It can be traced at least to Bronislaw Malinowski, who, in

---

[3] The way a mathematician talks about the world differs distinctly from the way a politician talks about it, even if both are American. Chemical engineers deal with a body of knowledge—complete with specialized terminology, unique uses of common language, and patterns of behavior—that is difficult for outsiders to understand even if they are members of the same culture. There are bodies of knowledge that are created within microcultures or by specialized subgroups within cultures that when learned, form unique ways of viewing and interacting with the surrounding world.

Coral Gardens, clearly shows that learning language and participating in a culture are related tasks: "I think that a complete knowledge of any native language is much more a matter of acquaintance with their social ways and cultural arrangements than of memorizing long lists of words or grasping the principles of grammar and syntax which in the case of Melanesian languages are appallingly simple" (1965, 453). Malinowski further advocated firsthand observation of culture and behavior, participation in the activities of the group of study, and repeated, long-term interaction.

In a group-oriented culture such as China's, syncing plays a much more obvious role than in the more individually-oriented culture of the United States. Chinese behavior is often determined by what others do or do not do. When asked about this tendency, one Chinese student of mine recently commented, "If others do something and I do not, it is not a good situation. I will think that I should be doing it as well." Living in Shandong Province exposed me to a related phenomenon that exemplifies this importance of adapting to the group. Rather than wanting to establish one's own niche or place in society, the tendency in Shandong is to conform to group expectations. Instead of displaying one's talents or expressing one's uniqueness, many people from Shandong fear having others view them as different, either positively or negatively. This is reflected in the local saying, "fear being a crane in a flock of chickens, *pà hè lì jīqún* (怕鹤立鸡群)."

One episode I observed hints at this cultural theme. A male student of mine at Yantai University confided in me that he wished to speak more in class, but was afraid of what his classmates would think of him for being different. Because no other students regularly spoke or expressed themselves, if he were to do so, he would be exposing himself to attacks from jealous classmates. He also expressed the feeling that he could confide in me things that he could not confide in his Chinese friends because I was an outsider who could not fully understand and therefore there would be no repercussions as a result of my knowing. A number of my professional acquaintances also went to extremes to ensure that their neighbors and friends were not aware of their successes, financial or otherwise. The following proverbs provide further evidence for the argument that Shandong people hold such a view:

- "Large trees attract the wind, *shù dà zhāofēng* (树大 招风)," meaning those who are well known are most likely to attract attention or meet unfortunate ends.
- "People fear becoming famous like pigs fear becoming fat, *rén pà chūmíng zhū pà pàng/zhuàng* (人怕出名猪怕胖／壮)," having obvious connotations.
- "If some wood is superior to the other trees in the forest, the wind will surely break it, *mù xiù yú lín, fēng bì cuī zhī* (木秀于林, 风必摧之)," meaning those who outperform the crowd will meet a bitter end.

These cultural themes underlie the rules that dictate the behavior of Chinese players as games unfold.

Although the foreign participant is extended additional leniency in such areas, a phenomenon such as the tendency to avoid standing out mentioned earlier is important for the language/culture learner to have integrated into his or her behavioral repertoire for a number of reasons. First, when interpreting the actions of the various people an individual comes into contact with, he or she must know their motivations. Disregard for these motivations could easily cause undo stress for native interlocutors. Had I shown excessive attention to a particular student, it would have resulted in additional pressures for that student, either personal or from peers. And had I called attention to the successes of my professional acquaintances mentioned earlier, unforeseen consequences might have resulted. By noting this cultural theme, adapting to it, and incorporating it into my bag of interaction tools, I increased the chances that my interlocutors would be willing to interact with me beyond the initial encounter. Finally, although the goal of the language learner is to become an accepted outsider, the group naturally tends to accept more quickly those who have characteristics similar to those of the group than those who have nothing in common with the group. If one realizes this point and is willing to make changes in behavior, it is then possible to sync with the group so that one does not stand out.

Returning now to the relationship between culture and communication, as already mentioned, all cultures provide rules for appropriate communicative interaction, defining behaviors that should occur, that may occur, and that should not occur in given contexts. These diverse rules are learned through formal and informal processes of socialization. Because culture is what people must know in particular social environments in order to operate efficiently and because, as Bruner (1990) claims, culture is the source of meanings and intentions, successful learning of communication without an understanding of the cultural rulebook members of a group are relying upon seems impossible. The examples provided earlier of Americans toasting at inappropriate times and refusing to participate in recognized modes support this idea. The behavioral rules dictated by Shandong culture are also critical in learning to communicate in the banquet context. The cultural rulebook defines (for informed participants) who talks to whom, when they talk, what they talk about, and how they say it. For example, men cannot simply talk to any woman present at a banquet without considering male-female relationships, and younger banquet participants typically speak only when spoken to. There are specific ways in which banquet speech must be conducted: younger participants must use titles and polite speech when speaking to elders; hosts talk more often than guests and attempt to talk in ways that enhance the atmosphere. There are also designated times that require hosts to speak, including initial and final toasts, as well as situations that require guests to speak—compliments and responses to toasts.

Learning to Navigate Events

In addition to roots connected to Malinowski (1922, 1965), the approach advocated here draws heavily on the work of Stephen Tyler (1969, 1978). First, Tyler noted the critical role of context in determining meaning and the need to account for nonverbal behavior and *the unsaid* when analyzing meaning. He suggests a more holistic view of situations: "our anticipation of speech as a sequence of events motivated by a guiding purpose and leading to a known or emergent goal or outcome, and our perception of a coherent pattern of co-occurrent relationships among significant components of style, situation, form, function, purpose, intention, participants, topics, and settings" (1978, 427).

Tyler also notes the distinction between declarative and procedural knowledge, or "knowing that" and "knowing how." The key for him was that *knowing how* "is often organized into units larger than propositions which comprise fixed sequences of propositions in the manner of a text or script or recipe. These larger schemata are predetermined episodic sequences or sets of instructions for such things as how to order a drink or a meal in a restaurant, how to buy drugs, how to grow crops, how to prune a plant, how to get from one place to another, how to poach a fish, how to perform a ceremony or play a role in one, and so on" (1978, 237). The notions of patterned scenarios, goal-oriented plans, and generalized schematic patterns used to express and interpret meaning have significantly influenced the shape of both cognitive anthropology and cultural psychology.

Anthony Wallace (2003) has provided us with the notions of society as a network of intercommunication and the possibility of multiple psychological realities. Psychological reality for Wallace is the world as he (an individual) perceives and knows it, in his own terms; it is his world of meanings. Wallace also suggested that culture is best viewed as providing a diverse range of choices to individuals rather than a single set of rules to which all members must conform. Moreover, Wallace suggests a focus on events in context similar to Tyler's in calling for a possible focus for what he calls "a science of human behavior." In addition to Tyler and Wallace, Charles O. Frake (1968, 436) similarly focused on context and situations by stating, "speech, noises and non-verbal behavior have meaning the segmenting of the behavior stream in such a way that culturally significant noises and movements are coded while the irrelevant is discarded."

Janet Dougherty and Charles Keller's (1985, 161) ethnographic study of blacksmithing adds to this mix the ideas that "a task at hand determines features of relevance for conceptualization" and "as strategies for action, organizations of knowledge are particularistically oriented." In other words, there are numerous ways in which relevant knowledge is organized and reorganized and that when creating meaning, people apply the one most relevant to the specific goal and event at hand. Finally, John Gatewood (1985) provides further evidence that human knowledge is linked to human action in his ethnographic study of salmon purse seining. [4] Gatewood demonstrated that in addition to verbally segmenting events, with experience or repeated encounters with a type of event, humans break down processes into events or episodes. Gatewood suggested the notion of segments as a descriptive for the units of behavior that organize small-scale actions such as the subroutines and small tasks that fishermen perform that make up the larger operation of seining. In the banquet context, introductions, the seating ritual, the opening ceremony, the free-flow toasting period, and the closing ceremony are all segments that make up the larger banquet activity. Following Gatewood's approach, each of these

---

[4] A seine is a large fishing net made to hang vertically in the water by weights at the lower edge and floats at the top. Seining is the operation of fishing with such nets.

units of behavior can be viewed as a separate segment of time and action that is made up of smaller-scale actions and behaviors. Toasts, for example, are composed of the physical act of standing, the verbal act of delivering the toast, the physical acts of tapping glasses (*pèngbēi*), the physical act of swallowing the contents of the glass, and displaying the empty glass (*liàngbēi*). For Gatewood, segments are psychological—not necessarily verbalized—units that are categories of time and action as well as a unified action mode with a characteristic emotional tone or ethos. Segments, in Gatewood's analysis, relate little tasks to large-scale tasks and understandings of the larger seining operation. As such, they facilitate comprehension of the temporal interrelations among different job routines on the same boat and thereby improve crew coordination.

The significance for learning culture is that learning the whole of a culture is an unrealistic task; if we focus instead on specific events, the task is both contextualized and more manageable. If we categorize knowledge based on specific tasks, as Dougherty and Keller (1985) suggest, and organize processes into smaller segments, as Gatewood (1985) posits, then a focus on developing specific abilities—the procedural knowledge of how to do these events— would facilitate our understanding of emic categorization[5] and segmenting as well as provide us with the skills necessary to accomplish specific things in our culture of study. Moreover, because cultures maintain schemas of knowledge and clusters of language and behaviors associated with specific events, these event schemas should be a focal point of study for learners of language and culture.

---

[5] "Emic" is an anthropological term that has come to mean "from a native's point of view." It contrasts with "etic," or "from an outsider's point of view." Kenneth Pike (1954) coined the terms based on the distinction made in linguistics between phon*emic*s and phon*etic*s. My use is similar to Pike's use meaning from the perspective of someone familiar with the way a system works. Thus, "emic categorization" refers to the ways those (typically natives) intimately familiar with a culture categorize their world.

In my estimation, schemas work on two levels: they can be personal and they can be shared. They can be a person's mental representations of events experienced or places visited that are constructed based on repeated encounters with a particular type of context or event. But following the idea mentioned earlier that we share in a "cognitive collectivity," I believe that schemas also can be shared—however incomplete that sharing may be. They can be collective constructs that members of a group build over time. This type of schema is a "cultural schema" and can be shared like other resources and artifacts created by the members of the culture. Learning about schemas provides context for understanding how to approach behaving in particular events, and learning how to *do* specific events provides a natural module for the focused study of deeply contextualized language and meaning.

Compiling Cultural Memory

Jerome Bruner (1990, 99) sees learning as "internalizing events into a storage system" and posits that memory "allows us to go beyond one encounter by providing us with the tools that allow us to make predictions and extrapolations from our stored model of the world." If this is the case, an understanding of memory and how culture knowledge is stored in memory—individual and collective—is vital to learning and teaching second cultures. Here, I do not claim a complete understanding of the concepts and processes involved in memory, but I attempt to connect the role of constructing memory and language learning.

Bruner (1990) argues that cultural scripts are received through experience and are disseminated to appropriate areas in the mind for proper analysis. This view allows us to consider memory as the process of storing information in the form of narratives or to the system with which we accomplish that process. Memory can be viewed as the tracking or guidance system that maps out the coordinates to and assigns a code to each memory. The memory system arranges narratives chronologically, spatially, through imagery, or through sensory perceptions. [6] Memory's encoding system utilizes key words, kinesic behavior, sounds, smells, or images that resemble a password to link stories stored in the subconscious portion of the brain.

Because memory is an interpretation of an experience, it is flexible, with a potential to be more or less accurate or inaccurate. It is a record of experience, which means that individuals may also store the same schema differently. Moreover, memory stores only a framework of an experience: our limited capacities permit us to store only a small portion of the information found in the flow of events, and individuals store different elements of the same event. When a password is entered, the system is activated much like the completion of a circuit, and the stored information can be called upon through the links created by memory narratives that are archived in the subconscious mind, bringing them into the active portion of the mind.

The key to memory, and thus for language learners (and teachers) developing memories of cultural events, lies in the way information is encoded. As Bruner (1990) argues, if it is encoded in narrative form, the opportunity for recall is much higher, and what is not structured together by narrative suffers loss in memory. This is simply because narrative supplies more ways of linking up with a particular piece of information. If we know how memory is structured and how it works, we can control how we go about conscious memory acts just as distance runners who understand the physiological make up of the body can take advantage of that information to focus training even though they cannot alter their own biological make up. Without narrative, individual pieces of data present limited numbers of links to reach that data. As a result, the

---

[6] Daniel Schacter's (1996) work on memory, which is based on extensive medical and psychological research, sheds light on the biological and psychological issues involved in how memory is constructed and stored in the brain.

information is more difficult to access. If people organize their knowledge and thoughts in narratives, as Bruner suggests, language should not be learned in ways contrary to the manner in which we organize our thoughts. As was pointed out in a previous chapter, learners cannot react if they do not know what to expect in a given situation. Knowing how thoughts and knowledge are organized—in narrative form—allows one to better predict the behaviors of others. Having memories of participation in given situations gives one the ability to react more efficiently and effectively in similar situations in subsequent events; these ideas should inform our pedagogical approaches to language and culture learning. Because information is encoded in memory in narrative form, if we learn it in this format, recall should be higher. If information is typically both presented and received in narrative form, narratives provide larger units of discourse—larger than individual words and sentences—to both learn and analyze.

Cole (1996) and Bruner (1990) also note the presence of both individual and cultural memory, asserting that memory is a way of recording sensations or experiences, which may or may not be accurate. Because individuals experience events from different vantage points, they may record a different perspective from that of others who experience a similar event. Cole views cultural memory as written information or systematic knowledge and holds that schools are enculturating institutions that deal in reified and codified speech structured in a fashion seen appropriate by the culture. He posits that this knowledge changes the mind once education begins.

Cole further suggests that cultural memory is heavily influential on all members of a culture. The way people view themselves and others is often dictated by cultural memory. So too is the way people, especially educated people, look at problems and go about analyzing questions. Their whole way of thinking is set for them without their realizing it. This is important for language learners to know for many reasons, one of the most important of which is that the way people of another culture perceive an outsider can often be found in the cultural memory of a particular group.

Identity Categories

On numerous occasions while interacting in Chinese cultures, I have heard that I am not like an American because Americans are...and then people would enumerate the characteristics that Chinese culture has stored about Americans; these often include directness, arrogance, casualness, and superficialness. During one encounter, a middle-aged woman I met on a train from Weifang to Qingdao told me that she felt talking with me changed her entire outlook on Americans. She explained that she felt much closer to Americans now because they were not as *different* from Chinese as what she had been taught in school and had read in newspapers. This would serve as further evidence that Chinese culture has a collective memory in which information about Americans has been recorded.[7]

During these and similar interactions in China, it became apparent to me that there was an expectation of what foreigners were and should be like. I learned what that foreigner stereotype, or artifact, in Cole's (1996) terminology, was every time I did not conform to it. The discrepancies pointed out to me between my behaviors and those of the typical foreigner in China include studying hard, avoiding bars and discos, dressing formally rather than in what has been described as tattered clothes, reciprocating, being more reserved in speech, and expressing a genuine interest in all Chinese people.

---

[7] EVERY culture constructs cultural memories that include perceptions (stereotypes) of people from other cultures; there is nothing special about Chinese culture in this aspect. Cultures have these shared resources and memories that the learner must be aware of when interacting in a nonnative culture. If we are going to *sync* with local behavioral patterns to reduce the workload of natives so that they will want to continue interacting with us, we need to know how they perceive us and what their expectations are for us.

Goffman (1959) has talked similarly about how "when an individual enters the presence of others, they seek to acquire information about that individual or to bring into play information about him already possessed." He lists factors such as socioeconomic status, self-conception, attitude, competence, and trustworthiness. This information about the individual "helps to define the situation, enabling others to know in advance what he will expect of them and what they may expect of him."

Goffman goes on to explain that there are many sources of such information (sign-vehicles) that convey this type of information. The key for our purposes, even though Goffman is not talking about interacting in a foreign culture, is "If unacquainted with the individual, observers can glean clues from his conduct and appearance which allow them to apply their previous experience with individuals roughly similar to the one before them or, more important, to apply untested stereotypes to him" (1). His terms for using these signs intentionally or unintentionally are "expressing" oneself and being "impressed" by others (2). He also distinguishes between the expression one "gives" (verbal cues) and the one that an individual "gives off" (wide range of action symptomatic of the actor) (2). Finally, Goffman differentiates the impression one thinks he is giving off and the one being received: "The others, in their turn, may be suitably impressed by the individual's efforts to convey something, or may misunderstand the situation and come to conclusions that are warranted neither by the individual's intent nor by the facts" (6). These characteristics of expressive behavior become more important when crossing cultural boundaries because when the interpretive framework shifts without a concurrent change in thinking and behavior, it is quite easy to give off an impression that does not match what is intended.

In his discussion of performances, Goffman (1959) deals with playing a part and the potential to be taken in by one's own performance; that is, to believe that "the impression of reality one is staging is the real reality" (17). He employs the term *front* for that part of the individual's performance, which defines the performance for those who observed it.

> When an actor takes on an established social role, usually he finds that a particular front has already been established for it. Whether his acquisition of the role was primarily motivated by a desire to perform the given task or by a desire to maintain the corresponding front, the actor will find that he must do both. Further, if the individual takes on a task that is not only new to him but also unestablished in the society, or if he attempts to change the light in which his task is viewed, he is likely to find that there are already several well-established fronts among which he must choose. Thus, when a task is given a new front we seldom find that the front it is given is itself new. Since fronts tend to be selected, not created, we may expect trouble to arise when those who perform a given task are forced to select a suitable front for themselves from among several quite dissimilar ones. (27-8)

Goffman was concerned mainly with American culture in this book, but the phenomena he discusses are relevant when interacting in a foreign culture. There are a limited number of fronts—for example, a young male may maintain a "student" front when interacting in certain circles, a "banqueter" front while in others, and "one of the boys" in still others—available[8] to the foreigner interacting in Chinese culture, especially when significant

---

[8] The same young man could maintain fronts as a "hard worker," as a "business-oriented person," as someone with "official connections," or as a "good friend." The key is that the culture dictates what fronts are possible for any person. A young man cannot maintain an "eminent scholar" front because of his young age and lack of experience. It is also difficult for a young man to maintain a front as "head/leader of an organization" for the same reason. Age, sex, appearance, societal position, speech, and behavior are some of the factors that influence the effectiveness of any front.

physiological or cultural differences exist between an individual and target culture members. Additionally, there is a role, "foreigner," which can facilitate or hinder one's movement within the culture. Finally, there are consequences for not conforming to the expectations a culture holds in its collective memory about a particular kind of person. This reinforces the notion that *who* a person is in another culture is, at least in part, determined by the culture. So, even when a nonnative does nothing at all while in Chinese culture, natives make guesses about what that outsider should be like based on both their individual and the group's prior knowledge of that "category" of person. When an American, who stands out because of physical differences, enters the cultural world of China, he or she is already an object of a culturally conditioned interpretation.

These observations about how the foreigner is perceived suggest the significance of reflexive work[9] in which the nonnative becomes acutely aware of how he or she is perceived, how he or she affects the game he or she is playing, and how to become comfortable with that position. When dealing with a nonnative culture, it is important that the learner know how people from his or her own culture, nation, or ethnic group are perceived by members of the target culture, because such knowledge may indicate how to transform interactions. The learner can then be prepared for some of the potential reactions to his or her presence and behavior such as the "performing monkey" phenomenon mentioned earlier. Additionally, being cognizant of successful and unsuccessful strategies for dealing with such aspects of the cultural memory of a group can both provide interaction equipment usable in games and raise the level of comfort a nonnative experiences while playing those second culture games.

---

[9] "Reflexive work" is a term frequently used by anthropologists to refer to conscious thinking about how the presence of the anthropologist affects the situations/cultures he or she is observing. I apply it to the language-learning context because learners must also be aware of how their presence alters events, interaction, behavior, and communication.

Developing Layers of Experience

Vygotsky's (Cole 1996) notion that word meanings develop over time and Schank's (1990) notion of dynamic memory support the view that language learners must gradually both compile individual memories of experiences in the target culture and access the memories shared by members of that culture. Building meaning for concepts is a part of a larger process of building stories, which is accomplished in a similar fashion and is discussed later. My personal learning experience serves as an example. I can place any given word in my Chinese lexicon into at least five levels of understanding. In some cases, several levels are acquired simultaneously, but many times my memory of a word remains at one level of understanding for a long period of time without advancing. Normally these levels of understanding occur in the following order, but they are not confined to this path of development.

In the early stages of learning Chinese, I frequently equated terms such as "relationship" and "*guānxi*" but as I encountered these terms in more and more contexts, I realized that I was dealing with different but related concepts. In some contexts, *guānxi* can be translated as relationship and has the exact same meaning as the English equivalent. In other contexts it has other meanings. It is this process of encountering the term on multiple occasions that allows us to construct a more and more complete understanding of the concept involved.

1. *Awareness:* This is the stage of initial contact with a concept or word. It is usually characterized by a realization of something new or something not comprehensible.
2. *Recognition:* I can pronounce the word or character upon contact. Even though I recognize a character or combination when I see or hear it, I may not be able to associate meaning to it.

3. *Context association:* Meaning is often equated to an already existing concept, but although I am able to recognize the new concept, I do not have the ability to employ it independently: I am dependent on reacting to native-speaker use of the concept. Another characteristic of this stage is that I know that the concept or word is found in a certain context. That is, I begin making a connection between the concept and the events in which it occurs.

4. *Internalization:* The new concept becomes a part of natural speech that can be employed independently. During this stage, I normally have a surface- or sentence-level understanding of the concept but am not necessarily aware of many of the private-code meanings associated with it and its uses.

5. *Manipulation:* I obtain cultural connotations associated with the word that enable me to manipulate or play with words for a desired effect. It is in this stage, or during use in the context of game play, that I am finally able to access deeper-level cultural knowledge not readily apparent in the public code.

Cole (1996) argues that such a process of cognitive development is at work on the concept level. In his study of language development among the Oriya people of Africa, the Oriya children were able to use *mara*—a term mothers use in the sense that they are "polluted" when menstruating—in conversation with adults long before they had adult concepts of the term. They began using the term when they had only a vague understanding of what *mara* involved while gradually filling in the gaps as they acquired new bits of information until they had a fully developed understanding of the notion.

Scripts

Cole (1996) notes one type of schema that seems to be equivalent to what Schank (1990) calls *scripts*. According to Cole's (1996, 126) description, a script is "an event schema that specifies the people who appropriately participate in an event, the social roles they play, the objects they use, and the sequence of actions and causal relations that applies." According to Schank (1990, 8) each culture has established means for interpreting situations; "there are rules to follow, the way things are supposed to be." These "sets of expectations about what will happen next in a well-understood situation" are called scripts and are a kind of memory structure. For Schank (1990, 7), "life experience means quite often knowing how to act and how others will act in given stereotypical situations. That knowledge is called a script." Scripts associated with cultural games both guide our actions in those games and are the means through which we store the knowledge that we encounter in them. (see chapter 4 for an example of a script associated with Shandong banquets) In Schank's terms, "They serve as a kind of storehouse of old experiences of a certain type in terms of which new experiences of the same type are encoded" (1990, 8). Scripts are learned bodies of shared cultural knowledge that allow us to predict what others will do and say by limiting the number of possibilities that may occur in a given situation. "Early education involves learning the scripts others expect us to follow…The more scripts you know, the more situations will exist in which you feel comfortable and capable of playing your role effectively" (Schank 1990, 8).

An example of the presence of a culturally coded script can be seen in the following dialogue between an elderly Chinese man and me that was subsequently clarified by the added comments a native observer made about the conversation. The event took place inside a small camera shop adjacent to Yantai University in 1996. The dialogue appears in a rough English equivalent that reflects speakers' intentions followed by the actual Chinese.

Shepherd: (Standing up from a small stool where I had been sitting and offering it to the elderly man who was walking past the open shop door) Uncle, please sit down.

Elderly Chinese man: (Refusing in a display of courtesy) No, sit down (don't get up on my account).

Shepherd: (After moving the stool into a position for the elderly man to sit and retrieving a second stool from the back of the store) Please, Uncle, have a seat.

Man: (Reluctantly, still refusing) Don't make such a fuss...ok, ok (sits).

Shepherd: Have you had lunch yet Uncle?

Man: Yes, I have.

Shepherd: How's your health?

Man: Just fine. Thank you for asking.

Shepherd: It's rather cold today.

Man: You're not wearing enough (clothes to keep you warm), you don't want to catch a cold.

Shepherd: (After several minutes of discussion about recent local happenings, rising) Uncle, I have something that I have to take care of, I need to be going now.

Man: If you have time, drop by our house.

Shepherd: (Exiting) I certainly will!

Man: Take care!

Shepherd: Good-bye!

Shepherd: *Jiùjiù, qǐng zuò.*

Man: *Zuò, nǐ zuò.*

Shepherd: *Jiùjiù. Qǐng zuò. Qǐng zuò.*

Man: *Tài máfán le....hǎo, hǎo.*

Shepherd:	*Chīfàn le ma?*
Man:	*Chī guò le.*
Shepherd:	*Nǐ shēntǐ hái hǎo ma?*
Man:	*Tǐng hǎo de, xièxie.*
Shepherd:	*Jīntiān tiānqi tǐng lěng de.*
Man:	*Xiǎo Xiè, nǐ chuān de tài shǎo le, bié gǎnmào.*
(duìhuà)	
Shepherd:	*Jiùjiù, wǒ yǒu diǎnr shìr, xiān zǒu le.*
Man:	*Xiǎo Xiè, yǒu kòng dào ǎn jiā lái zuò yī zuò.*
Shepherd:	*Yīdìng, yīdìng.*
Man:	*Màn zǒu.*
Shepherd:	*Zàijiàn.*

Shepherd:	舅舅， 请坐。
Man:	坐，你坐。
Shepherd:	舅舅，请坐。请坐。
Man:	太麻烦了……好，好。
Shepherd:	吃饭了吗？
Man:	吃过了。
Shepherd:	你身体还好吗？
Man:	挺好的，谢谢。
Shepherd:	今天天气挺冷的。
Man:	小谢，你穿得太少了，别感冒。
（对话）	
Shepherd:	舅舅，我有点儿事儿，先走了。
Man:	小谢，有空到俺家来坐一坐。
Shepherd:	一定，一定。
Man:	慢走。
Shepherd:	再见。

An American interpreting this exchange with his or her native interpretive framework might find the exchange unusual. The questions asked and the ways of asking them are not what is found in the American game of talking to older people. This exchange, although short, is loaded with game and culture-specific information that can be easily overlooked. In fact, it was not until a Chinese student who had been present at the dialogue made the comment, "You really understand how things work, *nǐ hěn dǒngshì* (你很懂事)," that I even reflected on what behaviors gave him that impression. When I asked what he meant, he replied that I had asked all of the questions that one *should* ask an older person. His response was a clear indication of the presence of a set expectations for linguistic and cultural behavior recognized and accepted by the group as the norm. In other words, there was an established formula for handling this very act of talking with an older person. There were certain moves that were expected of me in my role as a younger person when engaged in interaction with an elderly acquaintance. Although the language I used may not be the exact wording a native would use, this is an example of an accepted foreigner recognized by at least one player for following a culturally appropriate script.

The knowledge gained through the performance of this script and the subsequent discussion about it can then be applied to other encounters with elderly friends in Shandong: The event is interacting with an elderly person, and the key participants were a seventy-year-old man and me. The roles were determined by our ages and our previous interactions. From the terms of address, Uncle and Xiao Xie, it is apparent that we were familiar with one another and that this was not an initial encounter. The objects involved in this example consist solely of the stools in the store. The audience was my friend who later commented on the effectiveness of the performance.

In looking at the order of events and the causal relations involved, a detailed explication is required. I recognized my role as junior by smiling, standing up, and addressing my elderly friend by our previously established title when he entered the store. This was further reinforced when I gave up my stool for him. It was culturally expected that he would refuse my offer of the stool out of courtesy even if he wished to sit down. Recognizing that bit of hidden culture, I insisted and left him no option by obtaining another stool for myself.

After this opening, I employed what turned out to be a culturally appropriate set of questions that should be asked. By inquiring as to whether he had eaten and about the state of his health, I showed concern for my interlocutor's state of being. After that I broached a culturally appropriate topic of small talk, the weather. During the small talk that ensued, I allowed him to dictate the flow of conversation because of his status as an elder. When it was time to take leave, I used a common mechanism for disengaging oneself from conversation in Shandong, "I have some business to take care of."

Stories

A corollary of the view that knowledge and experience are organized into schemas and scripts is that thinking and memory involve the indexing of that information. We must have a way to label, record, and retrieve these knowledge structures in the mind. In explaining how we record and index memories of experiences, Schank (1990, 11), echoing Bruner, argues that memory is story based:

> Information without access to that information is not information at all. Memory, in order to be effective, must contain both specific experiences (memories) and labels (memory traces). The more information we are provided with about a situation, the more places we can attach it to in memory and the more ways it can be compared with other cases in memory. Thus, a story is useful because it comes with many indices.

For Schank (1990, 12–13), knowledge is based in experience, learning from experience depends on being able to communicate our experiences as stories to others, and communication is rooted in the number of stories we know how, when to tell them, and to whom.

> Telling our stories allows us to compile our personal mythology, and the collection of stories we have compiled is to some extent who we are, what we have to say about the world, and tells the world the state of our mental health.

> To some extent, our stories, because they are shaped by memory processes that do not always have their basis in hard fact, are all fictions. But these fictions are based on real experiences and are our only avenue to those experiences. We interpret reality through our stories and open our realities up to others when we tell our stories. (Schank 1990, 44)

In Schank's view of how memory and learning work, we extract the gist of stories for storage in memory, and understanding means being able to add information to memory. Thus, stories and memory operate on at least two levels: the individual or personal level and the group or cultural level. On the one hand, we have unique personal memories that are recorded in the form of stories and that allow us to remember who we are and what we have personally experienced. On the other hand, we have shared group memories, also recorded in story form, that allow us to know how to interpret the people and events we interact with. Oftentimes, the two are conflated or overlap in ways that we may not realize:

> We take the standard stories of our culture and interpret what happens to us in terms of such stories. In other words, often the stories we rely upon to help us reason and remember are not even our own. Knowing a culture means knowing the stories that the culture provides and observing how people interpret their own experiences and construct their

> own stories in terms of the standard story of the
> culture. (Schank 1990, 149)

In this view, we learn stories from and share stories with friends, family, schools, governments, media, and books, and by listening and watching those around us. It is in this sense that Schank's claim that "understanding in its deepest sense, depends on shared stories" (202) takes on significance for language learners and pedagogues. To truly understand and be understood by members of a target culture, learners must know how to access and communicate in the stories of that group.

Compilation

The question then arises of how to obtain and store these scripts and schemas. Walker's (2000) view is that through repeated performance in cultural games, we compile memories by building or expanding schemas. In one's first culture, adults control scripts, whereas in a second culture, natives of the host culture control them. Katherine Nelson (in Cole 1996) asserts that because the information in a child's script is less complete than that of an adult, adults try to fill in the gaps for the child, which influences the development of his or her thinking. Bruner (1990) holds that compilation occurs at the narrative level. He asserts that scripts are elements of a narrative (stories) that link events over time and lie at the heart of human thought. Narrative (stories) provides the frame (context), which enables humans to interpret their experiences and one another. They can be very rough frameworks at first and over time gradually fill in to become very detailed, complex narratives (stories). In familiar situations, individuals already have the schemas as a framework, but may not have the entire script memorized. Schank's (1990) notion of dynamic memory supports this view, as does Cole's (1996) rediscription experiment, in which each time the children described an event, their descriptions became more complex.

Compiling Second Culture Memories

Because acquiring a culture is a process of both enculturation and acculturation and because adult learners have already acquired scripts in one culture, first culture scripts often form a barrier to the acquisition of a second culture. Initially, learners are not capable of interpreting second-culture situations without influence from base-culture prior knowledge. This often causes misinterpretations, especially in areas where the hidden code differs across cultures. Through time, however, second culture scripts can be more deeply understood, if the learner is aware that he or she is interpreting them with first culture scripts and is willing to create new stories based on the target culture. This may require reassigning meanings to certain concepts already existing in first culture memories. Of course, the first and second cultures are not always in conflict. But sometimes conflict occurs, as in the case of certain ritualistic behaviors involving drinking and smoking in Chinese culture. As mentioned earlier, Americans interacting with people from Shandong in the banquet context may not wish to drink or smoke, but in Shandong, hosts have the responsibility to ensure that they take care of all guests. In Shandong culture, hosts work on the default assumption that guests will refuse (as a display of modesty and politeness) any offer made by the host, so they will continue to insist that guests drink and smoke even when they decline. Some Americans who do not realize that the game has changed do things—refuse because they do not want to drink or smoke—in the same way they would in the United States, which oftentimes offends hosts. I have also seen other Americans who were offended by the Chinese persistence in offering alcohol and cigarettes—what the Americans perceived as personal attacks or infringements on individual space but what the Chinese perceived as overtures of friendship and hospitality. These Americans refused in ways that would be deemed rude in American culture because they were offended themselves by what they deemed inconsiderate behavior on the part of their hosts. A third type of reaction to cultural conflict that I have observed is when American banquet participants have realized that something was different—drinking and smoking is important in banquets—but they misinterpreted the actual importance of these behaviors. These Americans—who thought the importance of banquets was in the drinking and smoking themselves—often drank too much (or smoked) when they did not want to or have to. In these situations, foreign participants have to make choices—when and if to participate and how far to go—about participating or acculturating where first and second cultures do not match. As stated earlier, learners can acculturate, which requires that they be willing to expand their worldviews, incorporating the new set of meanings encountered in a second culture.

However, when the choice is made not to sync with the target culture, there are often consequences for not participating on target culture terms, which have to be weighed in the learners' decisions. Americans who do not wish to participate in the ritual of drinking in Chinese culture are certainly perceived differently from those who do. Two examples of learners suffering consequences for not syncing are the many Chinese in the United States who isolate themselves from American cultural games and American businesspeople in China who spend the majority of their time in the bubbles of foreign cultural enclaves. A common result is that the foreigners develop the perception that the second culture is not willing to accept them, when in reality it is more likely that they are not willing to accept the second culture.

Cole (1996, 206) aptly characterizes the culture/language acquisition process:

> a culturally organized joint activity that incorporates the child into the scene as a novice participant is one necessary ingredient in language acquisition. As children in such activities struggle to understand objects and social relations in order to gain control

over their environment and themselves, they re-
create the culture into which they have been born,
even as they re-invent the language of their forebears.

Although the process is somewhat different for adult learners of a
foreign language, they still need to endure a similar process of
struggling for meaning and control over their environment. However,
they do not re-create a culture, but rather create a third or
metaculture, which is a combination of their first and second cultures.
This new way of organizing information, what Walker (2000) refers
to as a worldview, is obtained through negotiation between first and
second cultural group values.

Sagas and Cases

Walker (2000) also espouses the concept of a long series of stories
about places and people that he dubs *sagas*. Stories are narratives of
the events that take place in a game, but sagas are ongoing
compilations of stories that involve a number of actors. They can be
likened to a television series or a soap opera. If an analogy is made
between learning a saga of a new cultural group and watching a soap
opera for the first time, some of the difficulties facing culture
learners become obvious. When jumping into a saga in midstream,
the individual does not know what is going on or what has already
occurred; the same is true when watching a soap opera for the first
time. However, by associations to already existing sagas of
knowledge, the individual is able to gradually fill in gaps. Sagas
enable us to develop large, catch-all categories or cases that increase
our knowledge of a culture and, in turn, enhance our new worldview.
This does not necessarily affect an individual's persona, but changes
how he or she looks at the next batch of cultural knowledge.

Walker (2000) muses that language learners progress in
cycles, failing on higher levels as their knowledge becomes deeper
and wider; the higher the level, the more opportunities there are to
fail. This recalls the popular Michael Jordan television commercial

promoting the notion that failure is the mother of success. The key to success in language learning, or any endeavor, then, is *managed failure:* learners who are willing to fail but who possess the ability to understand the causes for that failure are then able to construct memories that include this new information that can be used in a subsequent encounter.

Culture Games and Learning

As key social activities necessary for successful integration into any community, games are an effective means for getting recognized by target culture members. As such, they should be the focus of language learners' attention from beginning stages and thus an area of emphasis for pedagogues as well. If instructors can identify and analyze the most commonly encountered games, modules of instruction based on game knowledge and interaction can be created. Additionally, and more importantly, learning and teaching approaches can be altered to incorporate a game approach. This is a fundamental shift in approach that changes what takes place both inside classrooms—rehearsing behaviors and skills necessary to participate in specific games—and outside classrooms—instructors identifying games and game skills and students rehearsing game skills—and that transforms the roles of instructors—who become coaches rather than disseminators of information—and learners— who become aspiring players rather than receivers of instruction. Video game theorist Espen Aarseth (cited in Wolf and Perron 2003, 198) describes video games activity as ergodic. "Ergodic phenomena are produced by some kind of cybernetic system, i.e. a machine (or human) that operates as an information feedback loop, which will generate a different semiotic sequence each time it is engaged." This kind of system has the potential for actualizing itself differently every time it is used and requires nontrivial work from participants— not strictly on the mental plane; an element of physical action is also present. Because culture games are similar systems and because game play is ergodic activity, there are significant advantages for using games as the contextual unit for learning activities.

First, culture games are special types of performances that present players with microworlds of ergodic activity that model both principles (declarative knowledge) and processes (procedural and intuitive knowledge) important for participation in the culture. By approaching learning how to interact in a second culture from the game perspective, learners are more likely to access deeper levels of cultural understanding and, in turn, ultimately achieve higher levels of proficiency. The notion of *game* requires learners to assume authentic cultural roles, conform to actual cultural rules, make moves that they will likely have to make repeatedly while participating in the target culture, establish intentions that fit a given cultural framework established by the game, and strive for authentic goals in the target culture. Therefore, learners engage in many of the processes involved in the actual social interactions encountered when in the target culture.

As highly contextualized and culturally significant events, games provide the opportunity to learn frequently encountered cultural themes, language, and behavior in action. Moreover, games typically revolve around domain-specific knowledge, which limits the amount of information a learner must attend to at any single time. That is, learners avoid many of the distractions associated with a holistic approach to learning culture. A game approach not only allows learners to be exposed to language in context but also provides them with resources (knowledge of the local area, traditions, shared topics of discussion, etc.) that facilitate conversation and promote interaction. Localizing learner focus also deepens interaction and increases the potential for the development of interpersonal bonds by providing learners with opportunities to engage in shared attentional experiences with members of the community.

Learning in culture games also involves multiple modes and sources of learning, which can enable multiple learning styles. That is, learners who are better at procedural, declarative, or visual tasks can all find ways of developing game competence. What's more, because the game community enables peer learning (from, by, and with other participants), it overcomes the limits of the dyadic nature of interaction in traditional learning formats. That is, game players are able to learn from peers, mentors, and patrons simultaneously. Because much of social interaction is conducted in formats that involve multiple interlocutors, learners must also learn how to communicate in multiparty situations rather than simply how to engage a single speaker in one-on-one exchanges.

In addition to being the locus of the generation of shared meanings, games are also where behaviors are defined and monitored, decision-making processes are engaged, and deeply contextualized language is relatively consistent. In this sense, games offer potential for exploration, discovery, and problem solving by the learner, which form the intrinsic rewards that foster motivation and drive additional learning. Games have embedded challenges that require learners to actively monitor their own performance; observe the events and players around them; hypothesize on the nature of the situation and the intentions, goals and moves of other players; make choices based on others' intentions and moves; employ courses of action; and reflect on the success or failure of such moves. Moreover, game play involves the risk of failure, which ups the ante and requires additional emotional involvement and commitment on the part of the learner. That is, becoming a cultural player requires intimate involvement by the learner without the unrealistic expectation of having to become a native. The feeling of accomplishment players get from discovering themes, goals, and successful moves and performance during the course of game activities tends to be a better intrinsic motivator than grades.

Learners who adopt such an approach focus their energies on practical, learnable behaviors that will facilitate their future movement in the target culture. By participating in the games of a local culture, learners gain access to firsthand knowledge of cultural meanings while they are able to construct an experientially based, emotionally encoded, long-term memory of the culture. Once learned, the process of learning a game can then be applied to any other game a learner encounters.

CHAPTER EIGHT

Becoming a Player

In this chapter, I address some of the most important issues that culture learners need to grapple with in their pursuit of becoming players in a given culture game. In so doing, I summarize some of the views stated earlier and provide one successful strategy for getting into socializing games found in China.

Reorganizing Your Worldview
We have shown that players from different cultures rely on distinctive frameworks of meaning and that to accurately interpret and establish intentions in a second culture, an individual must employ methods for establishing intentions that are recognizable in the target culture. The key for language learners, then, is twofold. They must first understand that it is important to establish recognizable intentions so that they can begin cultivating their own skills in organizing information in target culture modes. Second, they must be willing to make changes in their worldviews, taking into account the new information the target culture provides. Because of the discomfort such reorientation causes, it is something many learners are reluctant to do. Worldview reorganization requires the individual to reconsider notions taken as facts in his or her old worldview and to supplement them with those found in the new one.

This is a time-consuming process that involves both developing new behaviors based on target culture patterns and constructing new cognitive frameworks that are informed by, in this case, Chinese cognitive orientations. As stated earlier, this is in essence a process of constructing a new cultural memory. Learners must create personal memories of cultural games and game play while they tap into[1] shared group memories that inform behavior. Moreover, this should be done in such a manner that the new skills are stored in memory separately[2] and can be applied independently according to the game at hand. That is, the newly formed cognitive frameworks and cultural behaviors are informed by both the old and the new but the learner must be capable of distinguishing the two or be able to operate in them distinctly, without interference, depending on the cultural context.

The significant point for the learner is that this process of learning a new worldview is also a social process in that it cannot be done without the assistance of and participation with members of the target culture in shared attentional events: the learner must both

---

[1] There are multiple ways to tap into local shared memories. One can accomplish this through interaction with target culture members, by engaging target culture media—movies, television shows, radio, newspapers, Internet or books—and by participating in target culture activities. However, the most direct manner is through participation in target culture activities. Thus, the specifics of how to go about doing this differ from culture to culture. Tapping into shared memories is much more than asking questions. In fact, in many situations, asking questions is not effective: if the memories in question are aspects of the target culture that members do not typically share with outsiders—such as accounts of events that occurred during the Cultural Revolution in China and aspects of Chinese culture perceived by natives as negative—initially asking questions can actually hinder access to group memories.

[2] One of the points made in this book is that changing the basic approach to learning a second culture to a game approach will shift learners' focus, making them aware that something different is going on and that they must take measures to adapt to that new something. In many cases, this new focus of attention on the behavioral patterns of the target culture as something different and worthy of learning in their own right will foster conscious construction of different categories by learners. For other learners, it will take multiple encounters and repeated coaching before they are able to distinguish target culture behaviors from base culture ones. In any case, learning in the context of participation—in a meaningful role—in second culture games that involve natives in typical settings provides learners with opportunities to engage meanings and behaviors that are embedded in the larger framework of the events in which they occur. Learning in such a manner allows learners to create multiple links to memory for each behavior or bit of knowledge, which increases the likelihood of long-term retention.

engage in acculturation and be engaged by members of the target culture in enculturation. Worldview adjustment is a two-directional socialization process—being socialized by a community and learning how to socialize in a community. This process cannot be done by reading about the culture in the classroom; it requires engaging Chinese people on their terms.

Focusing on Microcultures

Because of the complexity of any given culture, it is impossible to know all of the information associated with a culture. Natives are not players in all of the games of their own culture and certainly are not proficient in all of the games in which they participate (Ochs and Schieffelin 1990). Microcultures, however, with their smaller number of players and available games, are significantly more manageable than sagas or entire cultures. Thus, if an individual learns to participate in the games of microcultures, one by one, compiling memories of each, he or she can expand the number of fields on which he or she can play to include a significant number of social arenas.

The question, then, becomes: How do learners know which microcultures to choose as their target of study? In many cases, this is not a matter of choice for the learner: generally speaking, the learner must sync with the microculture of his or her work unit or place of residence. However, language-learning activities can be designed around general types of microcultures, which permits learners to focus on the ones they are most likely to encounter. Examples include office culture, the culture found in various university departments, campus culture, laboratory culture, gym culture, coffee shop culture, and bookstore culture. By exposing learners to various types of frequently encountered microcultures, language teachers can assist them in developing initial narrative scripts about how to interact in those microcultures, which can later be used for reference when they encounter actual microcultures in China.

Getting into the Game

It is through participation in the games of a microculture that learners become recognized by local communities and begin socialization processes. To get into a game, one must first know something about the microcultures involved as well as the rules of the individual games one will play. In other words, learners must know how to score before they can become successful players. The prospective player must seek out information that is held in reified culture about the microcultures he or she will engage.

The memory of a culture provides a significant repository of cultural knowledge that can serve as both background knowledge and a potential key to entering in the game; this is pregame work in which the learner can be seen as fulfilling the role of a collector. Although this is often the work of language pedagogues, it is also an area in which good learners separate themselves from average learners. To again extend the sports metaphor, good players read scouting reports (in our case, things written by others who have been to Shandong or who have had banquet experiences), watch game films (watch scenes in movies or television shows that take place in banquet settings), and learn everything they can about the game (by asking natives, asking nonnatives who have been to Shandong, and engaging media about and by natives). The knowledge learned about the target community and its games serves as tools through which to participate, and attempts at play demonstrate to the members of the community that the learner is willing and able to play by the rules. A participant in the 1999 US/China Links program provides an example of successfully getting into the games of a microculture. Our student was interning at China Central Television Station, where he was initially ignored by his coworkers. After several weeks, a sinking feeling began setting in, so the intern decided to adapt to those around him because "they would not adapt to him." He adapted by establishing commonalities with each person that served as the foundation for relationships and further interaction. Among other things, he translated some of his mother's recipes into Chinese for friends interested in Western food and wrote e-mails in English for those who had poor English. In each case, he made overtures to his coworkers by assisting them in some way and in the process created a realm of shared interest with each one. Ultimately, this intern was quite successful at integrating himself into the group but expressed regrets about not having been more aggressive in his early stages in the new environment.

In addition to knowing something about target culture games, learners must also develop a "player" mentality. That is, learners must see themselves as legitimate players in target culture games and have playing in target culture games as their ultimate goal. If learners view themselves as students, Chinese players will not view them as legitimate players in meaningful games. Becoming a player, even shifting to a player perspective, just does not happen. Even when students say they are taking the player approach, many are not. On numerous occasions during US/China Links training, students made claims that they were players or that they were approaching interactions from the player perspective. However, because their actions were those of nonplayers, they were not recognized as players; as a result, their interactions remained at the superficial level. For instance, while the students were at work in their internship host companies, they did things that students do rather than what people in office settings do. Thus, they were perceived as "students." Examples of things our students did that sent the signal that they were students include carrying book bags, toting dictionaries in the office, and talking about personal matters rather than work-related affairs. In the context of Shandong office culture, new employees typically ask what can be done to help, they prepare and pour tea for superiors, they sweep the floor and straighten up the office without being told to do so, and they do things to make coworkers' jobs easier to do even if it involves doing what everyone else does not want to do. Because our students acted in "foreign student" ways rather than in "new employee" ways, they were categorized and reacted to in just this manner. In the Shandong office setting, "student" is not a role that is likely to be taken seriously. In the local view, students have no experience and are not yet capable of positively contributing to a professional organization; they need to be protected and taken care of and so can be seen as a burden in the business setting. Because our students were *foreign* students, they attracted attention initially but once the novelty of having a foreigner in the office wore off, students reported that coworkers gradually began to ignore them. Moreover, because US/CL students were foreign, they were often categorized as "guest," which meant that they were to be "taken care of" rather than "taken seriously."

To shift to the player perspective, learners must encounter incongruencies in cultural frameworks, they must recognize them, and then they must be willing to make adjustments to their own behavior and approach. Once they reach this point, they are ready to perform in the target culture. If students experience success while performing in the target culture, the target culture behaviors are then reinforced and the feeling of success motivates further attempts to perform. US/CL facilitates this process by conducting guided training in the target culture. Learners are primed for frequently encountered target culture games and behaviors. They are given the opportunity to see a contrast between American and Chinese behaviors in those contexts and are required to rehearse new behaviors. Then, they are placed into live target culture contexts in which they must perform. Finally, the learners return to group sessions during which they discuss and evaluate what occurred during performance. It is during this phase of training that learners often discover what they had actually been experiencing during performance and what behaviors or strategies would have best worked in such situations. One example of this process occurred during the 2004 program when we covered gift giving as a strategy for deepening relationships in Chinese culture. Program participants were required to memorize phrases used when presenting gifts, rehearsed the act of presenting gifts with Chinese peers, and discussed with instructors and native peers appropriate types of gifts and occasions when they could be given in Chinese culture. The participants were then asked to watch for opportunities to present gifts while they were working as interns in local companies. When the group went on a trip to Hangzhou, for example, an instructor told the participants that returning from a trip is an appropriate time to give a gift—something special from the place visited—to coworkers and friends in Chinese culture because it demonstrates that you were thinking of the person although you were not together. On the day that two of the interns returned to work after the trip, they entered the elevator at their work unit at the same time as a coworker. The coworker asked how the trip was, and the interns responded with positive comments about the place visited. They also seized the opportunity by presenting the coworker with some tea that they had bought while on the trip. Not long after the students had given the gift, their coworkers invited them to dinner—a banquet—to reciprocate. The interaction was their first outside of the work setting and served to deepen the bonds of friendship that had begun. The next time the interns were at work after the banquet, they discovered that their coworkers were willing to teach them more about the job, China, and Chinese culture than they had been previously because they had deepened the personal bonds with their coworkers during the social setting of a dinner banquet.

The idea is that to really engage the target culture in the player mode, learners must do things players do in game situations. In a banquet, for example, they could toast in a Shandong way, refill others' glasses before refilling their own—regardless of what the drink is—decline the seat of honor, or defer to someone else who is of higher status. A learner-player could also give gifts at appropriate times, remember birthdays, call associates on regular basis to ask about their welfare, or offer assistance to friends before being asked for it. As a foreign participant in Shandong culture, the key is for the learner to repeatedly perform such acts because the default assumption that natives work on is that foreigners cannot possibly play the game. Repeated performances indicate that the foreign learner is in fact actually capable of playing the game. If learners have learning about Chinese culture or learning Chinese language as their goal, they may learn some surface-level knowledge about Chinese culture and a limited amount of the linguistic code, but if they instead view themselves as players and are viewed as players in Chinese culture games, the likelihood of accessing deep cultural knowledge and a wider range of linguistic tools is greatly increased.

Playing the Game

If we follow Cole's (1996) notion that learners must participate in a language-learning activity in order to learn, developing the ability to play the game should include performing culture. In other words, the learner must participate in culture games, which entails establishing and interpreting intentions in a second culture. Such a proposition requires that learners see themselves as active players rather than fans or analysts who focus their energies not on performing for a culture, but on watching culture performances. A player might prepare for a banquet by reading a book so that he or she will have something interesting or useful to tell other participants. He or she may also prepare several toasts and/or a larger performance or two (e.g., a song in Chinese, a song in English, a story, a joke). Once at a banquet, a foreign player must do some of the things that natives do in banquets in order to ease the accommodative burden placed on natives and to indicate that he or she is able and willing to participate on local terms. That is, when others host you, you reciprocate by toasting them. When others make overtures to bridge the gap in feelings, you respond by acknowledging the overtures. The idea is that you play the game. That does not necessarily mean that you drink; rather, it means that you view and participate in the event in ways that natives might (i.e., you approach the event as an opportunity to meet people and become part of a network of relationships, you partake of the atmosphere, and after the banquet is over, you maintain relationships with the people you met at the banquet).

This philosophy must be used in creating pedagogical materials and activities and should be reinforced regularly when interacting with students. Activities developed around games and scripts give learners practice in skills needed during actual games; the image of the good player who reviews game films and hones skills in unscored practice performances comes to mind. However, each game and script is different. What the learner encounters in the target culture will never be the same as the scripts provided in pedagogical materials. As we have seen, knowing what to expect in games is half the battle. If a learner is aware of certain patterns of communication and what types of behaviors and stories are frequently found in a game, he or she can use that knowledge to make educated guesses about similar games. Learners who understand something about banquets also could handle any game that involves status, hierarchy, or interpersonal relationships. They would also possess skills that are useful in games that involve government officials, business negotiations, superior-subordinate relationships, face, and reciprocity.

Shandong banquets are an excellent training ground for language learners because of their performative and inclusive nature. All participants are forced to participate. As was explained earlier, the culture dictates that everyone must participate to give the host face and to ensure a positive atmosphere. For natives who do not actively participate, other participants take measures to force them to participate. For nonnatives, the same reaction occurs. However, when overtures fail, foreign participants are ignored and categorized as not worthy of further interaction or as not willing to participate on local terms, or they are forgotten altogether. The cultural themes that underlie and shape banquets, such as face, feelings, and being candid, are encountered in nearly every Shandong game that I have played. Furthermore, Shandong banquets are replete with performable culture such as displays of modesty, accepting and declining compliments, showing concern for other players, introductions, and ordering food. Strategies for recognizing and fulfilling roles that can be applied to nearly every Shandong context are repeatedly encountered in banquets. The skeptic may argue that the ordinary language learner does not have access to a Shandong banquet room, but much of what is encountered in this game is applicable to other Shandong games and can be re-created in the classroom. These bits of performed culture can be used to form the core of language-learning strategies, activities, and materials. A language program that is structured around the games learners will certainly encounter— banquets, interpersonal relationships, meetings, negotiations— although unable to construct an exact match to the actual game environment, can provide learners with rehearsal opportunities for behaviors while forcing them to construct target culture memories rather than base culture or classroom culture memories. To that end, language teachers should prepare activities that involve learners participating in culture games or simulated culture games that expose them to scripts that contain culturally coded patterns of communication, social roles they might encounter or be required to fulfill, and potential sequences of events. This means teaching lexicon and language structures as part of the larger contexts in which they are embedded and should be done from the initial stages of instruction. Such exposure to target culture behaviors in context allows learners to begin to develop mental frameworks of these events that they can apply to future encounters. It also fosters the player mind-set and makes attainable goals obvious to learners.

Footnote: Simulated game play is different from role plays used in many language programs. Role plays can be effective in teaching certain aspects of game play but because they are smaller segments of interaction that tend to be removed from larger interconnected events, the roles involved often become the focus of instruction. Moreover, because role plays are removed from broader contexts—and thus the learners do not readily see intended goals—and because most students do not approach them from player perspectives, role plays are often ineffective because students do not take them seriously. Role plays also need to be contextualized as part of part of something else to be effective.

Organizing the information found in games is most effectively done if these events are developed in target culture story form. In the game of banqueting, for instance, if instruction is conducted in China, teacher-coaches can take students to restaurants where much of the background information about games can be delivered and rehearsals involving setting and props can be conducted. This can be done in the United States as well so long as instructors inform learners that Chinese restaurants in this country involve different scripts than the ones found in China. In cases where conducting class in an actual restaurant is not feasible, teacher-coaches must create restaurantlike settings in the classroom using behaviors and props. Before performance-oriented courses such as this are delivered, it is most effective to have students already familiar with the various roles and scripts associated with the game at hand. Thus, in the case of banqueting, instruction should be designed so that student assignments require preparation of as much of the script as possible—that is, outside of class, students can be practicing commonly used lexicon and structures for the context to be performed, they can be reading background information about the context including roles, expectations, etc. The actual performance in different roles during class then enables students to internalize behaviors associated with those roles. The idea is that a basic story is provided to the learner, which with guided rehearsal is gradually built into a more and more elaborate one as the learner returns to the same context at higher and higher levels.

Learners must also be risk takers in that they must convince the target group that interpreting their intentions is a worthwhile proposition, which can be accomplished only through cultural performances of recognized roles. Groups normally assume that outsiders cannot play the game until they prove otherwise. To do this, an individual must perform culture that other players can recognize, which further suggests that learners in training should have extensive opportunities to perform for audiences. Ideally, audiences used in rehearsals should include natives of the target culture, who can comment on the effectiveness of those performances. We accomplish this in US/China Links programs through two major techniques. First, all classes are team taught by one native of the target culture and one nonnative experienced in interacting in the target culture. Second, Chinese and American students attend classes together. This also provides the added benefits of having natives who can perform as models as well as multiple native perspectives.

Using the Environment

To find ways to perform, learners should turn to their environment. In other words, they should be using all available resources. In Shandong culture, interlocutor reprimand, in which players offer overt corrective feedback to indicate when a player has done something incorrectly, is one obvious source that learners can turn to. They must also develop the ability to read native responses to their speech and behaviors that are not so explicit. Most important, language learners must know how to develop peer and mentor relationships with natives of the target community through whom they can continue to learn. Active consultation with members of the target community is itself one form of participation in the culture. Of course, the onus is on the learner to create and develop such opportunities rather than on the members of the target culture.

As players, they must both play in the conventional modes associated with a particular game and follow the rules that make that game possible. In the case of Shandong banquets, this necessitates that learners approach interaction in an affective style overtly attending to the needs of the players around them and that learners focus energy and action heavily on interpersonal feelings. Competent communicators in these contexts both carefully monitor verbal and nonverbal displays and make moves based on the information gathered through such monitoring. Banquet players note and remember what other players (with whom they want to continue relationships) like to eat so that when they have the chance, they can order for them; they help other players solve problems; when they are not with those players, they buy things for them or do things that show that they were thinking of those people; and they reveal personal information to other players. The act of committing something of oneself to the relationship signifies the importance of the relationship as well as an individual's sincerity toward that relationship, both of which are keys to remaining in the game.

Experimental Thinking
If no model for moves in a game exists—that is, learners have no previous experience with a game and they have no story of game play built in memory—the individual must engage in experimental thinking. Learners still must engage in game play through attempts at meaning making based on existing or previous knowledge combined with information found in the environment. This type of behavior should be fostered in the language classroom so that learners' interpretive skills are developed. As previously noted, learners need to struggle for meaning in order to learn. If everything is provided for the learner, he or she will not have the personal experience of having done something and thus will not develop the memory of how

to do that event. The idea is to equip learners with the basic skills necessary to participate in game play but to allow them to gain a feel for game play themselves through actual experience. In the case of banquets, that means putting learners in banquet contexts that allow them to see exactly what to say, when to say it, what will happen, and when. Then the game experience must be followed by guided postgame review sessions. Learners must have their own stories to tell and their own memories to rely upon in order to successfully function in the target culture. This means that the role of the teacher is not to pass knowledge of games on to the learner or to teach the rules of cultural games by citing the rules to the learner, but rather to construct accurate cultural environments in which learners can extract their own stories and develop their own memories of having been in that situation. Moreover, in live culture games, foreign participants rarely, if ever, possess all of the information available to native players; often they must make educated guesses based on their personal experience with that type or similar types of target culture game. Thus, language learning activities should be designed with this fact in mind so that learners develop the skills required to handle situations in which they have only partial knowledge.

Re-mediation

The process of determining which behaviors are acceptable followed by a reassessment of meaning adding the newly acquired information can be seen as a form of what Cole (1996, 285) refers to as re-mediation. If learning culture were viewed in this manner, it would suggest that newcomers must constantly adjust to the group while the group adjusts to them. US/China Links utilizes two primary techniques to accomplish this goal. First, we place learners in live cultural games,[3] so that they can participate in real-life situations. We

---

[3] We have someone observe them periodically during interaction, and we have them participate in games with us. When we are invited to a banquet, we have a student go along. If we have negotiations, we have a student go along. If we are holding an

then follow these events with periods of review of the events and people involved in those games. Second, we require learners to keep two journals, one for linguistic structures and vocabulary and the other for experiences. The act of recording experiences in writing fosters metalevel thinking about those experiences and enhances the memories of those events by beginning the story-building process. It also forces learners to evaluate their own performance in those experiences. Whether it is through classroom activities or through engaging in metadiscourses with natives about the game, these principles can be applied to other language-learning situations as well.

Finding a Comfort Zone

Not possessing all of the information necessary to negotiate an encounter naturally makes learner uneasy. Success, to a certain extent, can be said to hinge upon what the individual does in response to that uneasiness. There are at least three possible responses

1. *The learner does not know how to deal with this fear created by a lack of information.* As a result, he or she withdraws from play in culture games and avoids exposing him- or herself to this type of situation.

2. *The learner feeds off of the adventure of trying to figure out what information is missing, and therefore enjoys putting him- or herself in that uncomfortable situation.* By taking this risk, this type of learner is participating in cultural performances, a prerequisite for learning.

---

event such as a large-scale "thank you" banquet, we make the students do most of the preparations. When we are printing business cards, we have students do it. We always have experienced faculty available for advice on how to go about accomplishing these tasks, but the students must carry them out themselves.

3. *The learner does not necessarily enjoy the feeling associated with a lack of information surrounding an event, but is able to manage that uneasiness.*

The critical point is that to be successful, learners must develop a certain level of comfort in target culture games, and that success can be achieved only through actual play. Learners must repeatedly engage in game play to develop sufficient experience with that particular game before they can achieve a zone of comfort that facilitates further development.

Gap Filling

How do you know that what you are doing is accurate? In this sense, learners must be analysts. We have shown that to accurately assess the intentions of players, learners have to become acute observers of culture, people, speech, and behavior. While doing so, learners need to assume that cross-cultural discourse is not necessarily proleptic—that is, that the listener may not understand what the speaker is intending. Pedagogues need to develop activities that teach learners to read clues in the listener's reactions to ascertain whether comprehension is occurring. [4] This is an extremely difficult proposition even in one's own culture, where the number of devices one possesses to handle such checking is infinitely larger. However, approaching cross-cultural encounters from this perspective will require the individual to be on the lookout for signs of "malfunction of intentions." This particular point tends to be particularly difficult for native instructors of the language of study to enforce. When

---

[4] The teacher's reaction is critical. If a teacher just understands and reacts to what the learners "meant" rather than what they actually said or did, learners will not realize that their speech or behavior did not conform to target culture norms. Instructors can directly point out appropriate performances or instructors or other students can model correct behaviors, but an effective means is to react in a way that a native might to what was actually said so that a breakdown in communication becomes apparent to the learner.

learners make mistakes, the natural tendency is for the instructor to understand what the learner means—even if what the learner says or does is not acceptable behavior in the target culture—and then react to what the learner meant rather than what the learner said or did. Such a reaction does not enhance the learner's ability to read cues that signal communication problems. The reaction that is of most help to the student is to react in a natural way to what the learner did or said rather than what was "meant."

Incorporation

Another key to becoming a successful communicator in a nonnative culture is becoming incorporated into the group. Cole (1996) notes that even a child must make him- or herself welcome when entering his or her own culture. [5] It would hold, then, that to become competent players, learners must make themselves welcome in their second culture. Knowing what behaviors are more likely to produce positive reactions in the target culture is critical for any learner's ultimate success. Furthermore, it is significant to note that all groups are more reluctant to accept outsiders if they have nothing in common with the group members. This necessitates that learners find something in common with the group members so that they can enter and remain in the game. A primary goal of the second language learner becomes syncing to the extent that he becomes an accepted outsider. Each individual of the new culture holds a different perception of the learner's stage in the enculturation process, which means that the learner is constantly required to make moves that demonstrate his ability to play. For instance, when at a banquet with locals who have not met me, I have to demonstrate that I, in fact, understand the banquet context and how to behave in such a setting. I

---

[5] I am following Cole's idea that entry into culture occurs later than birth. Culture is not just there when we come into the world and we somehow automatically become a part of it when we come out of the womb. If that were the case, why would we need to learn it? We are socialized into culture at some later point that begins with adults' speech, behaviors, and reactions to us.

do this by participating in introductions and exchanges of business cards according to local norms. In some cases, this is sufficient to signal to the participants that I am capable of participating in local games. When it is not, I must demonstrate my playing ability by showing that I understand where and when to sit, when to tap glasses, how to drink in appropriate way, how to react to or deliver a toast, or through any other recognizable move found in the banqueting game.

Making oneself welcome in a culture includes both acting in culturally appropriate ways and avoiding cultural taboos and stigmas. It also involves making oneself less of an accommodative burden. We have noted that in the early stages of game play, other players must accommodate newcomers. By syncing with the group, learners can make themselves less of a cultural burden on the other players involved. Syncing involves finding one's role in each communicative event, which may differ in each performance, and fulfilling the expectations associated with that role. By finding the appropriate role the culture establishes in each encounter and by fulfilling that role to the expectations of the group members, the learner lightens the burden of accommodation on the other players and increases the likelihood that they will want to interact with the learner beyond that one encounter.

Creating a Persona

Fulfilling culturally accepted roles in order to become a player in cultural games involves creating a persona in the target culture. By persona, I follow Walker (2000) in referring to what an individual allows an audience to know about him or her. Creating a persona involves negotiation with the group because the culture has and will accept only certain personas. We cannot simply assume the same persona we have in our base culture and expect to be successful in a second culture. The individual must observe other players in the game to see how people react to certain behaviors and ascertain which personas are desirable in a particular culture. Then, as

Goffman (1959) has shown about American culture, the individual must consciously manipulate his or her behavior to fulfill the expectations of that persona in the context at hand. This conscious manipulation of behavior to fit a persona among those available in society is what allows us to be individuals in our own culture. Thus, it should not seem to be less than candid to do so in a learned culture because it is how individuals are who they are in any culture.

Afterword

Ski Colorado
Surf Hawaii
Eat Shandong

The tourism boards of especially well-endowed geographical regions attract practitioners of popular sports to take advantage of their natural environments. Eric Shepherd in a like manner invites us to join in an activity that is particularly appropriate for the cultural environment of Shandong, namely eating in groups. All of these activities—skiing, surfing, and eating—are everyday activities that can lead to undesirable consequences. Without the element of expertise, skiing is simply a matter of getting down a cold mountain without a broken body, surfing is either floating or trolling for sharks. Eating is the basic activity for maintaining one's existence; but, if done poorly, it can result in distorting one's shape and shortening one's life span. Doing these well are performances that lead to grace and glory. Doing them poorly leads to ignominy and even premature death. All are performances that can be converted into games: skiing, by keeping time and devising style points; surfing, by judging waves and devising style points, eating by counting hotdogs, or *jiǎozi*, or jalapenos. I do not recall style points in eating contests.

These slogans convey the idea that locality is an important aspect in the quality of the experience. The assumption being that we might be more proficient in the activity if we are in the right place. In the narration of his journey toward expertise in banqueting in Shandong, Eric Shepherd has shown us how a foreigner can learn to negotiate local customs and participate in an activity that to a significant degree defines membership to a culture. He gives an insider's view of the process. Then he explains how to convert that experience to an apperception of culture and the construction of a pedagogy.

The most significant contribution of Eric Shepherd's study is its application to the pedagogy of advanced skills. He has learned to participate in banquets in Shandong by study, practice, and, most importantly, earning the trust of people in Shandong for whom banqueting is important. Combining the results of his study of language and culture with this trust, he was able to gain mentors and participate frequently enough to be coached to a level of acknowledged expertise. Within a relatively short period of time, he moved from being invited because he was a novelty to being invited because he could contribute to the purpose of the event. Although Eric Shepherd is physically distinct from Chinese and he can never pass as a native, he is accepted as a player in a distinctly Shandong social environment. This approach to the study of a culture is a clear remove from the omniscient base-culture scholar working with target-culture native informants to produce narrative interpretations for the base culture.

The model of advanced learner that Eric Shepherd gives us is that of someone who is willing to work hard to become a student of the culture. Although he has done his share of teaching and advising in China, he does not approach China or the Chinese as if he had much to contribute. When he is in China, he is there to learn and his attention and work are pointed in that direction. Over the years that we have been training young Americans to participate in organizations in China, I have been surprised at the number of young American college graduates who are convinced they can make significant contributions to China. I have, however, not been surprised at the reaction of the Chinese who after all can tolerate such attitudes for only a certain amount of time. And I am sure that clinging to such an attitude has impeded many a young person's progress toward gaining advanced skills in Chinese. Eric Shepherd demonstrates that an important step in reaching expertise in a foreign culture is cultivating a genuine humility in the company of other people's cultures.

Finally, Eric Shepherd has challenged us to identify other key cultural activities through which we can learn to participate in Chinese culture. Banqueting—an activity that sustains a huge food service industry—cuts across many divisions of wealth and power. It is both a venue for displaying and rubbing up against these desired qualities. Conversely, there are many equally admirable individuals who do not participate in banqueting precisely because of the blatant exercise of power relationships. If we knew more about activities or sets of activities that would introduce us to non-banqueters or other groups, perhaps we could formulate pedagogies that would place students of Chinese in richer learning environments sooner rather than later in their learning careers.

Galal Walker

References and Further Reading

Aarseth, Espen. 1997. *Cybertext: Perspectives on Ergodic Literature*. Baltimore: Johns Hopkins University Press.

Agar, Michael. 1969. "Game Rules and the Rules of Culture." *Game Theory in the Behavioral Sciences*, I. R. Buchler and H. G. Nutini, eds. Pittsburgh: University of Pittsburgh Press.

-----. 1986. *Speaking of Ethnography*. London: Sage Publications.

-----. 1994. *Language Shock: Understanding the Culture of Conversation*. New York: William Morrow and Company.

Anderson, E.N. 1988. *The Food of China*. New Haven: Yale University Press.

Andrews, Larry. 1997. *Language Exploration and Awareness: A Resource Book for Teachers*. New Jersey: Lawrence Erlbaum Associates.

Apte, Mahadev. 1992. "Humor." *Folklore, Cultural Performances, and Popular Entertainments*. Richard Baumann, ed. New York: Oxford University Press.

Austin, J.L. 1960. *How to Do Things With Words*. Oxford: Clarendon Press.

-----. 1962. *Sense and Sensibilia*. London: Oxford University Press.

Avedon, Elliot and Brian Sutton-Smith. 1971. *The Study of Games*. New York: John Wiley and Sons.

Babcock, Barbara. 1977. "Metanarrative." *Verbal Art as Performance*. Richard Bauman. Prospect Heights: Waveland Press.

Bachnik, Jane and Charles Quinn. 1994. *Situated Meaning: Inside and Outside in Japanese Self, Society, and Language*. New Jersey: Princeton University Press.

Bakhurst, David and Stuart Shanker. 2001. *Jerome Bruner: Language, Culture, Self*. London: Sage Publications.

Barme, Geremie. 1999. *In the Red: On Contemporary Chinese Culture*. New York: Columbia University Press.

Barnouw, Eric and Catherine Kirkland. 1992. "Entertainment." *Folklore, Cultural Performances, and Popular Entertainments*. Richard Baumann, ed. New York: Oxford University Press.

Barro, Anna, Mike Byram, Hanns Grimm, Carol Morgan, and Celia Roberts. 1993. "Cultural Studies for Advanced Language Learners," *Language and Culture*. British Association of Applied Linguistics. Clevedon: Multilingual Matters.

Bartlett, Frederic. 1932. *Remembering, A Study in Experimental and Social Psychology*. Cambridge: Cambridge University Press.

Bateson, Gregory. 1972. "A Theory of Play and Fantasy," *Steps to an Ecology of Mind*, New York: Ballantine: 177-93.

Bauman, Richard. 1977. *Verbal Art as Performance*. Prospect Heights: Waveland Press.

-----. 1986. *Story, Performance, and Event: Contextual Studies of Oral Narrative*. New York: Cambridge University Press.

-----, ed. 1992. *Folklore, Cultural Performances, and Popular Entertainments*. New York: Oxford University Press.

Ben-Amos, Dan. 1976. *Folklore Genres*. Austin: University of Texas Press.

Bender, Mark. 1989. "Suzhou Tanci: Keys to Performance." MA Thesis, The Ohio State University.

-----. 1995. "Zaisheng Yuan and Meng Lijun: Performance, Context, and Form of Two Tanci." Diss., The Ohio State University.

-----. 1996. "Keys to Performance in Kunming Pingshu." *Chinoperl Papers* 19 (1996): 21-37.

-----. 1998. "Oral Performance and Orally Related Literature in China." *Teaching Oral Traditions*. John Foley, ed. New York: Modern Language Association of America.

-----. 1999. "Shifting and performance in Suzhou Chantefable." *The Eternal Storyteller: Oral literature in modern China*. Vibeke Bordahl, ed. Nordic Institute of Asian Studies. Surrey: Curzon Press, 181-96.

-----. 2001. "A Description of Jiangjing (Telling Scriptures) Services in Jingjiang, China." *Asian Folklore Studies*, 60 (2001): 101-133.

-----. 2003. *Plum and Bamboo*. Urbana: University of Illinois Press.

Berne, Eric. 1963. *The Structure and Dynamics of Organizations and Groups*. Philadelphia: J.B. Lippincott Company.

-----. 1964. *Games People Play: The Psychology of Human Relationships*. New York: Grove Press.

-----. 1976. *Beyond Games and Scripts*. New York: Grove Press.

Bernstein, B. 1968. "Some Sociological Determinants of Perception. An Inquiry into Sub-Cultural Differences." *Readings in the Sociology of Language*. Joshua Fishman, ed. The Hague: Mouton, 223-239.

Birdwhistell, Ray. 1954. "Kinesics." *Explorations*. E.S. Carpenter, ed. Toronto: University of Toronto, 31-45.

-----. 1970. *Kinesics and Context*. Philadelphia: University of Pennsylvania Press.

Birrell, Anne. 1988. *Popular Songs and Ballads of Han China*. London: Unwin Hyman.

Boas, Franz. 1911a. *The Mind of Primitive Man*. New York: The Macmillan Company.

-----. 1911b. Introduction to the *Handbook of American Indian Languages*. Franz Boas, ed. Washington DC: Government Printing Office.

-----. 1962. *Anthropology and Modern Life*. New York: Norton.

Bock, Philip. 1968. "Social Structure and Language Structure." *Readings in the Sociology of Language*. Joshua Fishman, ed. The Hague: Mouton.

Boltz, Judith. 1996. "Singing to the Spirits of the Dead: A Daoist Ritual of Salvation." *Harmony and Counterpoint: Ritual Music in Chinese Context*. Bell Yung, Evelyn S. Rawski and Rubie S. Watson, eds. Stanford: Stanford University Press, 177-225, 258-260.

Bond, Michael Harris, ed. 1988. *The Psychology of the Chinese People*. Hong Kong: Oxford University Press.

-----. 1991. *Beyond the Chinese Face: Insights from Psychology*. Hong Kong: Oxford University Press.

Bonvillain, Nancy. 1993. *Language, Culture, and Communication*. Englewood Cliffs: Prentice Hall.

Bordahl, Vibeke. 1996. *The Oral Tradition of Yangzhou Storytelling*. Surrey: Curson Press.

-----. 1998. *The Eternal Storyteller*. Surrey: Curzon Press.

----- and Jette Ross. 2002. *Chinese Storytellers: Life and Art in the Yangzhou Tradition*. Boston: Cheng and Tsui.

Briggs, Charles. 1986. *Learning How to Ask: A Sociolinguistic Appraisal of the Role of the Interview in Social Science Research*. New York: Cambridge University Press.

----- and Richard Bauman. 1990. "Poetics and Performance as Critical Perspectives on Language and Social Life." *Annual Review of Anthropology*. Vol. 19: 59-88.

Bright, Jane and William Bright. 1969. "Semantic Structures in Northwestern California and the Sapir-Whorf Hypothesis." *Cognitive Anthropology*. Stephen Tyler, ed. New York: Holt, Rinehart and Winston, Inc.

Brittan, Arthur and Mary Maynard. 1984. *Sexism, Racism, and Oppression*. New York: Basil Blackwell.

Bruner, Jerome. 1956. *Contemporary Approaches to Cognition*. Cambridge: Harvard University Press.

-----. 1962. *A Study of Thinking*. New York: Science Editions, Inc.

-----. 1966. *Toward a Theory of Instruction*. New York: W.W. Norton.

-----. 1986. *Actual Minds, Possible Worlds*. Cambridge: Harvard University Press.

-----. 1990. *Acts of Meaning*. Cambridge: Harvard University Press.

-----. 1996. "Frames for Thinking: Ways of Making Meaning." *Modes of Thought: Explorations in Culture and Cognition*. David R. Olson and Nancy Torrance, eds. New York: Cambridge University Press.

Bruner, Jerome, Jacqueline J. Goodnow, and George A. Austin. 1956. *A Study of Thinking*. New York: Wiley.

Buonanno, Michael. 1996. "The Genius of Palermo." *The World Observed*. Bruce Jackson and Edward D. Ives, eds. Chicago: The University of Illinois Press, 84-99.

Burke, Kenneth. 1950. *A Rhetoric of Motives*. New York, Prentice-Hall.

-----. 1966. *Language as Symbolic Action: Essays on Life, Literature, and Method*. Berkeley: University of California Press.

Caillois, Roger. 1979. *Man, Play, and Games*. New York: Schocken Books.

Cao, Tiansheng 曹天生. 1997. *Zhongguo shangren* 中国商人. Lanzhou: Gansu renmin chubanshe.

Carlson, Marvin. 1996. *Performance: A Critical Introduction*. New York: Routledge.

Chang, Kwang-Chih. 1977. *Food in Chinese Culture*. New Haven: Yale University Press.

Chase, David. 1983. "Video Game Play and the Flow Model." *The Many Faces of Play*. Kendall Blanchard, ed. Champaign: Human Kinetics Publishers, 208-217.

Chen, Ling. 1994. "How We Know What We Know About Americans: Chinese Sojourners Account for Their Experience." *Our Voices: Essays in Culture, Ethnicity, and Communication*. Alberto Gonzalez, Marsha Houston and Victoria Chen, eds. Los Angeles: Roxbury Pub. Co.

Chen, Si 陈思. 1996. *Richang shiyong yingchou daquan* 日常实用应酬大全. Guangzhou: Guangdong jingji chubanshe.

Chomsky, Noam. 1993. *Language and Thought*. London: Moyer Bell.

Clayton, Jacklyn. 1996. *Your Land, My Land: Children in the Process of Acculturation*. Portsmouth, NH: Heinemann.

Cole, Michael. 1996. *Cultural Psychology: A Once and Future Discipline*. Cambridge: Harvard University Press.

Cole, Michael and Sylvia Scribner. 1974. *Culture and Thought: A Psychological Introduction*. New York: John Wiley and Sons.

Csikszentmihalyi, Mihalyi. 1990. *Flow: The Psychology of Optimal Experience*. New York: Haper Collins.

Davis, Patricia. 1991.*Cognition and Learning*. Texas: The Summer Institute of Linguistics.

D'Andrade, Roy. 1995. *The Growth of Cognitive Anthropology*. New York: Cambridge University Press.

----- and Claudia Strauss, eds. 1992. *Human Motives and Cultural Models*. New York: Cambridge University Press.

De Keijer, Arne J. 1992. *China: Business Strategies for the '90s*. Berkeley: Pacific View Press.

De Koven, Bernard. 1984. "Video Games: At Play in the Virtual World." *Cultural Dimensions of Play, Games, and Sport*. Bernard Mergen, ed. Champaign: Human Kinetics Publishers, 115-120.

De Mente, Boye Lafayette. 1994. *Chinese Etiquette & Ethics in Business*. Lincolnwood, IL: NTC Business Books.

Dorson, Richard. 1983. *Handbook of American Folklore*. Bloomington: Indiana University Press.

Dougherty, Janet. 1985. *Directions in Cognitive Anthropology*. Urbana: University of Illinois Press.

Dougherty, Janet and James Fernandez. 1981. Introduction and Afterward. *American Ethnologist*, Vol. 9, No. 4, Symbolism and Cognition II, 820-832.

Dougherty, Janet and Charles Keller. 1985. "Taskonomy: A Practical Approach to Knowledge Structures." *Directions in Cognitive Anthropology*. Urbana: University of Illinois Press.

Douglas, Jack. 1970. *Understanding Everyday Life*. Chicago: Aldine Publishing Company.

Dundes, Alan. 1971. "Folk Ideas as Units of Worldview," *Journal of American Folklore* 84: 331: 93-103.

-----. 1999. *International Folkloristics: Classic Contributions by the Founders of Folklore*. Oxford: Rowman and Littlefield Publishers, Inc.

Duranti, Alessandro. 1981. *The Samoan Fono: A Sociolinguistic Study*. Pacific Linguistics Monographs, Series B. Vol. 80. Canberra: Australian National University, Department of Linguistics, Research School of Pacific Studies.

-----. 1997. *Linguistic Anthropology*. Cambridge: Cambridge University Press.

-----. 2001. *Linguistic Anthropology: A Reader*. Malden: Blackwell Publishers.

Durkheim, Emile. 1995. *The Elementary Forms of Religious Life*. New York: The Free Press.

Elkind, David and John Flavell. 1969. *Studies in Cognitive Development: Essays in Honor of Jean Piaget*. New York: Oxford University Press.

Eskelinen, Markku. 2001. "The Gaming Situation," *Game Studies*, Issue 1 Volume 1. www.gamestudies.org.

Fang, Tony. 1999. *Chinese business Negotiating Style*. Thousand Oaks, CA: Sage Publications.

Farb, Peter. 1973. *Word Play: What Happens When People Talk*. New York: Alfred Knopf.

Fei, Faye Chunfang. 1999. *Chinese Theories of Theatre and Performance from Confucius to the Present*. Ann Arbor: University of Michigan Press.

Foley, John Miles. 1990. *Traditional Oral Epic*. Berkeley: University of California Press.

-----. 1991. *Immanent Art: From Structure to Meaning in Traditional Oral Epic*. Bloomington: Indiana University Press.

-----. 1995. *The Singer of Tales in Performance*. Bloomington: Indiana University Press.

-----. 1998. *Teaching Oral Traditions*. New York: Modern Language Association of America.

-----. 2002. *How to Read an Oral Poem*. Urbana: University of Illinois Press.

Frake, Charles. 1964. "How to Ask for a Drink in Subanun." The Ethnography of Communication. John Gumperz and Dell Hymes, eds. *The American Anthropologist* 66 (6), 2: 127-132.

-----. 1968. "The Ethnographic Study of Cognitive Systems." *Readings in the Sociology of Language*. Joshua Fishman, ed. The Hague: Mouton, 434-446.

Frank, Arthur. 1979. "Reality Construction in Interaction." *Annual Review of Sociology*, Vol. 5: 167-191.

Gao, Ge and Stella Ting-Toomey. 1998. *Communicating Effectively with the Chinese*. Thousand Oaks, CA: Sage Publications.

Gardner, Howard. 1984. "The Development of Competence in Culturally Defined Domains." *Culture Theory: Essays on Mind, Self, and Emotion*. Richard Shweder and Robert LeVine, eds. New York: Cambridge University Press, 257-275.

Gatewood, John. 1985. *Directions in Cognitive Anthropology*. Janet Dougherty, ed. Urbana: University of Illinois Press.

Gee, James. 2003. *What Video Games Have to Teach Us About Learning and Literacy*. New York: Palgrave Macmillan.

Geertz, Clifford. 1968. "Linguistic Etiquette." *Readings in the Sociology of Language*. Joshua Fishman, ed. The Hague: Mouton, 282-295.

-----. 1973. *The Interpretation of Cultures*. New York: Basic Books.

-----. 1983. *Local Knowledge: Further Essays in Interpretive Anthropology*. New York: Basic Books.

Geirsson, Heimir and Michael Losonsky, eds. 1996. *Readings on Language and Mind*. Cambridge: Blackwell Publishers.

Geis, Michael. 1995. *Speech Acts and Conversational Interaction*. New York: Cambridge University Press.

Glassie, Henry. 1968. *Pattern in the Material Folk Culture of the Eastern United States*. Philadelphia: University of Pennsylvania Press.

Goffman, Erving. 1959. *The Presentation of the Self in Everyday Life*. New York: Anchor Books.

-----. 1961. *Encounters: Two Studies in the Sociology of Interaction*. Indianapolis: Bobbs-Merrill.

-----. 1963a. *Behavior in Public Places: Notes on the Social Organization of Gatherings*. New York: The Free Press.

-----. 1963b. *Stigma: Notes on the Management of Spoiled Identity*. Englewood Cliffs: Prentice Hall.

-----. 1964. "The Neglected Situation", *American Anthropologist* 66: 6: 133-136.

-----. 1967. *Interaction Ritual: Essays on Face-to-Face Behavior*. New York: Pantheon Books.

-----. 1969. *Strategic Interaction*. Philadelphia: University of Pennsylvania Press.

-----. 1974. *Frame Analysis: An Essay on the Organization of Experience.* Boston: Northeastern University Press.

Goodenough, Ward. 1957. "Cultural Anthropology and Linguistics." Report of the seventh annual round table meeting on linguistics and language study. Georgetown University Monograph Series on Language and Linguistics No. 9.

-----. 1964. *Explorations in Cultural Anthropology.* New York: McGraw Hill.

Goodman, Nelson. 1968. *Languages of Art: An Approach to the Theory of Symbols.* Indianapolis: Bobbs-Merrill.

-----. 1978. *Ways of Worldmaking.* Indianapolis: Hackett Publishing Company.

-----. 1984. *Of Mind and Other Matters.* Cambridge: Harvard University Press.

Grice, H.P. 1971. "Meaning." *Semantics: An Interdisciplinary Reader in Philosophy, Linguistics, and Psychology.* D. D. Steinberg and L.A. Jakobovits, eds. Cambridge: Cambridge University Press, 53-59.

-----. 1975. "Logic and Conversation." *Syntax and Semantics*, Vol. 3, *Speech Acts.* New York: Academic Press, 43-58.

Gumperz, John. 1968. "Types of Linguistic Communities." *Readings in the Sociology of Language.* Joshua Fishman, ed. The Hague: Mouton, 460-472.

-----. 1984. Introduction to *Crosstalk and Culture in Sino-American Communication.* New York: Cambridge University Press by Linda Young.

Hall, Edward. 1959. *The Silent Language.* Garden City, NY: Doubleday.

-----. 1966. *The Hidden Dimension.* Garden City, NY: Doubleday.

-----. 1976. *Beyond Culture.* Garden City, NY: Anchor Press.

Halliday, M. A. K. 1968. "The Users and Uses of Language." *Readings in the Sociology of Language*. Joshua Fishman, ed. The Hague: Mouton, 139-169.

Hallowell, Irving. 1955. *Culture and Experience*. Philadelphia: University of Pennsylvania Press.

Hammerly, Hector. 1982. *Synthesis in Second Language Teaching*. Blaine, Washington: Second Language Publications.

-----. 1991. *Fluency and Accuracy*. Multilingual Matters 73, Multilingual Matters, Clevedon.

Hammersley, Martyn and Paul Atkinson. 1983. *Ethnography: Principles in Practice*. London: Tavistock Publications.

Hammonds, Charles. 1992. "Americans in China: The Individualist Meets the Collective," *Journal of the Chinese Language Teachers Association* 27: 55-69.

Hart, Marie and Susan Birrell, eds. 1972. *Sport in the Sociocultural Process*. Dubuque, Iowa: William C. Brown Company Publishers.

Ho, David. 1986. "Chinese Patterns of Socialization: a Critical Review," *The Psychology of the Chinese People*. Michael Harris Bond, ed. Stanford: Stanford University Press.

Holowchak, M. Andrew. 2002. *Philosophy of Sport: Critical Readings, Crucial Issues*. Upper Saddle River, NJ: Prentice Hall.

Hu, Wenzhong and Cornelius Grove. 1999. *Encountering the Chinese: A Guide for Americans*. 2nd Edition. Yarmouth, ME: Intercultural Press.

Hughes, Everett, Buford Junker, Ray Gold, and Dorothy Kittel. 1952. *Cases on Field Work*. Chicago: The University of Chicago Press.

Huizinga, Johan. 1980. *Homo Ludens: A Study of the Play-Element in Culture*. London: Routledge and Kegan Paul.

Hymes, Dell. 1964. *Language in Culture and Society*. Dell Hymes, ed. New York: Harper and Row.

-----. 1968. "The Ethnography of Speaking." *Readings in the Sociology of Language*. Joshua Fishman, ed. The Hague: Mouton, 99-138.

-----. 1974. *Foundations in Sociolinguistics*. Philadelphia: University of Pennsylvania Press.

-----. 1975. "Breakthrough into Performance." *Folklore: Performance, and Communication*. Dan Ben-Amos and Kenneth Goldstein, eds. The Hague: Mouton.

-----. 1983. *Essays in the History of Linguistic Anthropology*. Philadelphia: J. Benjamins.

Jackson, Bruce. 1987. *Fieldwork*. Chicago: University of Illinois Press.

-----. 1996. *The World Observed: Reflections on the Fieldwork Process*. Urbana: University of Illinois Press.

Jia, Wenshan. 2001. *The Remaking of the Chinese Character and Identity in the 21st Century: The Chinese Face Practices*. West Point, CT: Ablex Publishing.

Jian, Xiaobin and Eric Shepherd. Forthcoming. "Playing the Game of Interpersonal Communication In Chinese Culture: The 'Rules' and the Moves." Columbus: The Ohio State University National East Asian Languages Resource Center.

Jones, Stephanie. 1997. *Managing in China: An Executive Survival Guide*. Singapore: Butterworth-Heinemann Asia.

Kalow, Nancy. 1996. "Living Dolls." *The World Observed*. Bruce Jackson and Edward D. Ives, eds. Chicago: The University of Illinois Press, 60-71.

Kasper, Gabriele. 1995. *Pragmatics of Chinese as Native and Target Language*. Honolulu: University of Hawai'i Press.

Kipnis, Adrew. 1997. *Producing Guanxi : sentiment, self, and subculture in a North China village*. Durham: Duke University Press.

Kripke, Saul. 1982. *Wittgenstein on Rules and Private Language*. Oxford: Blackwell.

Labov, William. "The Reflection of Linguistic Processes in Linguistic Structures." *Readings in the Sociology of Language*. Joshua Fishman, ed. The Hague: Mouton, 240-251.

Leaver, Betty Lou and Boris Shekhtman, eds. 2002. *Developing Professional-Level Language Proficiency*. Cambridge: Cambridge University Press.

Lin, Yutang. 1935. *My Country, My People*. New York: Reynal and Hitchcock.

Liu, Dezeng 刘德增. 1997. *Shandongren* 山东人. Jinan: Shandong renmin chubanshe.

Liu, Hongbin 刘洪滨 and Liu Xuezhi, eds. 1995. *Shandong kuaishu youmo xiao duan xuan* 山东快书幽默小段选. Beijing: Beijing Yanshan chubanshe, 138–142.

Loftus, Geoffrey and Elizbeth Loftus. 1983. *Mind at Play: The Psychology of Video Games*. New York: Basic Books.

Lounsbury, Floyd. 1968. "Linguistics and Psychology." *Readings in the Sociology of Language*. Ed. Joshua Fishman. The Hague: Mouton, 38-67.

Lu, Xun 鲁迅. 1994. *Lu Xun xiaoshuo quanji* 鲁迅小说全集. Xinyang: Henan renmin chubanshe.

Lyotard, Jean-Francois. 1979. *The Postmodern Condition: A Report on Knowledge*. Translated by Geoff Bennington and Brain Massumi. Minneapolis: University of Minnesota Press.

Malinowski, Branislow. 1922. *Argonauts of the Western Pacific*. New York: Dutton.

-----. 1965. *Coral Gardens and Their Magic*. Bloomington: Indiana University Press.

-----. 1967. *A Diary in the Strict Sense of the Term*. New York: Harcourt, Brace, and World.

McDowell, John. 1992. "Speech Play." *Folklore, Cultural Performances, and Popular Entertainments*. Richard Baumann, ed. New York: Oxford University Press.

Minami, Masahiko. 2002. *Culture-Specific Language Styles*. Multilingual Matters, Clevedon.

Mitchell, Rosamon and Florence Myles. 1998. *Second Language Learning Theories*. London: Arnold Publishers.

Morgan, William and Klaus Meier, eds. 1988. *Philosophic Inquiry in Sport*. Chicago: Human Kinetics Publishers.

Mueggler, Erik. 2001. *The Age of Wild Ghosts: Memory, Violence and Place in Southwest China*. Berkeley: University of California Press.

Mullen, Patrick. 1978. *I Heard the Old Fisherman Say*. Austin: University of Texas Press.

Nisbett, Richard. 2003. *The Geography of Thought: How Asians and Westerners Think Differently and Why*. New York: The Free Press.

Noyes, Dorothy. 1995. "Group," *Journal of American Folklore* 108: 449-478.

Nunan, David. 1991. *Research Methods in Language Learning*. New York: Cambridge University Press.

Ochs, Elinor and Bambi Schieffelen. 1990. "Language Socialization." *Cultural Psychology: Essays on Comparative Human Development*, Richard Shweder, ed. New York: Cambridge University Press.

Parkin, David, ed. 1982. *Semantic Anthropology*. New York: Academic Press.

Phinney, Jean. 2003. "Ethnic Identity and Acculturation." *Acculturation: Advances in Theory, Measurement, and Applied Research*. Kevin Chun, Pamela Balls Organista, and Gerardo Marin, eds. Washington, DC: American Psychological Association.

Piaget. 1963. *The Origins of Intelligence in Children*. Margaret Cook, trans. New York: W. W. Norton.

Pike, Kenneth. 1954. *Language in Relation to a Unified Theory of Structure of Human Behavior*. Glendale, California: Summer Institute of Linguistics.

Posen, I. Sheldon. 1988. *For Singing and Dancing and all Sorts of Fun: The Story of the Ottawa Valley's Most Famous Song The Chapeau Boys*. Toronto: Deneau Publishers.

Pye, Lucian W. 1992. *Chinese Negotiating Style: Commercial Approaches and Cultural Principles*. Revised Edition. New York: Quorurm Books.

Quinn, Charles Jr. 1994. "The Terms uchi and soto as Windows on a World." *Situated Meaning: Inside and Outside in Japanese Self, Society, and Language*. Jane Bachnik and Charles Quinn Jr, eds. Princeton: Princeton University Press.

Riezler, Kurt. 1941. "Play and Seriousness." *The Journal of Philosophy*. Volume 38, Issue 19: 505-517.

Ren, Jingsheng 任京生. 2003. *Cong dong dao xi kan guanxi* 从东到西看关系. Guangzhou: Nanfang ribao chubanshe.

Reynolds, Dwight F. 1996. "Crossing and Recrossing the Line and Other Moments of Understanding." *The World Observed*. Bruce Jackson and Edward D. Ives, eds. Chicago: The University of Illinois Press, 100-117.

Sapir, Edward. 1921. *Language: An Introduction to the Study of Speech*. New York: Harcourt, Brace and Company.

-----. 1949. *Selected Writings in Language, Culture and Personality*. David Mandelbaum, ed. Berkeley: University of California Press.

Saville-Troike, Muriel. 1982. *The Ethnography of Communication: An Introduction*. Oxford: Basil Blackwell.

Schacter, Daniel. 1996. *Searching for Memory*. New York: Basic Books.

Schank, Roger. 1990. *Tell Me a Story: A New Look at Real and Artificial Memory*. New York: Scribner.

----- and Robert Abelson. 1977. *Scripts, Plans, Goals, and Understanding: An Inquiry into Human Knowledge Structures.* Hillsdale, NJ: Lawrence Erlbaum Associates.

Schechner, Richard and Willa Appel. 1990. *By Means of Performance: Intercultural Studies of Theatre and Ritual.* New York: Cambridge University Press.

Schegloff, Emanuel. 1996. "Confirming Allusions: Toward an Empirical Account of Action." *The American Journal of Sociology,* Vol. 102, No. 1: 161-216.

Schumann, John. 1978. *The Pidginization Process: A Model for Second Language Acquisition.* Rowley, MA: Newbury House Publishers.

Schutz, Alfred. 1945. *The Problem of Social Reality.* The Hague: M. Nijhoff.

Searle, John. 1969. *Speech Acts: An Essay in the Philosophy of Language.* Cambridge: Cambridge University Press.

Seligman, Scott D. 1999. *Chinese Business Etiquette: A Guide to Protocol, Manners, and Culture in the People's Republic of China.* New York: Warner Books.

Shepherd, Eric. 1998. "Playing Their Game: Banqueting in Shandong." MA Thesis, The Ohio State University.

-----. 2002. "Qingke: Guest Hospitality." *Encyclopedia of Modern Asia.* Karen Christensen and David Levinson, eds. Great Barrington, MA: Berkshire Publishing Group.

Shore, Bradd. 1996. *Culture in Mind: Cognition, Culture, and the Problem of Meaning.* New York: Oxford University Press.

Shubik, Martin. 1975. *Games for Society, Business and War.* New York: Elsevier.

Shuman, Amy. 1986. *Storytelling Rights: The Uses of Oral and Written Texts by Urban Adolescents.* New York: Cambridge University Press.

Shweder, Richard. 1990. *Cultural Psychology: Essays on Comparative Human Development*. New York: Cambridge University Press.

-----. 1991.*Thinking Through Cultures: Expeditions in Cultural Psychology*. Cambridge: Harvard University Press.

Simoons, Frederick. 1991. *Food in China*. Boca Raton: CRC Press.

Smith, Barbara Hernstein. 1988. *Contingencies of Value: Alternative Perspectives for Critical Theory*. Cambridge: Harvard University Press.

Spradley, James. 1970. *You Owe Yourself a Drunk: An Ethnography of Urban Nomads*. Boston: Little, Brown, and Company.

-----. 1972. *Culture and Cognition: Rules, Maps and Plans*. San Francisco: Chandler Publishing Company.

Stover, Leon. 1974. *The Cultural Ecology of Chinese Civilization: Peasants and Elites in the Last of the Agrarian States*. New York: Pica Press.

Straub, William and Jean Williams, eds. 1984. *Cognitive Sport Psychology*. Lansing, NY: Sport Science Associates.

Suits, Bernard. 1967a. "What is a game?" *Philosophy of Science* 34: 2: 148-156.

-----. 1967b. "Is Life a Game We are Playing?" *Ethics* 77: 3: 209-213.

-----. 1969. "Games and Paradox." *Philosophy of Science* 36: 3: 316-321.

-----. 1978. *The Grasshopper: Games, Life, and Utopia*. Toronto: University of Toronto Press.

Taylor, Talbot J. 1992. *Mutual Misunderstanding: Scepticism and the Theorizing of Language and Interpretation*. Durham and London: Duke University Press.

Ting-Toomey, Stella. 1994. *The Challenge of Facework*. Albany, NY: State University of New York Press.

Tomasello, Michael. 1999. *The Cultural Origins of Human Cognition*. Cambridge: Harvard University Press.

Torres, Cesar. 2002. "Play As Expression: An Analysis Based On The Philosophy Of Maurice Merleau-Ponty." Diss. Penn State University.

Turner, Mark. 2001. *Cognitive Dimensions of Social Science*. New York: Oxford University Press.

Turner, Victor. 1987. *The Anthropology of Performance*. New York: PAJ Publications.

-----. 1982. *From Ritual to Theatre: The Human Seriousness of Play*. New York: PAJ Publications.

----- and Edward Bruner, eds. 1986. *The Anthropology of Experience*. Urbana: University of Illinois Press.

Tyler, Stephen. 1969. *Cognitive Anthropology*. New York: Holt, Rinehart and Winston.

-----. 1978. *The Said and the Unsaid: Mind, Meaning and Culture*. New York: Academic Press.

Van Maanen, John. 1988. *Tales of the Field: On Writing Ethnography*. Chicago: The University of Chicago Press.

Vygotsky, Lev. 1962. *Thought and Language*. Eugenia Hanfmann and Gertrude Vakar, trans. and eds. Cambridge: M. I. T. Press.

Walker, Galal. 2000. "Performed Culture: Learning to Participate in Another Culture." *Language Policy and Pedagogy*. Richard D. Lambert and Elana Shohamy, eds. Philadelphia: John Benjamins Publishing Company, 221-236.

----- and Mari Noda. 2000. "Remembering the Future: Compiling Knowledge of Another Culture." *Reflecting on the Past to Shape the Future* (ACTFL Foreign Language Education Series). Diane W. Birckbichler and Robert M. Terry, eds. Lincolnwood, IL: National Textbook Co., 187-212.

Wallace, Anthony F. C. 1961. *Culture and Personality*. New York: Random House.

-----. 2003. *Revitalizations and Mazeways: Essays on Culture and Change*, Volume 1. Robert Grumet, ed. Lincoln: University of Nebraska Press.

Wallace, Anthony and John Atkins. 1960. "The Meaning of Kinship Terms." *American Anthropologist* 62:58-80.

Wang, Mary Margaret et al. 2000. *Turning Bricks into Jade: Critical Incidents for Mutual Understanding among Chinese and Americans*. Yarmouth, ME: Intercultural Press.

Watson, Rubie. 1996. "Chinese Bridal Laments: The Claims of a Dutiful Daughter." *Harmony and Counterpoint: Ritual in Chinese Context*. Bell Yung, Evelyn Rawski, and Rubie Watson, eds. Stanford: Stanford University Press.

Wertz, Spencer. 1991. *Talking a Good Game: Inquiries into the Principles of Sport*. Dallas: Southern Methodist University Press.

Wittgentstein, Ludvig. 1958. *Philosophical Investigations*. New York: Macmillan.

Wolf, Arthur, ed. 1974. *Religion and Ritual in Chinese Society*. Stanford: Stanford University Press.

Wolf, Margery. 1985. *Revolution Postponed: Women in Contemporary China*. Stanford: Stanford University Press.

Wolf, Mark and Bernard Perron, eds. 2003. *The Video Game Theory Reader*. New York: Routledge.

Xi, Changsheng. 1996. "Individualism and Collectivism in American and Chinese Societies," *Traversing Cultural Paths*.

Yamada, Haru. 1997. *Different Games, Different Rules: Why Americans and Japanese Misunderstand Each Other*. New York and Oxford: Oxford University.

Yang, Bojun 杨伯峻. 1990. *Chun qiu Zuo zhuan zhu (xiuding ben)* 春秋左传注(修订本). Beijing: Zhonghua shuju.

Yang, Mayfair Mei-hui. 1994. *Gifts, Favors & Banquets: The Art of Social Relationships in China*. Ithaca, NY: Cornel University Press.

Ye, Lei. 1995. "Complimenting in Mandarin Chinese." *Pragmatics of Chinese as Native and Target Language*. Gabriele Kasper, ed. Honolulu: University of Hawai'i Press, 207-296.

Yeung, Irene and Rosalie Tung. 1996. "Achieving Business Success in Confucian Societies: The Importance of Guanxi (Connections)." *Organizational Dynamics* Autumn, 1996: 54-65.

Young, Linda. 1994. *Crosstalk and Culture in Sino-American Communication*. New York: Cambridge University Press.

Yung, Bell, Evelyn Rawski, and Rubie Watson. 1996. *Harmony and Counterpoint: Ritual in Chinese Context*. Stanford: Stanford University Press.

Zhang, Yanyin. 1995. "Indirectness in Chinese Requesting." *Pragmatics of Chinese as Native and Target Language*. Gabriele Kasper, ed. Honolulu: University of Hawai'i Press, 69-118.

Zhou, Jingfang 周景芳, 1996. *Zhongguo si da gudian xiaoshuo* 中国四大古典小说. Shenzhen: Haitian chubanshe.

Zhu, Yunxia. 1999. *Business Communication in China*. Commack, NJ: Nova Science.

INDEX